NET Strategy

CHARTING THE DIGITAL COURSE FOR YOUR COMPANY'S GROWTH

Robert Spiegel

DEARBORN™
TRADE

A **Kaplan Professional** Company

HD
30.7
.S68
2000

This publication is designed to provide accurate and authoritative information in regard to the subject matter covered. It is sold with the understanding that the publisher is not engaged in rendering legal, accounting, or other professional service. If legal advice or other expert assistance is required, the services of a competent professional should be sought.

Publisher: Cynthia A. Zigmund
Acquisitions Editor: Jean Iversen Cook
Managing Editor: Jack Kiburz
Project Editor: Trey Thoelcke
Interior Design: Lucy Jenkins
Cover Design: Jody Billert, Billert Communications
Typesetting: the dotted i

© 2000 by Dearborn Financial Publishing, Inc.

Published by Dearborn Trade, A Kaplan Professional Company

All rights reserved. The text of this publication, or any part thereof, may not be reproduced in any manner whatsoever without written permission from the publisher.

Printed in the United States of America

00 01 02 10 9 8 7 6 5 4 3 2 1

Library of Congress Cataloging-in-Publication Data
Spiegel, Robert.
    Net strategy : charting the digital course for your company's growth / Robert Spiegel.
       p.   cm.
    Includes bibliographical references and index.
    ISBN 0-7931-3866-3
    1. Business enterprises—Computer networks.   2. Electronic commerce.
3. Internet.   I. Title.
HD30.7 .S68 2000
658.8'4—dc21
                                                      00-011409

Dearborn books are available at special quantity discounts to use as premiums and sales promotions, or for use in corporate training programs. For more information, please call the Special Sales Manager at 800-621-9621, ext. 4514, or write to Dearborn Financial Publishing, Inc., 155 N. Wacker Drive, Chicago, IL 60606-1719.

DEDICATION

To Thomas Spiegel because the greatest dad on earth should have a book dedicated to him.

CONTENTS

Introduction: Net Strategy or Else xi

1. The Warm Revolution 1
Welcome to the brave new world 4
A generation of creative thinkers 5
Charting the future 6
Hop on the new train 9

2. Dot-Coms and Net Plays 13
The Internet company is born 16
The magazine model online 19
The catalog model online 21
The brilliant Christmas of '98 23
Dot-coms change like quicksilver 25
The day of the Net play 27
Bricks begin to learn 29
The virtual world needs real-world roots 31
Everyone becomes a Net company 34

3. E-commerce 39
The boom in sleaze 44
Scams and spam 46
The Web site explosion 48
Online brokerage 50
Wireless e-commerce 51

E-commerce security issues   53
Tooling the globe   55
The sleepy B2B giant   57
The birth of e-marketplaces   60

4. E-tailing   65

Categories: the e-tail winners and losers   68
Trouble in the online mall   71
Travel agent in a can   73
eBay and the land of retail auctions   76
The sticky wicket of apparel   78
Virtual health care   80
Financial services: the mouse as ATM   82
Security issues   84
The future of Internet retailing   86

5. Net Consumers: Brands and Loyalty   91

The Internet family   94
The Internet generations   97
Internet shopping by gender and income   99
Branding on the Internet   101
Loyalty strategies   104
Building loyalty with service   107
The power of content   110

6. Entertainment   115

Cheap channels mean content wins   117
The broadband audience is already waiting   120
The Web stimulates traditional entertainment   121
Music: a world of downloads   122
Movies: promotion on the Net   125
Sports: the teams go electronic   127
Global gaming   130
Television: bracing for the changes   131

7. E-mail and Click Throughs   135

Internet advertising is a growth industry   137
Web advertising: from banners to webcasts   140
Viral marketing   141
Banner exchanges   144
Affiliation marketing   145
Permission marketing   147
The statistics on permission programs   149

CONTENTS   vii

    The growth of e-mail marketing   151
    Successful e-mail marketing techniques   153
    The future of Internet marketing   156

8. B2B: The Nimble Giant   161

    The Internet makes procurement efficient   165
    The bigger they come, the better they get it   168
    Online procurement heats up   170
    A B2B smorgasbord   171
    To dot-com or dot-corp   174
    Software giants: four horsemen ride the wild race   177
    Exchanges and auctions: Internet flea markets for big junk   179
    E-marketplaces: the world shopping bazaar   182

9. E-marketplaces   187

    A paradigm shift in an eye's blink   190
    Auctions, exchanges, e-marketplaces, and information flow   193
    The models for online exchanges   195
    Vertical, horizontal, or geographic?   198
    Software makers deal themselves in   201
    Shakeout? It's not as crowded as it looks   203
    The coming IPO boom for exchanges   205

10. Global Reach   209

    Europe: taking notes from U.S. development   212
    European e-marketplaces   214
    The Asia-Pacific Rim   216
    Latin America's slow emergence   218
    Is English the only language of e-commerce?   220

11. Venture Capital and Incubators: Funding the Next World   223

    The venture capital market   224
    The top venture capital firms for Internet companies   226
    Incubators: a slingshot to launch   230
    New models for Net incubators   231
    The cornucopia of hatcheries   237

12. Business-to-Government: Finally Some Efficiencies   241

    The first movers: city, county, and state governments   244
    The big government hurdle: resistance to change   246
    VCs turn their support to e-government companies   248
    Auctions and exchanges   249

Citizen payments and permits   249
Government ramps up for e-spending   250
B2G e-marketplaces   251

13. The Future's Future   255

Singing the middleman blues   257
Internet health care: a phoneline to a healthy life   260
The passing of the industrial age   262
The culture changes   265

14. Your Comprehensive Net Strategy   271

Remember business 101   272
You will buy and sell online   273
The customer is king   274
The visible company   275
The revolution will change our lives   275

Resources   277
Bibliography   283
Index   293

ACKNOWLEDGMENTS

Thanks to all those who helped me put this book together. Jeremy Solomon, my agent, encouraged the concept. Jean Iversen Cook, my editor, helped me to focus the book. Lester Craft, Jr., editor-in-chief of *eCommerce Business Weekly,* has been a constant source of perspective, knowledge, encouragement, and continual good will.

Thanks to my kids, Jesse, Mari, and Connie, who had to put up with dad playing on the computer when it was really time to go swimming.

INTRODUCTION

NET STRATEGY OR ELSE

I live in Albuquerque, New Mexico, a city that has three business sections. There's Old Town, down by the river. There's Downtown a couple of miles away. And there's Uptown. Like tree rings that mark each year of growth, these sections mark shifts in commerce. When the railroad came through in the late 1800s, commerce left the river and moved to the tracks, forming Downtown. As the population shifted to suburban areas, business left Downtown and moved near the malls. Most cities have similar markings. Now a new shift has occurred that won't leave a physical mark, but its effect is more profound than any of the earlier changes.

The shift is the move to the Internet. Most of the cliches about the changes the Internet will bring about are true. Here are a few:

- The Internet has ushered in a transformation of business that is as vast as our move from agrarian commerce to industrial business.

- This new Information Age will alter our communities and our nations.

- It will challenge the concept of national borders as online communities take a larger role in people's lives than national identity.

- Companies that fail to find a place online will lose their markets.
- "Get it," or you're lost.

One cliche that is particularly relevant to this book is that keeping up with Internet business changes is like drinking from a fire hose. As a business journalist, I have covered e-commerce every day since 1998. Prior to that, I covered Internet business regularly. I started writing about the online world back in the early 1980s, during the days of Dialog and VuText. There was no World Wide Web and no America Online (AOL). The online customers were research librarians trained in Boolean literature searches. I remember how exciting it was when Prodigy and CompuServe appeared, giving information access directly to professionals without the need of an intermediary librarian. Back then, it was easy to keep up with the changes.

The Early Online Days

Knight Rider's VuText experiment in delivering electronic news directly to consumers failed in Florida. The disaster confirmed the widespread doubts about consumer acceptance of electronic information delivery. Clearly consumers were not interested in electronic information. Who wants to read news on a computer screen, especially when it takes 28 to 30 seconds for each page of text to appear? Advertising took even longer to "paint" on the screen. The industry was growing, but it was growing very slowly. I remember Jean-Paul Emard, the editor of *Online Review,* telling me, "We're a toddler industry now. We're not very big, but we're not going to go away." Back then, you could forget the online world for weeks at a time, then check back in and find not much had changed. I found I could catch up with the changes in a couple of days of research.

The pace of changes moved at a reasonable pace for many years. Even when an advertisement for America Online appeared on television, shocking me, the growth moved at a comprehensible rate. When I pitched this book idea in 1996, my agent told me that most of the business on the Internet was porn and get-rich-quick schemes, and thus there was no market for a book about Internet commerce.

The comment contained some truth. So I concentrated on magazine writing about Internet business. The really big shift began sometime in 1998. Interest in the Internet started to grow among professionals, and I suddenly found that all my writing clients wanted stories about e-business. Within weeks I found I was writing about nothing but e-commerce.

Living on Internet Time

In 1999 I started a weekly column called *eBiz*. Then I started a second fortnightly column, *Shoestring eBiz*. I took a job writing two stories a day about e-commerce for the daily Internet news service *E-Commerce Times*. A few months later, I took a job as senior editor for Cahners' *eCommerce Business*. I live it and breathe it daily, and I can't keep up with the changes. At first, industry insiders said Internet companies were changing and growing at four times the rate of offline businesses. By 1999 they were saying the rate was ten times the speed of traditional commerce. I don't know how you can possibly clock the speed of business that's moving faster than the brain can comprehend.

Back in 1998, the *Wall Street Journal* smugly called the Internet an "economic pipsqueak." I would imagine the editors see the Internet differently now. Yet reading their pages, you don't get the full impact of the changes. The *Wall Street Journal* gives more coverage to e-commerce than it did in the past, but the inches devoted to the Internet are small compared with the actual changes out on the streets of global commerce. When you read the *Wall Street Journal*, the Internet seems downright comprehensible. Yet look at the ads in the paper. The shift to Internet advertising in the WSJ is startling. In reality, the transformation to e-commerce is widespread, and it runs deep into every conceivable industry and business sector.

Watching the Tech Leader Moves

As I cover e-commerce, I have a regular experience that is quite disturbing. As I begin research on a story about a new business concept, I uncover rocks here and there, trying to find just the nugget that will illustrate the significance of the new enterprise. I lift a rock, and instead of finding a nugget, I find a whole new world of changes that I had previously not seen. I scramble to incorporate the breaking information into my story, only to find the new information leads to newer information, and the next pocket negates my original concept. The new story is even more compelling than my original idea, but now I'm on deadline.

This occurred when I covered Ariba, Commerce One, Oracle, and i2, the e-marketplace software companies. I happily began a story on how they derive their revenue. Unlike many companies that license the use of their platforms and offer consulting services to support the new system, these companies started taking equity positions in the hubs they were building. They also grabbed a percentage of every transaction that passed through the marketplace. While reading the press releases about each of the marketplace launches, it was hard to see the undercurrent. The software companies were holding their industry partners hostage with a multi-source revenue model.

Their industry partners had nowhere to turn, but they were not overly concerned anyway. The software providers were the only game in town on building e-marketplaces, and the industry partners couldn't wait for new players like Microsoft to develop alternative applications. If you want to be first to market with your sector's e-marketplace, you better make your pact with the devil. So the big software makers called the shots, taking licensing fees, consulting fees, transaction fees, and an equity position in the new business. Not bad for selling technology you've already developed.

I called an analyst in frustration, asking, "When did these companies start this bizarre revenue mix?"

"Oh, about five weeks back," she answered. In Internet time that might as well be years ago. Pay attention to the flood of new e-marketplaces, and you'll miss the underlying story. Pay attention to the underlying story, and you'll miss the notices of new launches. Watch business-to-business (B2B) developments, and you'll miss the new twists and turns of retail (B2C). Keep an eye on both B2B and B2C, and you'll miss the birth of B2G (business-to-government). It's a fire hose. Open your mouth and you'll drown.

INTRODUCTION

Trying to See the Forest

Even though it's fruitless to keep up with the details of the swirling changes, the concepts still come through. They arrive with a force that alters even the oldest and most staid businesses. Shippers who never made the transition from logbooks to computers (or even typewriters!) are now going straight to Net. Steel, auto, and petroleum companies that seemed immune to change just months ago are turning their companies upside-down to take advantage of e-commerce. It's not just Nasdaq that's reaping the Net rewards, the bricks and the smokestacks are getting in on the game, and they stand more to gain, since their inefficiencies add up to billions.

The basic Internet concept is not complicated at all. The Net allows consumers and businesses to gain a wider choice of goods and services at lower prices. That's the heart of the Internet's success, and it's the reason e-commerce will continue to grow at a dizzying rate. What company wants to wait even the shortest second before taking savings on previously fixed expenses? The reasons you need a Net strategy for your company is to take the savings available to you, to keep your market, and to extend your market by offering new savings to your customers and clients.

The Net Touches Everyone

I've tried to think of a company that is not part of this business revolution on either the sell or buy side. Local businesses came to mind. How about my primary care physician? Surely doctoring is still an offline business. Well, his practice buys supplies through physician sites, and he can take odd symptoms and send them through the Internet for a backup opinion. His accounting systems, records management, and HMO or Medicare billings and reimbursements will likely be online by the time you read this book. And just why would my doctor be so aggressive about getting on the Internet? Because it will add thousands of dollars to his annual income almost immediately. He may never buy a CD or book from Amazon.com because he is timid with his Visa card, yet he'll get very bold with online procurement.

I tried to think of another local business that doesn't need the Net. How about my natural foods store? Turns out my local store is part of a chain of 23 stores in five states. The company's accounting and inventory system is patched into an online Intranet. Fresh seafood is purchased through the e-marketplace, Gofish.com, which reduces the cost of seafood while giving the store more choices among fish farms and fishing outfits. The result is a wider variety of products, fresher seafood, and lower costs. And why is my local store so quick to the Net? Because the savings goes to the store's bottom line immediately. That's motivation enough, without taking into account that the seafood is fresher and customers get a wider selection.

There's much more to the story for both the physician and the natural foods store. The physician has access to research way beyond the sources of most doctors just two or three years ago. That physician can easily search medical data without the help of a librarian, and connectivity to others in the field is greatly enhanced. At the natural foods store, e-marketplaces help with the purchase of organic vegetables as well as packaged goods. The store can tie into online consulting services and business applications to get help with retail promotions as well as employee compensation packages and liability insurance choices. Each one of these services can trim the company's expenses.

What's Your Net Strategy?

I gave up trying to find a business that can't be improved through Internet connectivity. The Internet can benefit every business. In order to compete in this new business world that's evolving at bewildering speed, you need a Net strategy. You need it to extend your business. You need it to defend your business. It doesn't matter if you sell oranges or cartoons. It doesn't matter if your customers are around the corner or in Antarctica. You need to develop an e-commerce strategy because there are consumers or businesses out there that need or want your products and services. If you don't deliver over the Internet, someone will step in and take your place.

You also need a Net strategy to trim your business expenses. You need to buy over the Net because it will give you enhanced choices while saving money. If you don't buy over the Internet, your competitors will. It doesn't matter if you buy steel or consulting services. It doesn't matter if you purchase from local vendors or manufacturers in Guatemala. Buying on the Internet will make your business more efficient and more competitive.

Alan Greenspan almost seemed surprised in mid-1999 when he confessed that part of the reason we were experiencing fast-paced growth without inflation is because computers were finally delivering productivity gains. The gains are coming from the Internet. If you can deliver solutions to your customers that allow them to take a savings and enhance their choices and quality through purchasing your goods or services online, you'll put the sell side of your Net strategy in place. Adding Internet procurement is even easier, since many of the traditional suppliers are already rushing to the Net.

Want a winning Net strategy? Go to the Internet and look for ways to help consumers or businesses save money, widen their choices, and lift quality. If you look hard enough, you'll find opportunities whether you're selling nails or pizza. Comb the Internet for ideas on how to improve your products and services while fulfilling them more efficiently. Look for the savings. If you can deliver the savings to your market, you'll have all the Net strategy you'll need. This book offers examples of how companies are doing this in all areas of business, from books and CDs to Mickey Mouse cruises and market research reports.

CHAPTER 1

THE WARM REVOLUTION

Because no businesses are immune to the developments of the Internet, every company needs to make moves into the online world. This includes buying, selling, and working with partners. The move to the Internet will eventually involve all aspects of your organization's operations, from sales management to procurement and even human resources. Some companies will move fast. Some will adopt transitory solutions just to get started. Some companies will drag their collective feet. But all organizations will eventually move their processes and communications online.

This evolution to the Internet cannot be avoided, so it's best to accept the fact that major changes are ahead for the next few years. It is also wise to begin assessing your opportunities immediately and begin the process of learning how the Web affects your market or business community. You also need to brace for a rough ride as some constituencies within your organization meet these changes with fear and resistance. The top level will likely get it before the middle levels of management in large organizations. So be prepared to argue for change and reassure all players that the move to the Internet benefits everyone.

There is no change in our history that compares with the alteration the Internet brings to our working lives. The opportunities presented to us by evolving technology far outpace our ability to change our behavior. This means the biggest challenge to our companies isn't simply choosing the right technology partners to make your Net strategy effective, it also involves changing how all the members of a company work, from the CEO to the sales team to the company's individual buyers. This is not the French Revolution. Heads won't roll like they did during downsizing. It's a warm revolution, but like all revolutions, it will change the landscape forever.

Peter Drucker's 1970s Prediction

No one living today saw the birth of the last business revolution, the Industrial Age. That transformation of commerce took a lifetime, stretching from the mid-1800s to the early 1900s. Our revolution is moving at 20 to 30 times the rate of the development of manufacturing. Where the industrial revolution took 70 years to gain its full impact, the information age or Internet revolution is only taking three or four years to begin seriously changing the way we do business and the way we work and play.

A couple of decades ago, Peter Drucker predicted the coming of an Information Age that would end the Industrial Age. He stated these predictions long before the Internet appeared. He pictured a world in which the Soviet Union would collapse under the weight of its own inefficiencies and the economies of the democratic countries would shift from a reliance on capital and heavy infrastructure to an economy based on information. The new capital would be knowledge, and knowledge workers would replace managers and executives as the most valuable population in the business community. The leaders of this new economy would be those with the greatest access to information as opposed to those with the greatest access to capital.

Drucker also predicted a change in the way we lived and conducted our work lives. The new knowledge workers would not be managed in the same manner as workers in the hierarchical Industrial Age. Instead of reporting to work and following directives from above, the knowledge workers would deliver information in much the same manner as a professional or small business owner delivers work to a client. Drucker predicted management would lose its central position as the hub of power. Instead, power would be distributed across a wide range of people with knowledge and information. Thus a corporation would buy information from knowledge workers rather than hire workers and manage their tasks.

Without the golden assets of infrastructure or capital, what would information-based corporations own? Patents, information systems, and distribution networks would become the new knowledge-based assets. This corporate property would be valued at a higher level than the old corporate assets of capital, factories, and physical distribution systems. Like the Soviet Union collapsing under its own weight, the relics of the Industrial Age would become marginalized and eventually fail from the burden of their own inefficiencies.

I find it a great pleasure that Mr. Drucker has lived to see our new age. Drucker gained fame, ironically, as a leading management philosopher during the absolute height of the Industrial Age, from the mid-1950s through the 1970s. He predicted the end of his own age with stunning precision. Never regarded as a futurist, Drucker's picture of the world ahead gleams with pinpoint accuracy. Drucker didn't give a timeline for his predicted changes. I would guess he is surprised at the rapidity of the transformation of our economy. If you look at the time it took for Microsoft to rise from start-up to the world's largest company, it is lightning-fast by the old industrial standards. But the speed at which it moved from top dog into irrelevancy is even more amazing. The startling thing about Microsoft's technological stumble is that the company was not asleep at the wheel. The company was fully engaged and driving at breakneck speed when it took a wrong turn on the Internet.

Microsoft Admits Missing the Online Boat

Bill Gates admitted in 1995 that the Internet's fast development took his company by surprise. He further admitted that Microsoft was late to the game and that catching up would be tricky. Gates may be one of the few people who truly understands the depth of Microsoft's miscalulation. It's a cruel irony that Gates is forced to defend his company's monopolistic practices at a time when Microsoft is pedaling as fast as it can and is still falling behind. Another cruel twist is that Microsoft probably only missed its chance to dominate the Internet by a few months.

Drucker's vision of the Information Age has come to fruition in a half-dozen years at longest estimate. The only one of his points that hits slightly off the mark is his underestimation of our cunning industrial giants. After watching Ford and GM stagger from the hits delivered by Japanese auto makers in the mid-1970s, it's easy to see why he thought they would crumble under the more formidable challenge of a full-scale economic shift. Who could have predicted that smokestacks such as Ford, GE, and GM would eventually be led by executives who embrace the information-based economy? How could anyone foresee that knowledge workers would rise to the top of these corporations and turn the old stalwarts upside-down and inside-out in pursuit of information-based efficiencies.

Drucker was certainly right. The very nature of our business world has changed, and the future isn't what it used to be. It is not the Internet gimmicks that will alter our lives. Internet-connected refrigerators, on-demand movies, and Net-ordered pizza are not particularly meaningful to our future. Those changes will happen, and they will be trivial and fun. But the real change will come in the form of prolonged economic growth and short, shallow recessions. The Internet will help us control inventory and streamline commerce. The productivity gains have just begun. We've lived for a couple of decades with a 1.5 percent average gain in productivity. Now we'll get a chance to see what prolonged gains in excess of 2, 2.5, even 3 percent can mean to our economy and ultimately to us individually. There's no Internet gadget that can compare with the possibilities of those little productivity percentages.

WELCOME TO THE BRAVE NEW WORLD

Some economists wonder if we've reached a point where we can leave the economic cycle behind. Maybe we've seen our last recession, they say. Fat chance. In a world where a positive perception bears some of the heavy lifting required to keep our economy on its toes, we'll see plenty of new recessions. But now we have a lighter, more nimble economy based on information exchange. Our ability to adapt to change is enhanced. This new dexterity is likely to give our system more bounce when it hits a rough patch.

However you view the Internet, and whatever its implication for the very nature of economics, it's a big story. I remember a humorous column by Michael Parsons, deputy editor of the *Industry Standard* magazine. With all the wild new Net plays occuring in the magazine's home town of San Francisco, he fantasized his staff brainstorming a great Internet idea and pitching it to a venture group for funding. Why not? Journalists know a silly idea is capable of rounding up $10 million in venture capital and angel dollars. He takes the dream a step further and imagines his staff weathering an instant IPO and becoming quick millionaires. When he comes back to the office Monday morning expecting that everyone has departed for the Greek Islands, he instead finds his crew fully at work. He asks why all these instant Net-wealthy moguls would show up for work. "No matter how wealthy we may be, we can't pass up the chance to cover the business story of the century," says one of his staff writers. The others nod in agreement.

I'm not sure what century this business story fits into, but Parsons's fantasy is correct in that we've entered a very fascinating era. As we move deeper and deeper into this Internet transformation, it gets clearer and clearer that the economic changes are deep and complete. We may not know exactly where the online economy is taking us, but it's becoming obvious that the old world is gone. We've reached the turning point where the former economy is no longer available should we stumble along our new path. That's just as well. The old economy was rife with arbitrary hierarchy and implicit class distinctions. Let it go. I'd rather place my democratic, capitalistic bet on an economy that rewards the quick and creative.

A GENERATION OF CREATIVE THINKERS

One of the reasons the switch to an information economy has moved with such speed is that it has attracted the best and brightest from at least two generations, the late boomers and Generation X. In past ages, each generation's smart and creative thinkers shied away from business in favor of the arts, sciences, education, and politics. Business leadership was often viewed as territory for a ruthless lot who viewed creative thinking and innovation a distraction from the pure discipline of market domination. To this crew, a concept such as "coopitition" was wasteful blather. They viewed intellectuals and creative souls as weak.

When you think of the great creative thinkers of the past, Lincoln, Tolstoy, Darwin, and Picasso may come to mind. Business leaders don't usually make the list of the most admired leaders in a given generation. The territory of organizational leadership has traditionally been very restrictive. Few creative thinkers would consider taking such a brain-numbing course. Even the great American inventors such as Edison shunned the role of organizational leadership. Perhaps only Henry Ford was able to mix an innovative nature with the cold-steel ruthlessness needed to beat back union workers during the early stages of industry.

The Information Age has brought about a few changes. Can you image Bill Gates sending in thugs to beat strikers? For Generation X and its descendents, business may be the most creative avenue available. Each century has produced a dominant art form. The 18th century was dominated by music. During the 19th century, the novel was the leading creative art form. During the 20th century, the visual arts in the form of photography, film, and television dominated. For the 21st century, the leading creative avenue for bright minds may be business. Aside from the lure of riches, running an Internet start-up could be the single greatest creative challenge facing the generation now reaching adulthood. Dreaming up the next Net play is perhaps a more attractive prospect than writing a screenplay or forming a rock and roll band.

CHARTING THE FUTURE

The future for Internet commerce looks exceedingly positive even if there are some predictable and unpredictable bumps coming along the way. Here are the projections given by Forrester Research, a company with a reputation as the leading research firm in Internet forecasts. This chart shows the outlook for consumer and business-to-business e-commerce:

	Retail Projections	Business-to-Business Projections
1997	$2.9 billion	$18.6 billion
1998	$8.0 billion	$43.1 billion
1999	$20.2 billion	$109.3 billion
2000	$38.8 billion	$406.2 billion
2001	$64.2 billion	$716.6 billion
2002	$101.1 billion	$1.2 trillion
2003	$143.8 billion	$1.8 trillion
2004	$184.5 billion	$2.7 trillion

Looking at the figures, it's not surprising that in mid-2000 Internet experts stopped talking about AOL and Amazon.com and started concentrating on the business-to-business (B2B) action. Between 1999 and 2000, retail Internet sales failed to double, while B2B began to skyrocket. For the remaining years in the projection, B2B sales exceed consumer sales by at least tenfold. These figures become even more intriguing when you consider that many Internet watchers believe the retail figures are probably right and the B2B numbers are a very conservative estimate. The Gartner Group projects B2B will exceed seven trillion dollars by 2004.

If B2B isn't enough to get your attention, there is a corner of e-commerce that hasn't yet been tapped, business-to-government (B2G). It may not seem very sexy to sell goods and services to the federal government over the Internet, but the total government procurement machine that is expected to move online during the early years of the 21st century will reach $800 billion. This figure doesn't count local and state governments.

These numbers will alter our economy drastically. No matter how many books and CDs you purchase online, the world won't change much. The B2B changes, however, will directly affect your life. For one, the B2B efficiencies allow companies to absorb inflation. The main reason companies are rushing to Internet commerce is because it saves money. Ariba, one of the leading e-marketplace builders, estimates that the average corporation will save from 8 to 20 percent by moving its procurement to the Internet. Those savings go straight to the company's bottom line, which allows it to pay higher labor costs in a tight job market while still delivering higher profits. Thus, no increase in the price of the company's goods.

The Game Where Everybody Wins

The odd thing about B2B commerce is that the seller also takes a savings. The lower costs on the procurement side do not simply mean that the buyer uses the Internet to beat the seller into a lower price. Instead, it means both the buyer and the seller can negotiate their transaction online while keeping the transaction data online, thus eliminating billions of dollars in paperwork processing. Even as the seller lowers the cost of goods on the exchange, the lower price comes with a greater quantity of goods sold to a wider group of buyers. This allows the both the seller and the buyer to maintain smaller inventories. Both sides of the transaction benefit financially through the online connection.

This means that corporations can increase their profits while simultaneously paying the higher cost for labor that comes in a boom cycle's labor market. This model for greater efficiency is not just available to heavy manufacturing such as autos, steel, and industrial chemicals. The savings can be taken by every business sector, from health and steel to oil and convenience-store retail product purchasing. The smallest company and the largest company can both take the savings. It doesn't take long for the efficiencies to produce positive results. Ariba says that in some cases they move clients onto a procurement hub in two weeks, and the savings come just as soon as the transactions begin. There's no waiting period. No sweating out the return on investment.

While we wait to see whether Amazon.com will ever be profitable, the largest chunk of Internet business, B2B e-commerce, is reaping rewards from ubiquitous connectivity. Even as online retail sales are getting called into question, business commerce is proving itself transaction by transaction. In the past, a Net strategy meant you had a plan to sell something to somebody over the Internet. But with the advent of Internet-based marketplaces, a Net strategy can just as easily be a means for improving your business by shifting procurement online and taking an 8 to 20 percent savings.

HOP ON THE NEW TRAIN

Oddly enough, the shift of commerce to the Internet may bear some resemblance to the development of the train. When the train system was first implemented in England in the mid-1800s, most people believed it would be used primarily to transport passengers across the country. In the beginning, freight was a second thought. The shipping industry had the freight business well under control. But within a few years it became obvious that freight was more efficiently sent by train. Trains could reach inland, and the light weight of the train saved both energy and labor. In a few quick years, the majority of England's freight moved onto trains. At that point, the passenger traffic become a secondary consideration.

The change brought about in England as a result of trains carrying freight was profound economically. The effect of passengers using trains had a much smaller overall effect on the country. The situation with the Internet may be analogous. It very well could be that the Internet, which was once viewed as a great way to get news and buy a book, may actually have a more profound effect on our lives when the companies around us use it to streamline their buying and selling. The retail side of the Internet may be fun and exciting, especially as broadband allows entertainment to proliferate, but the real power of the Internet is likely to be in the Net strategies of companies that push large portions of their transactions into electronic form.

YOUR NET STRATEGY:

The Internet is bringing about major shifts in the way business is conducted, and those changes are coming about very quickly. Your company will eventually be involved with the Internet on both the sell side and the buy side. The question is not whether you will shift to e-commerce, but how that change will take place. Even more important than getting involved in the Internet, it's important to enter this cyber-territory effectively. In the not-too-distant future, we will see lists of the Net strategies that failed. They will seem humorous in retrospect, but they will have seemed perfectly legitimate at the time.

In the haste to get involved one way or another, many traditional companies have set out on a handful of conflicting strategies simultaneously. The concept is similar to the horse racing enthusiast who bets on every entry in the field in hope that one of them wins. The smart gambler who is unsure of a race will select the three or four horses that collectively have more than a 95 percent chance to win. The next step is to determine the odds to see if the payoff of each individual horse exceeds the total bet. If the numbers are not favorable, the smart gambler will wait.

Can you wait out the Internet? Certainly speed to market is a serious consideration if waiting means that a competitor can enter your business space and grab portions of your market share. Yet waiting is often preferable to moving ahead with a faulty strategy. It takes great discipline for the horse bettor to sit out a confusing race. Sometimes hesitancy is the best strategy. Whatever strategy you finally embrace, it should be well considered. An e-procurement business consultant once said, "It doesn't do any good to speed up a process that you shouldn't be doing at all."

Consider Multiple Strategies

Some of our largest companies have taken the multi-horse approach to their Net strategies, implementing a number of conflicting solutions for selling and buying in the belief that they will be ahead of the game no matter how things develop. This is a reasonable approach if you have the resources and your cost-of-losing is greater than the cost of multiple strategies. Most Fortune 100 companies know they need to get the Internet right, so they invest in a number of approaches to make sure they don't get it wrong.

If you're not blessed with the resources to back every horse in the race, you're wise to spend more time pouring over the racing form until the likely winner becomes clear. Even then, keep some resources in check in case your industry takes an abrupt shift away from your horse. Urgency is hard to discount when your competitors are rushing into your space. Yet you need to educate yourself before jumping to a counter move. Use knowledge as your rudder to make sure you move consistently in the right direction.

Read the trades; read the e-commerce magazines; go to conferences; read books. Pay particular attention to the quotes from actual practitioners. Analysts and software company CEOs wax eloquent on the future, but it's your fellow business people whose comments are of greatest consequence. As you educate yourself, go to conferences within your industry as well as Internet conferences. You need to hear your fellow business leaders explain what works for business more than you need to hear the Net companies give their pitches.

Second-to-market with the right technology beats first-to-market with failed technology.

CHAPTER 2

DOT-COMS AND NET PLAYS

The New Economy

There really is a new economy. And with this new economy, there comes a cultural shift in the way business is conducted. If anything, the new economy is marked by a business's ability to become more responsive to the needs of its customers and clients. The connectivity of the Internet allows companies to deliver products and services faster and more efficiently. Internet technology also helps a company tailor its products and services more effectively to its customers's individual needs. If Internet companies are better at responding to the needs of their customers, then the distinction between Internet enterprises and brick companies is only temporary. If a new way of doing business is a superior way of doing business, it will soon become the only way of doing business. In as much as the new economy increases operational efficiency and improves a company's ability to respond to its customers and clients, it will not long be the new economy. It will quickly become the only economy.

We are clearly headed toward a fully integrated Internet-based economy, but in the meantime, there are some business distinctions between companies that launch and live on the Internet versus the traditional companies that are struggling to learn how to become effective with electronic connectivity. These distinctions are as much cultural as they are technical. Terms like *dot-com* and *Net play* are still useful just to show the difference in approach between those companies that live through e-commerce and those businesses working to incorporate e-commerce into a system run by managers who are accustomed to doing business in more traditional ways.

A dot-com is a company that is created for the Internet and launched on the Internet. A Net play is a common term for the Internet component or division within an offline business. These terms are arbitrary and often misleading. As Internet trade expands, online companies are developing considerable offline activities in service, warehousing, and fulfillment. Likewise, traditional brick-and-mortar companies are quickly expanding their Net sales and service. As Internet usage proliferates over the next few years, the distinction between a dot-com and an offline company's Net activities will become meaningless.

So far, though, there is still a great cultural difference between companies born on the Net and the Net strategies of traditional companies. This cultural difference is profound in business-to-consumer companies as well as business-to-business enterprises. During the late 1990s, this difference was striking, as dot-coms carried the attitude that their offline counterpoints just didn't "get it" when it came to Internet business. Early online ventures were hip, savvy, smart, and smug. The offline world was more or less bewildered.

Quick-to-Change Is Paramount

The biggest difference underlying all this attitude was the dot-com's ability to innovate and change. Early online companies were designed and managed from the assumption that the company's services and products would change continually. This is true of companies as diverse as AOL, Yahoo!, and Amazon.com. Even as these companies grew and added armies of employees, innovation and change stayed at the top of the venture's priority list. Definitions such as retailer, entertainer, service provider, or news service blended as each company turned itself inside-out trying to find new ways to grab and hold customers.

Early on, AOL charged for Internet access by the hour. When the company faced competition from providers who offered monthly fees for unlimited access, the company switched its pricing structure overnight. This was no small move, as the switch at first meant a sudden shift from a profitable pricing structure to a questionable pricing structure. Yet the company also saw that without a switch it could quickly fall on the trash heap of service providers like Prodigy. What the heck, let's change. The new pricing structure was a smash hit, and AOL phone lines turned into constant busy signals as millions rushed to the new pricing structure.

When Amazon.com faced a competitive challenge from office book giant Barnes & Noble, it lowered its prices. This may have seemed a bold move from a company that was already bleeding by the bucketful, but the company knew its audience and also understood what was at stake on the Internet. As much as the customers may love Amazon.com's search engine and interactive book reviews, if a competitor offered a better price, the customer would search Amazon.com, then buy from the discounter. Amazon.com knew it had to be the best and the cheapest.

Amazon.com also understood what was at stake in its race to the dominant spot as leading Internet book retailer. The company understood that it couldn't let a competitor get close, especially one with the clout and resources of Barnes & Noble. If the offline giant came within 10 or 20 points, it could quickly catch up. Just catching up could give Barnes & Noble that leverage to ring the death knell for Amazon.com. So Amazon used its dot-com nimbleness to give its customers a great experience on the site, low prices and the best service on the Internet. The company also launched an affiliate program that changed the way Internet companies related to each other. Within a year, you could find Amazon's search engine on over 350,000 Web sites. The clunky Barnes & Noble couldn't keep up.

Change Is the Assumption

When facing competitive challenges, the Internet companies that succeed are those that can make sweeping changes overnight. As companies like AOL and Amazon.com alter their very pricing structure in the face of competition, there's a go-for-broke quality that can look reckless from the outside. Traditional companies test new pricing models in selected geographical territories or in isolated portions of their product lines before overhauling the entire company. Dot-coms don't have the heavy layers of management caution to stop them from bold moves. From the perspective of AOL and Amazon.com, I'm sure these moves seemed obvious and relatively safe. The assumption is that doing nothing in the face of competition is much more dangerous than a bold move.

To a dot-com, change is assumed. To a traditional company, change is disruptive. To a dot-com, change is exciting, stimulating. In a traditional company, change is threatening. In a dot-com, management discourages the formation of long-term political factions that can sabotage change. In a traditional company, change usually requires a huge effort to build the support of deeply entrenched factions. In order to gain this support, the intended change is often compromised or mitigated. The resulting change is frequently delayed or weakened. The early Net plays by traditional companies were usually half-hearted attempts to get "something up there." They were commonly directed by a small group of bright, young employees sequestered in the basement of the corporation. Even if the team received adequate funding, it likely had little clout within the company.

The young, bright kids are often the owners at dot-coms. They're entrepreneurial by instinct. They don't sit behind desks saying "nay-nay" to the wild suggestions coming from the trenches. Instead, they're trying to figure out how to encourage their trench staff to propose more solutions. The CEOs of dot-coms understand that their chance for success is entirely dependent on their ability to get their brand or their model established on the Internet before the large corporations wake up. Thinking outside the box is not just management seminar puff; it's a mandate that echoes throughout the company.

THE INTERNET COMPANY IS BORN

The first online companies go back to the early 1980s with Dialog Information Services and a legion of other document search-and-delivery companies including Lexis-Nexis and Find/SVP. Many of the early companies, such as the ones I mentioned, still exist, though most have been bought and sold a few times as the information stocks grew in respectability and financial value. The early service providers didn't fare as well. Does anyone remember Prodigy? VuText? eWorld? But as the online world became the Internet world, electronic commerce began to change. The biggest change that came with the World Wide Web was that librarians were no longer the intermediaries between information and the end user.

For most early Internet users, the fun began at work. Early Internet consumers were often researchers, engineers, and other technical or business workers who had access to the Internet during work hours and began to explore the Web at their desks. Before the proliferation of desktop computers, these information workers had to march down to the corporate library for their information requests. But when the search capability moved to the private desktop, the whole world began to change. For one thing, the financial services professional who started to use the Internet to track stocks also found out he could learn a lot about his number one passion, fly fishing, by going to fishing sites and chatting, usually by message board, with other enthusiasts.

A Playground for Enthusiasts

The Web as we know it was pushed forward by enthusiasts. Mostly men at first, they used the Internet at work and at home to learn more about their hobbies and to connect with other enthusiasts. This is the consumer core that supported the early Web sites based on collecting information on individual topics. These sites also offered their members the ability to connect with each other through e-mail, newsgroups, and chats. These sites were almost always free. Few carried advertising, and fewer had products for sale. Most were run by fellow enthusiasts who devoted their time to creating and maintaining a hub of special interest information.

Magazine companies were some of the first companies to develop special interest sites in earnest. Magazine publishers felt a real ownership over their special interest information. They rightfully felt threatened that their readers were going online to get fresh information and connect with other enthusiasts. I was a special interest publisher at the time the Internet started to attract consumers with a passion for a subject. I published *Chile Pepper,* a small magazine covering hot foods. The whole magazine industry began to experience the creepy feeling that its readers were getting together and sharing information all by themselves. Up until those days in the early 1990s, magazines were very accustomed to their position at the very center of their subject areas. Then the center began to shift.

The Web Site as Magazine

Thousands of magazines simultaneously looked at the Internet and thought, "Hey, this is a no-brainer. We'll simply put our information online and sell advertising around it." Magazines certainly looked like the companies that were best poised to take advantage of the Internet. They were already in the business of gathering information of their subject. Their editors were the subject's experts. They knew all of the players in their subject, and they also knew all the advertisers in their given market. On first glance, the Internet looked like it would accommodate the magazine model of delivering information to attract enough readers to build an audience for advertisers.

It was roundly a disaster. Looking back, we can see that magazine publishers made every mistake in the book during their efforts to take their rightful place at the center of their subject in the new technology. Yet all the mistakes they made were perfectly logical moves at the time. Take your editorial and put it up on the Web. Go to your advertisers and sell them some banner ads. Let your readers know how to get to your Web site. Sell subscriptions online to those who do not already subscribe to your print publication. Do some specialized research and sell it online to your most devout readers. Hire a webmaster to run the Web site and provide an empty office back by the mail room.

The concept seemed natural. The magazine company owned the best information on its subject. The magazine company hired the best graphic artists in the subject, and those artists were already computer literate. The magazine also had the credible brand in the market. *Condé Nast* could have beat Travelocity to the travel consumers. *Rolling Stone* certainly had an opportunity to be the source of both CD purchases online as well as music downloads. Almost any trade magazine knows its given industry better than the new e-marketplaces that are setting up shop at the center of individual industries. The problem isn't with the magazine's position in an industry or subject area. The problem lies with how the magazine company sees itself.

THE MAGAZINE MODEL ONLINE

If ever an industry didn't "get it," it was the magazine industry during the early days of consumer growth on the Internet. Their print advertisers were reluctant to pay for the unknown qualities of banner advertising. Plus, their ad sales reps didn't like the new medium. In these early stages, magazine were not about to hire new reps to sell the banner ads, since it would cause confusion to have two sets of sales reps call on the same customers. Most magazines decided to give away banner advertising to print advertisers as a value-added benefit. This move, of course, eroded any value the banners might have had in the eyes of the print advertising market.

The Web sites themselves also posed a problem for magazine publishers. Because print publishers were accustomed to biweekly, monthly, or every bimonthly print schedules, the sites would often go without updates between issues. Publishers also worried about losing subscribers to a free Web site that contained the magazine's editorial, so most magazines posted only portions of each publication's content. Magazine sites generally contained weak content that was updated infrequently by Net standards. For the sites, this meant poor traffic and weak click-throughs on the banner advertising. The result was widespread losses throughout the magazine industry.

A New Model Emerges

The missed opportunities were so abundant, that *Condé Nast* bragged when it reached breakeven with its food-content Web site, Epicurious. The *Condé Nast* site broke with the losing pattern of magazine sites. For one, the site didn't carry either of the strong brand names the publisher owned in print, *Bon Appetit* and *Gourmet*. Epicurious was not designed to attract magazine readers. It was created with the Net visitor in mind. The company gave the site its own editorial and creative staff and placed them outside the magazine offices. The editorial was aimed at Internet users, and a full 95 percent of it was original. Visitors were able to order *Bon Appetit* and *Gourmet* at the site, but the tie between the site and the magazine was not heavily promoted.

The core attraction of the site was its searchable file of two million recipes. The site also posted extensive cooking and entertaining instruction, a territory that is not prevalent in either of the print publications. The site was also updated with recipes and new information on a daily basis. As a result of these efforts to create an Internet-based experience, Epicurious became the leading food Web site for unique visits each month. Since the company had a new brand on its hands, it quickly took the Epicurious brand and created an offline weekly television program. The traffic allowed Epicurious to sell enough advertising to pull out of the red. The profits didn't come until the site's next move.

In 1998, Epicurious signed a deal to sell Williams-Sonoma kitchen products on the site. Since Epicurious was already at breakeven, the products' sales led the site into the black. A magazine company had finally figured out a model that worked online. Yet the model is not one that fits easily into the heart of a magazine company. It's one thing to sell advertising. It's quite another to team up with your advertisers and sell products. Given the weakness and difficulties of banner sales, most magazines have not bothered to develop successful Net strategies. Instead they use their Web sites as brochures, showing off a limited amount of free content.

Some Net companies have experimented with creating a magazine online in the belief that if a magazine was created online specifically for the Net visitor, it could attract enough traffic to make banner ad sales profitable. Microsoft launched *Slate* hoping to sell subscriptions and advertising. The company hired a respected and well-known editor, Michael Kinsley, to lead the launch. Subscription sales were weak, so the company quickly switched to free access to build traffic. The jury is still out on whether this business model will be profitable.

Another Web-based magazine launch, *Salon,* is attempting to create a model similar to *Slate. Salon* at this writing is struggling with red ink in spite of strong visitor traffic, excellent editorial content, and a strong reputation. The only companies that seem to be able make a profit by selling advertising to those who come to read are news services. A number of business information services are creating profits by posting breaking news on stocks, Internet business, and e-commerce. These operations have limited editorial staffs that produce little more than a stream of breaking stories. They obtain traffic by affiliating with Internet service providers.

THE CATALOG MODEL ONLINE

Internet consumers go to Web sites for their content and once there, they are willing to buy products or services. To a small extent, they are willing to view advertising or click through to an advertiser's site. They are rarely willing to pay for content. The deep resistance to paying for content online may have come from the fact that the Internet began as an information network for librarians and researchers. Perhaps the reluctance developed because free information is so plentiful. The only content that consumers are willing to buy is specialized financial information and pornography. The first movements in e-commerce came not from the purchase of content, but from the sale of products and services.

As consumers began to buy online is small numbers, it became clear they were comfortable buying many of the same products they often purchased through catalogs and other direct sales vehicles. This included books, videos, CDs, and specialty products related to the special interests that attracted Internet buyers. Catalog companies soon found they were actually better structured than magazines to take advantage of consumer e-commerce, even though they were not in the information business. Aside from the ability to produce content, consumer catalog companies had all the other attributes that supported a successful Net venture:

- A direct marketer's ability to segment the market. Catalog companies are accustomed to think of customers in terms of demographic and psychographic groups. This give catalogs an edge in finding the right online communities to market to.

- Marketing and merchandising techniques that encourage repeat purchases. Catalog companies know how to create product lines that encourage repeat purchases. They also have a deep understanding of how to get the optimum repeat business from their existing customers.

- A fulfillment operation that can quickly move from order to shipment. Many Internet companies fell apart on fulfillment. Some failed because they were new to fulfillment. Others had trouble finding fulfillment vendors that could turn around delivery at speeds that satisfied Internet customers.

- The service structure to respond rapidly to a wide range of customer requests. This is another area of great trouble for dot-coms. Catalog companies have well-developed service support systems that can solve customers's problems and use the service arm as a source of information to improve all areas of the operation.

What About Content?

The one area of weakness for catalog companies is content. Some catalog companies didn't have to correct this deficiency when they launched online because their brands were strong enough to attract buyers even without building a content-based site. Companies such as Lands' End, J. Crew, and L.L. Bean didn't need to add content in order to attract Web visits. It did, however, take these companies some time to create Web sites that offered customers more than an alternative to calling an 800 number. Most of these catalogs launched with nothing more than Web presentations of their catalog pages.

In time, Lands' End, J. Crew, and L.L. Bean began to tailor their Web sites to the needs and preferences of Internet shoppers, which meant a larger selection, preloaded purchase information for past customers, e-mail notices of sales and closeouts, and e-mail alerts to upcoming anniversaries and birthdays to customers who have given gifts in the past. When catalog companies shifted from posted catalog pages to developing Web sites with a wide range of choices and interactivity, they began to gain customers from the Internet venture itself. Previously, they were attracting mostly their own catalog buyers.

Williams-Sonoma solved its lack of content by partnering with *Condé Nast*'s Epicurious food-based Web site. *Reader's Digest* leveraged the partnership advantages of magazines and catalogs by acquiring a catalog company, The Good Catalog, then adding components to the catalog to fill in product sectors to fit the needs of its readership and Web visitor audience. The magazine and catalog partnership needs to be augmented with interactive Web techniques such as personalized e-mail communication to customers. A wide selection and constant updates in products and information also need to be added to the site to attract Net visitors and turn those visitors into repeat customers. These Web-oriented features are not difficult to add to a magazine and catalog partnership, because the content, product line, and service structures are already in place.

THE BRILLIANT CHRISTMAS OF '98

In mid-1998, the *Wall Street Journal* called the Internet an "economic pipsqueak." Web site owners may have been disappointed by the smug dismissal of an emerging new market, but the comment was not unwarranted. At the time, online sales were barely 1 percent of consumer sales. There was serious doubt about whether consumers would overcome their natural reluctance to type a credit card number onto their computer screen, then click it across the country. They were certainly not afraid to read it over the phone to a complete stranger at a catalog call center. Nor were they worried about handing it to a waiter, who took it around the corner to the card machine and had it long enough to make a copy of the number and expiration date. Still, something about the Internet made consumers nervous.

That all changed during the Christmas season of 1998. That season was the first time Net consumers spent in large numbers. Some analysts believe that consumers were so far behind in their shopping that the fear of credit card theft was overruled by the fear of not buying a present on time. Whatever the reason, Forrester Research reported holiday consumer e-commerce soared 230 percent over 1997, reaching almost $5 billion for the 1998 season. These sales encompassed a wide range of consumer goods, including consumer electronics, books, CDs, videos, toys, and apparel.

The Net Goes Mainstream

The Christmas season of 1998 marked the beginning of the mainstreaming of the Internet. Suddenly companies like Toys 'R' Us, Wal-Mart, and Kmart began to realize they needed a stronger presence online. The Internet was no longer just for geeks, porn mongers, and stock traders. All of the data coming in from the '98 Christmas season indicated that middle-class Americans were logging on and shopping. They were reporting that they enjoyed the Internet shopping experience. Forrester's research also indicated that consumers did not view the Web as just a novelty. More than 60 percent of online buyers planned to buy again during the coming year.

Another surprise of the 1998 Christmas season was the shift in the Internet's consumer demographic. Previously, Net consumers mostly consisted of highly educated men who were very comfortable with technology. Beginning with the holiday season of '98, the percentage of women Internet buyers started catching up with men. By mid-1999, the number of women consumers would reach 50 percent. For e-tailers this was particularly good news, since women are stronger consumers than men. Women buy or influence the buying decision on over 70 percent of the purchases of consumer goods. If the Internet had a chance to become a strong consumer market, women would have to come out in big numbers. Christmas '98 gave indications that women were ready for the Net.

If you can find one moment when it sank in that the Internet was going to change the landscape of consumer purchasing, it's the holiday buying season of 1998. You can watch the flurry of dot-com launches and Net plays by brick-and-mortar retailers during 1999 and trace it back to Christmas '98. By mid-1999, more than half of all venture capital in the United States was pouring into new Internet companies, selling everything from wine to couches. It set up a big year for Nasdaq as well as a big year in partnerships between dot-coms and brick companies. The holiday season of 1998 set off an unparalleled scramble to the Net.

With all the excitement, one little statistic received very little play. The $5 billion in Christmas shopping during November and December of 1998 added up to less than 2 percent of overall U.S. consumer spending for the season. Internet purchases totaled up to less than the consumer growth for 1998's holiday spending, which came in around 3 percent. Another story that was underplayed during the excitement of consumer Internet spending was that most of the dot-coms that were receiving the holiday orders were losing money in the process. Even if the losses were mentioned, they were not given much attention. A widespread belief at the time was that once an Internet company established itself in a consumer sector, it could dominate that sector and become an international brand. Who cares if eToys is losing money? It's beating Toys 'R' Us on the Net. That thinking would change by the end of 1999.

DOT-COMS CHANGE LIKE QUICKSILVER

One of the most striking qualities of an Internet company is its ability to change rapidly. Prior to the 1998 Christmas consumer surge, most dot-coms were very experimental. Different companies experimented with new models for doing business, from eBay's consumer auction play to 1-800-FLOWERS.com service of sending e-mail reminders of your mom's birthday, to Music Blvd.'s ability to let you create your own e-mail flow of music information on your favorite artists or genre of music. Most of these twists on consumer services went unnoticed by the business world at large, though other dot-com companies paid attention to each other's experiments if they happened to look up from their own frantic experimentation.

By 1999, these little marketing and shopping tricks began to gain some attention. Dot-coms began to develop connectivity configurations in earnest, sending off for patents as quickly as they attempted a new pricing or purchasing scheme. Tricks that were as basic as Priceline.com's reverse auction or Amazon.com one-click purchase technology were granted patents and those patents were upheld in copyright violation lawsuits. All of a sudden, the smallest new Internet trick became worthy of a patent application. Within days of a company using a new trick to attract visitors or encourage shoppers to return, all of its competitors would also begin using the tactic. Sales techniques such as free shipping or cash drawings for site registrants would spread through the Internet like wildfire.

Keeping Up with the Buzz

Whole marketing concepts spread across the e-tailing community at bewildering speed. One day you would hear the word *sticky* (the use of Web site techniques to encourage visitors to stick around). The next day it was part of everyone's conversation. Two days later the term was so common people no longer bothered to explain its meaning. Other words would appear; e.g., *viral* (a site's ability to encourage its visitors to spread the news to their friends), and *one-to-one* (marketing techniques utilizing personalization). It didn't matter if you were in San Jose or Little Rock, the entire Internet business community was speaking the same new language.

The fun part of this rush to new business models is that the feedback from consumers is instantaneous. The intense connectivity with customers works to encourage further experimentation. Teams of Internet entrepreneurs would sequester themselves for a three-day weekend just to try to come up with a new business concept. If they found a good idea, within a few weeks their prototype was up and they were meeting with major venture capitalists. The three friends who launched Accompany.com came up with their idea of collecting handfuls of buyers to purchase quantities of products such as Palm Pilots at low prices during one such weekend. Kris Hagerman walked the beaches near Mountain View, California, racking his brains for a business idea, when the concept that became Affinia.com popped up. Affinia.com gives away free Web storefronts stocked with goods from Affinia.com's collection of 2,000 vendors.

Goofy Ideas Proliferate

Concepts came so fast, it was hard to tell the good from the bad. As an April Fool's joke in 2000, *Esquire* magazine ran a spoof on an Internet-based business idea called FreeWheelz.com. The imaginary Net company was giving away cars that were completely covered with advertising inside and out. When the writer shared his spoof with some venture capitalists who were over at his home for dinner, two of them mentioned they had recently seen similar proposals. When the article ran in the magazine, *Esquire* was inundated with calls from people who wanted a free car. They set up a spoof Web site and received 5,000 hits per day. One entrepreneur called in saying he was about to launch a similar concept. He was surprised and distressed that FreeWheelz.com had beaten him to the Net.

In an environment where hundreds of wild ideas were getting funded with good chunks of capital, new ideas were swirling. Even existing dot-coms were frantically wrapping themselves in new concepts. Everything was possible on the consumer scene during 1999. Why shouldn't Amazon.com sell housewares and toys? Why shouldn't AOL create an army of storefronts? Why shouldn't Priceline.com let its customers bid on groceries? As long as the investment dollars were flowing and nobody was watching the bottom line, why not reinvent your company fast as quicksilver?

THE DAY OF THE NET PLAY

As the dot-coms began exploding online, the brick-and-mortar retailers started to get nervous. For the most part, the dot-coms were taking only a very small piece of the American retail pie. And most dot-coms were far from profitable. Yet in some sectors the slices were growing. By the end of 1999, Amazon.com became the leading bookseller offline or online. Another surprise from Amazon.com came with the company's 1999 fourth quarter returns. Though famous for its bleeding ink, the company showed a profit in its book sales. The traditional retailers responded by launching plays against the dot-coms.

The Net plays by traditional companies met with mixed results. The Internet troubles of Toys 'R' Us became legendary. The company teamed up with Benchmark Capital, a leading venture capital firm, to launch a Web site that could put eToys in its place. The result was a grand disaster. Six months out from Christmas in the summer of 1999, Toys 'R' Us pulled out of the deal. The site was expected to be a complete disaster going into 1999's holiday season. With the Net play in pieces, Toys 'R' Us was getting disparaging press from all sides. Even its strong offline chain business was in question. Yet when holiday 1999 rolled in, it began to look like the revenge of the bricks. Though the site received criticism among the Net savvy, consumers flocked to it in great numbers.

Battle of the Toy Titans

For all the fumbles along the way, the Toys 'R' Us site gave eToys a neck-to-neck race all through the gift-giving season. The race became one of the great lessons of Internet retailing. You can't count out the strength of an offline brand. If Christmas '98 brought a surprise showing by Internet companies, 1999 displayed the inherent strength of branding. In addition to the strong showing of Toys 'R' Us, J.C. Penney's site came in strong, as did Barnes & Noble, which came in third behind Amazon's first place showing for total sales during the season. The Net plays by offline companies were tagged brick-and-clicks.

Consumers indicated that trust was one of the reasons they chose the brick-and-clicks. Another factor was confidence in the exchange and return ease of Web sites that have stores throughout the country. Other studies showed that a good portion of Net surfers made their shopping decisions online, then took the gift list to the mall. The brick-and-clicks in the apparel industry did particularly well during the holiday season. Analysts attributed this to the discomfort consumers had with the idea of buying clothes from an unknown online retailer. Size variations were also a factor. Consumers know their Gap sizes, but were not so sure the clothing from the dot-coms was going to fit, and neither were they sure exchanges would work easily.

To Brick or to Click?

Even though many of the Net plays by bricks-and-clicks were successful in selling goods over the Internet, these operations were not so easy for the companies internally. Wal-Mart found they could attract customers on the Internet because of the powerful brand, but the discounter also found great difficulty in building an Internet division that could be managed effectively from the company's headquarters in Arkansas. For one thing, Wal-Mart wasn't able to attract the talent required for the type of site worthy of the world's largest retailer. In mid-1999, Wal-Mart gave it up and launched a Wal-Mart.com in Silicon Valley, where experienced Net players were plentiful and the company could grow outside the shadow of its huge brick parent. Industry watchers still contend the site is a dud, but the concept of launching a Net play in outside offices became a widely used alternative to the conflicts between Net staff and the company's existing management.

Other solutions to the difficulty of creating a credible Internet division within a traditional company included the formation of dot-corps. Like the Wal-Mart solution, this often included the formation of a new entity with its own strategy, its own budget, and its own marketing goals. This independent dot-corps would also often have a Web-savvy partner. Some corporations found this solution threatening to the management of the parent, since divided marketing strategies could quickly put the brick and the click components of a corporation in competition with each other. So far, no widespread model had evolved to solve the conflicts between the old and new worlds.

BRICKS BEGIN TO LEARN

Even if there are unanswered questions about how a traditional retailer reconciles itself to its Web site launch, one thing has become apparent—brick retailers are beginning to "get it" about selling over the Internet. Online retail sales may be a small portion of overall consumer spending, but traditional companies don't intend to be left behind. The prevailing attitude is summed up in the question, "Why should we give up any of our marketshare to dot-coms?" The great variety of Internet start-ups may be impressive, but equally impressive is the wide variety of traditional companies finding ways to use the Internet to enter new markets and connect with existing customers. The first rush of bricks to the Web were those who were acting defensively to ward off dot-com competition. Soon after that flurry of defensive moves, a wide array of traditional companies started to use the Internet in more interesting ways.

Albertson's grocery chain launched a grocery shopping service close to the same time WebVan began its Internet grocery service. The airline industry has banded together to give online travel services a run for their money. As the airline industry watches sites like Travelocity and Expedia, they begin to wonder why they should allow a switch from one intermediary to another. In 1999, 2,000 travel agencies went out of business as the online travel sites surged. The airlines are attempting to go straight to the consumers. Industry watchers question whether the combined site created by the major airlines will be successful. But almost as interesting is the airlines's indifference to their intermediaries, which include both the traditional travel agents and the online travel services. The airline industry is one of the few sectors that is showing indifference to its middlemen.

The Old Car Dog Learns New Tricks

The auto industry has been surprisingly agile in its Internet activities. Ford partnered with Yahoo! to provide online services to its vehicle owners. At the same time, GM struck a deal with America Online to create an auto channel for car shopping. These moves come after both companies have worked hard to push their procurement online. Even before Ford and GM partnered with Daimler-Chrysler to create Covisint, both auto makers dragged their vendors and suppliers online to take advantage of the efficiencies of Internet procurement.

Notably, the auto makers have been very careful not to burn bridges with their intermediaries, the auto dealers. As Ford and GM take steps toward online car shopping, they have been very clear about including dealers in the process. Consumers have long been understandably frustrated with the traditional process for buying new cars. The high-pressure negotiation tactics are particularly unpleasant for women. Internet car shopping sites are the consumer's revenge on unpleasant car salespeople. Yet Ford and GM make sure the cars are picked up at the dealer and the dealer is still in on the service contract. When Ford teamed up with Yahoo! and GM made its deal with AOL, both companies put their local dealers at the center of the online sales effort.

Another offline business surprise on the Internet is that local companies are using the Net to interact with their customers. You can now use AOL to buy tickets to General Cinema theaters. You can click onto Dominos.com and peruse the menu after searching for the closest outlet. You can go online to find a handful of local remodelers and request bids for a kitchen remodel. You can go to Autos.com and shop for a used car locally. In order to emphasize the widespread availability of products and services online, both nationally and locally, a number of people have sequestered themselves inside and filled all of their needs through e-commerce.

Living the Cyber-Life

The latest of these is DotComGuy, a young man formerly known as Mitch Maddox. Maddox legally changed his name to DotComGuy on January 1 of 2000 and began a year in cyberspace. DotComGuy walked into an empty house in Dallas that New Year's Day armed only with a telephone. Cameras were placed throughout the home so viewers could go to dotcomguy.com and watch DotComGuy buy himself a life over the Internet. In press coverage of the stunt, no reporter has questioned whether there were some needed items that are unavailable over the Internet. It is clear to everyone now that a life in cyberspace may be tedious, but it certainly wouldn't involve deprivation.

THE VIRTUAL WORLD NEEDS REAL-WORLD ROOTS

The advantages of a brick-and-click are clear enough that many dot-coms are creating stronger brick components. Both bricks and clicks clearly see they need to add components of each other's strengths to their own business structure. Offline companies see the Net's advantages of connectivity, community, and one-to-one interaction with a large number of customers. Dot-coms have come to respect the need for a substantial service component in their businesses. Amazon.com justifies its years of red ink as the price it must pay to make sure its service backbone is strong enough to hold its customer base in place.

If dot-coms have an Achilles's heel, it's offline service and support. Forrester Research reports that 90 percent of online shoppers consider good customer service to be critical when they choose a Web merchant. Service is particularly important to online shoppers because it is only a touch away, so it is heavily used. Forty two percent of online shoppers use a Web site's service more than they would an offline store's service because it is easier to use than the service department within a brick store. Internet buyers also use service more online because they can do it from home and because they consider online shopping more difficult than offline purchasing.

Don't Forget the Customer

Although Web sites commonly provide sections of frequently asked questions (FAQs) to address the most obvious service needs, customers want a real-world response vehicle available while they're shopping online. E-mail and telephone are the preferred forms of support for shoppers. To a dot-com, this means real world facilities in the form of call centers. Consumers report that if they had to choose one channel for service, 46 percent would choose e-mail, while another 41 percent indicated a preference for telephone service.

The cost of obtaining an Internet customer can run as high as $60. With this expensive customer acquisition cost, loyalty programs become critical to an online retailer's success. Forrester reports that over 90 percent of satisfied consumers are likely to visit a site again, while only 9 percent of unsatisfied customers will come back. The first rule of satisfying online service is providing a well-staffed service center. Lands' End and L.L. Bean have both invested heavily in making sure their online customers receive quick responses to both e-mail and telephone questions. In addition to a quick response, other factors that affect consumer satisfaction are a simple return process and easy order tracking.

The Gift-Giver Nightmare

The single biggest mistake a retailer can make is getting a gift order fouled up. Consumers find it personally distressing when they discover a gift failed to arrive on time, or failed to arrive at all. Toys 'R' Us made some aggressive delivery claims on its Web site late in the Christmas season in 1999. When the fulfillment system failed to meet the promises, the company received a flood of well-publicized ire from frustrated Internet consumers. One disgruntled gift-giver brought a class-action suit against the company for failing to meet its promises.

A strong, predictable fulfillment operation is critical to an online merchant's success. Many merchants have used drop-shipping, which involves paying the manufacturer to ship products directly to customers. The drop-shipping system saves the merchant the trouble of creating a warehouse and shipping operation, but it takes control away from the merchant. If there are problems with the merchandise or a mistake in fulfillment, the merchant has to resolve the problem through the manufacturer. With the drop-shipping system, the merchant has no consistent control over turnaround times on fulfillment and shipping.

Figure Out Who's in Charge

One popular solution is to use the services of a third-party fulfillment service. A merchant can negotiate turnaround targets with the service to bring fulfillment into a consistent territory. For small merchants who can't afford to set up their own backend operation, the service vendor may be the best resort to avoid the inconsistencies of drop-shipping. Major retailers such as Amazon.com see no alternative to creating a large warehouse and fulfillment operation.

Because repeat visits are essential to making an online retailer profitable, control over the back end ensures that repeat visits are not lost due to factors out of the retailer's control.

This means a successful Internet retail operation requires deep backend roots. Online merchants need to compensate for the fact they don't have a brick store with a stockroom by creating a responsive call and e-mail center and a fulfillment operation that can deliver orders accurately with a fast turnaround. As venture capitalists scour the plains for new Net enterprises, the strategy for creating a very real world back end and service support operation has become as important as the dazzling frontend marketing tactics.

EVERYONE BECOMES A NET COMPANY

Within the next few years the distinctions between Internet companies and traditional companies will blur. This process has already started. Even companies with no Web-based marketing and sales effort are moving their procurement activities online. There is a chunk of savings companies can take by purchasing online. E-commerce is producing efficiencies that can't be ignored by any company. The Internet is also becoming increasingly easy to use, which make the business move to e-commerce that much more assured. No matter what business you are in, your clients and customers expect you to have the interconnectivity of the Internet.

Consumers are also coming to expect the businesses they buy from to have an Internet component, even if it's a local company. Consumers have become very Net savvy. If they go to a merchant's site and find an unsophisticated system for service and shopping, it reflects poorly on the company. It doesn't matter any more whether the company is an Internet-based company or a traditional company. Consumers are losing patience with companies that haven't moved into the new economy. Over a few quick years, the business world has shifted so dramatically that any company that has not struggled to remake its operation is beginning to appear hopelessly archaic.

Webifying Traditional Companies

Just as an out-of-date tie can make a new suit look like it belongs on a Goodwill rack, a company with a static brochure-style Web site can appear out of touch. Both business and retail consumers seek quality. One major aspect of quality is technological proficiency. It doesn't matter if you're not a dot-com. Your Net presence needs to match or exceed your competition's Net presence, whether your competitors are based online or offline. The distinctions between dot-coms and traditional companies have blurred to the point that it may not matter whether you're competing with online or offline companies, since all companies now have Net components. In this new business world, you need to make sure your customers notice that you have both feet all the way in the new world.

YOUR NET STRATEGY:

The company of the future will be a blend of the innovative strengths of dot-coms and the hard-rooted, brand-centric world of traditional companies. If you're a dot-com, you need to go back to that business school you dropped out of and get your MBA. If you're a traditional company, you need to take off your tie and encourage innovation. The innovation, however, needs to be tied to improving the basic functions of a successful business. The Internet doesn't defy gravity. Its speed, community and connectivity do not enhance a business unless online functions are integrated with sound business methods and practices.

Consider this: it's easier to teach the brick company how to dance a jig than it is to teach the dot-com how to build a house. Or, it's easier to take off your tie than it is to set up a rock-solid accounting department. Through the early years of the Internet, traditional companies were thrown off their game. Their response to dot-coms was either confusion or denial. Dot-coms entered traditional markets with verve and arrogance, stating that they owned the future while smugly insisting that bricks just don't get it. The

Net companies owned the first peek at a new world, but the sight of a new world alone doesn't provide you with sound business skills and the understanding of how markets work.

Traditional Companies Need to Partner and Change

As bricks regain their confidence, they are naturally beginning to take the lead within their industries. The dot-coms will have to struggle to keep up. Many will forge partnerships with brick companies. Marketplace-maker, Ventro, succeeded in this strategy, bringing in domain partners as it entered each industry—DuPont here, American Express there. These partnerships helped Ventro deliver a highly-functioning business at great speed. The brick companies delivered a massive customer base, while Ventro brought its experience in running an Internet company. Without Ventro, DuPont and American Express might have spent years developing the appropriate technology to build a smoothly operating online marketplace. Without DuPont and American Express, Ventro might not have been able to sustain a business.

An additional difficulty for traditional companies will be to encourage a change in behavior to that necessary to integrate e-commerce effectively. When an existing company adopts Internet methods, whether in sales, procurement, or in-between, it means people within the organization have to do something differently than they've been doing it for 10, 20, or even 30 years. No matter how obvious the benefit, getting people to change is a slow and difficult process. Companies around the world are finding they need to change at a quicker pace than in the past.

They are also finding that the clear need to change doesn't bring about change. Effective change requires management strategies that reward changed behavior without instilling fear. There is a generation of middle-management workers who are still smarting from downsizing, and they see change as a threat to their jobs. One of the biggest challenges for traditional companies will be to get these people to do their jobs differently without triggering a natural defensiveness and resistance that is part of the culture of post-downsized corporations.

Identifying and encouraging change leaders within each level of the organization is the practical way to move a traditional company into the Internet world. It may be the only way to bring about widespread change. A CEO screaming, "Change, change, change," from the top has only limited effectiveness. The change-leader process, though, is slow. Some say it takes five years. If that's what it takes, you might as well get on with it.

So if you're a brick, already up and running as a business, you have the option of entering the Internet market by finding the right dot-com for partnership. You also have the option of hiring technical support and building your own. Your most difficult job will probably be managing change within your organization. Or more correctly, managing the resistance to change. If you're a dot-com, your options are probably more limited. You will need to build a business around your Net expertise. You can do a good portion of this by allying with a brick company that is already established in a market and has a functioning and stable business base.

CHAPTER 3

E-COMMERCE

Electronic information processing took an abrupt and dramatic shift in the late 1990s. Commerce began to occur over the Internet. Companies had long been using electronic date interchange (EDI) to pass financial and contract documents back and forth, but e-commerce was something new. All EDI did was allow a customer and vendor to share documents in electronic form. E-commerce allows consumers and companies alike to meet new vendors, reach new customers, share project or product information, negotiate prices, determine logistics, and follow up on orders without driving to a store or picking up the phone.

Each one of these aspects of business, whether it's sourcing a new supplier or passing a contract back and forth over the Internet, is a profound change in business behavior. There are huge efficiencies to be taken when you automate any of these processes. In the past, these business tasks were done over the phone, by mail, and in person. Suddenly a process that used to take weeks can get done in hours, whether it is contract negotiation, searching for overseas vendors, or designing an engine part for a Ford Explorer. It is hard to imagine a business process, from inventory control to shipping, that will not be affected by e-commerce.

This may sound simple, and conceptually it is not particularly complex, but it will turn business worldwide completely on its head. We have barely started the process of automating our traditional commercial interactions, and already the change has started to shift fortunes. Right now there is a tremendous emphasis on speed. That anxiety will begin to diminish as we get used to the idea that business change is widespread and unstoppable. Then we'll get a head for the evolution of e-commerce, and we'll begin to pick and choose our adoption in a less desperate manner than we saw at the end of the last century.

The World before E-transactions

There was a time when the Internet was not about commerce. For years, the online universe was a world of information services. Document search and retrieval were the primary functions online. Users paid for access and they often paid for documents, but they didn't conduct financial transactions over the telephone lines. The early forms of e-commerce were little more than online catalog pages posted by offline catalog companies. Consumers could buy from a merchant by calling a 1-800 number or sending an e-mail with the credit card number. E-commerce as we know it is a very recent development.

E-commerce now takes on a wide range of transactions, including retail trade in books and CDs, insurance policies, online banking, gaming, entertainment, automobiles, pornography, used toys, airline tickets, pharmaceutical drugs, even a jet. The business-to-business side of e-commerce started gaining speed in 1998 and quickly outgrew retail e-commerce by tenfold—electric energy, industrial chemicals, heavy equipment maintenance and repair, medical research, even grapes and corks for wineries. The connectivity of the Internet gives consumers and businesses an astonishing number of choices in goods and services.

It's about Convenience, Price, and Choice

Consumers turn to the Internet to make purchases for a variety of reasons, and there are some overriding advantages to online buying that ensure e-commerce is here to stay. Repeated studies show that convenience is the most compelling reason consumers buy online. The secondary reason in most studies is price. The third reason is choice. The reasons stack up in a different order depending on the type of product. Price advantage is the number-one reason consumers go to Priceline.com. Convenience is why that the same consumer logs on to Preview Travel for airline tickets. Fear of embarrassment is assumed to be the prevailing reason so many men go to pharmaceutical sites for Viagra. MotherNature.com receives its traffic for vitamins because of wide choices and detailed information. Wide selection and expert information drives hot sauce lovers to MoHotta.com.

The prevailing reason a consumer types in a credit card number changes from site to site, product to product. If price was the only driving force behind Internet shopping, Web sites like MoHotta.com would never get off the ground. The owners of MoHotta.com knew their customers wanted a place they could find every hot sauce on the planet. These enthusiasts wanted a wide range of choices and plentiful information on the use of hot foods, from cooking with hot sauces to growing peppers. The entrepreneurs at MoHotta.com understood from day one that their customers were seeking a one-stop shop for an extensive line of products and expert information.

For other products, price remains the controlling factor. Amazon.com knows that it can't relax its aggressive discounting of books. The discounting keeps Barnesandnoble.com at bay, and it has helped to destroy most of the niche competition in books. Some analysts question Amazon.com's long-term prospects. If Amazon.com uses discounting to keep its edge as an e-commerce retail leader, will it ever be able to create and sustain profits? Amazon.com struggles to make superior service its competitive edge, but the site may never fully emerge from under the weight of price competition, because book buyers will quickly give up superior service for adequate service if they can get a better deal at another site. After all, book buyers don't visit Amazon.com for the latté.

B2B Will Slowly Swallow the World

The B2B story is completely different. In 1998, B2B e-commerce hit $43 billion. That same year, retail online trade reached $8 billion. Yet retail e-commerce received most of the press because it was far more visible than B2B's trade in auto parts and industrial chemicals. In the early days, B2B e-commerce was conducted between large corporations and their regular vendors or suppliers. The big corporations moved their procurement online because it was far more efficient than the traditional purchasing process that included meetings, phone calls, and faxes.

Most of the early B2B e-commerce was stealthy. Consumers had little idea that the greatest benefit from this new Information Age might not be cheap stock trading or great buys from eBay. The most significant result of the Internet connectivity might be the simple efficiency of a corporation's Internet procurement. This efficiency can allow a corporation to pay higher wages in a tight job market without raising its cost of goods. It doesn't sound like much, but when you extend this efficiency across all industries, you find an economy that can expand beyond 3 percent per year without igniting inflation. This, of course, gives the online consumer more funds to buy online stocks.

It's about the Productivity

Federal Reserve Chief Alan Greenspan noted this increased productivity in 1999, commenting publicly that computers were finally delivering on their promise of productivity gains. He was right. It was because of computers. The sustained productivity gains derived from increased efficiencies in major corporations were delivering high economic growth without inflation. But it was specifically Internet transactions by these corporations that started putting dark black ink on the bottom of annual reports. And interestingly, it was not high-tech companies that were receiving the major benefits of B2B e-commerce. The smokestack industries had the largest inefficiencies in their awkward procurement systems, and thus they had the most to gain from Internet purchasing.

Even as investors drove profitless dot-coms into the valuation stratosphere on the Nasdaq, the stodgy old blue chips were quietly reaping serious financial benefits from Internet commerce. The crafty investors who read the analysts's reports on B2B e-commerce still missed much of the point. They invested in the companies that were taking the smokestacks into the digital age, while the smokestack industries themselves were remaking their companies into sleek, nimble, and efficient profit-generating machines.

E-marketplace builders benefited from the Internet stock boom even though most of them had yet to deliver black ink on the bottom line. The darlings of B2B have been the infrastructure providers such as Ariba, Commerce One, VerticalNet, and i2. Yet the big profit winners in early B2B e-commerce come with mundane names like Ford, GE, GM, Dow Chemical, and Boeing.

Retail E-commerce Will Be Limited

As for retail, the Internet players face a decline in the rate of expansion of consumers to the Net. Europe and the rest of the world may yet be rushing online in big numbers, but the prime U.S. market is mostly there. This means that Internet retailers cannot depend on the ever-growing online audience to push them into the volume purchasing they need to reach profitability. Nor can they depend on their existing customers to increase their online purchases year in and year out. If the market were to level out right now, most online retailers would fail. Their business models depend on significantly more growth in order to reach simple viability.

Even the most optimistic projections show that only 10 percent of the U.S. consumer dollar will go into retail e-commerce during the early years of the 21st century. Meanwhile, competition is forcing up customer acquisition costs at Web sites. Super Bowl ads are great for reaching the very center of the U.S. consumer market, but these ads certainly don't help the cost for acquiring new customers. Internet retailers have the additional challenge of getting their customers to return. Sites that sell CDs, for example, often spend up to $60 to gain a new customer. With CD sales returning less than $10 per unit, it takes an unrealistic number of repeat sales to justify the acquisition cost. The calculation looks dim even before you factor in discounts, sales, and the growing market for music downloads.

Retail Continues to Sort Out Its Models

The future of B2B e-commerce is ensured by the powerful procurement efficiencies available on the Internet. The future for consumer e-commerce is a mixed-up bag. CDs don't look promising. Books look okay. Flowers look okay. Travel looks great, but it is getting close to saturation. Brokerage looks good if the market stays strong. Auctions look good, but future growth is slowing. Outlet sites are coming on strong. Online banking, loans, and mortgages may have to wait a full generation (and they'll have to deal with the nasty problem of multiple loan applications giving credit reports a scare). Pharmaceutical drug sites look great (if the government goes easy on regulation).

Niche sites based on personal passions such as fly fishing, hot sauces, or wildflower seeds continue to look wonderful, even if they're modest in volume. There has never been any question over whether niche sites would succeed online. Retail e-commerce began life as a niche market. The question at the heart of retail e-commerce has always been about mainstream consumer viability. Though some mainstream sites such as Amazon.com, Priceline, and eBay have become household names, the basic questions about which business model works for mainstream Internet retailing remain unanswered.

Some big consumer companies, such as Disney, have decided to take a back seat and let others forge the model. Others, such as Wal-Mart and Kmart, are fishing around for a model, seemingly in the belief that when the model appears, they intend to be close at hand. Early online players Amazon.com and America Online are clearly working to create and control the model. But Amazon.com can't turn a profit, and America Online still gains its bread from access fees, which have a questionable future. Chances are, we're not seeing the successful model yet, and the future may belong to companies that are yet to form.

THE BOOM IN SLEAZE

Porn was the first truly successful model online, even though it lives outside the mainstream of Internet commerce. *Playboy* and

E-COMMERCE 45

Penthouse have been able to reach and sustain respectability in the financial community. Virtually all other pornography companies live outside the world of venture capitalists, Internet partnerships, and initial public offerings (IPOs) that characterize the business world of e-commerce. Yet in the early days of online commerce, porn dominated. In the mid-1990s, ignoring porn while talking about e-commerce was like a party of socialites failing to acknowledge the entrance of Groucho Marx and his frisky brothers. You can pretend they're not there, but they will still control the gathering like a force of nature. Like it or not, the sale of porn online was the first successful retail business model.

The success of porn made it difficult for legitimate Internet retailers during the early days. Ubiquitous porn caused millions of parents to recoil from the Internet in horror. The efforts to block children from the onslaught of porn promotions was often weak and ineffective. I remember standing over my 11-year-old son's shoulder as he participated in his first online chat. He was connected to America Online and Sega Dreamcast was the subject. Seemed safe, but I watched to make sure. Sure enough, the chat deteriorated into foul language and explicit sexual references. We departed quickly only to find that 15 minutes in the chat room resulted in a dozen explicit e-mail porn solicitations.

The Internet Provides a Brown Wrapper

Porn has reached considerable success on the Internet because its merchants can give the audience a new level or privacy. No brown-wrapped packages delivered to the home. No creepy XXX room at the local book or video store. No out-front parking at the all-XXX store. The porn lover has never experienced such complete anonymity. Porn exploded on the Internet almost from the beginning. Yet it remains an underground business, shunned by the legitimate business world.

For the mainstream business community, the presence of porn on the Internet threatens e-commerce. Yet rather than fighting porn directly, mainstream Internet retailers have tried to ignore it and outgrow it. Turning to the government to bring pressure down on porn has been out of the question for most online merchants and service providers. The prevailing belief is that when you invite the government in to help solve a problem, the government never goes away. To online companies, the idea of permanent government oversight is more frightening than the pesky and obnoxious porn industry.

Most observers believe the porn industry is inherently limited. They believe that because of the Internet privacy advantages, porn reached full saturation early. Full saturation early on gave the impression that the audience for porn is larger than it actually is. The early proliferation also created the illusion that porn would continue to grow, giving the Internet a long-term smutty feel. But porn on the Internet stayed true to its offline pattern. It has a limited audience, and once that audience is involved, growth levels off and simmers at a relatively constant level.

SCAMS AND SPAM

Like porn, Internet scams and e-mail spam gave the Internet a decidedly non-mainstream feel during its early days. The presence of this huckster element continues to plague e-commerce. Also like porn, the proliferation of scams and spam was disproportional to legitimate e-commerce in the beginning of online retailing. As e-commerce grows, this seamier side of online commerce begins to seem less overwhelming. It will never be gone altogether. As one e-mail marketing specialist noted, as long as there are people who will fall for scams, the swindlers will continue to run their phony come-ons.

Spam is essentially just unsolicited e-mail. It's the junk mail of Internet communication. Much of spamming is no different from sloppy direct mail. The old direct mail adage is that junk mail is simply a direct mail solicitation that went to the wrong name. Spam continues to proliferate because it is cheap; it doesn't take much of a response to encourage its use. Scams are something different. A scam is defined by some level of fraud. Some e-mail solicitations are outright illegal, while others live within the boundaries of legality even as they mislead their recipients into believing they will receive benefits that are not forthcoming. Business opportunities and stock offers are common scams on the Internet. Others involve charitable pitches, e-mail chain letters, and pyramid marketing schemes.

Too Much Junk E-mail

Direct mail has always suffered its share of illicit promotions and fraud packages. Yet the legitimate direct mail practitioners outnumber the sleaze factor, which keeps this medium of advertising effective for mainstream consumers. The Internet scams and e-mail spam look out of proportion with legitimate offers, but like direct mail, this is a temporary situation. A legitimate e-mail marketing industry is forming, and its practices are taking direct e-mail in a direction that is resulting in effective ways to communicate with consumers and business customers. Eventually, scams and spam will be appropriately relegated to the margins of e-mail communication.

In the meantime, it becomes a challenge to legitimate companies to explore ways to use the powerful and inexpensive e-mail medium to create marketing communications that are effective with consumers and business customers. Marketing companies are working vigorously to develop interactive e-mail communication tools that provide recipients with useful and welcome e-mails. Terms like *one-to-one*, *opt-in*, and *permission marketing* are defining strategies for communicating with consumers and businesses.

Marketing companies are developing these tools to look characteristically different from spam and scams. Because of this, the illicit solicitations are appearing more and more obvious. Spam can't follow along as legitimate e-mail communication grows more sophisticated, because legitimate efforts involve the recipient and usually require the recipient to choose, step-by-step, what type of communication they receive, whether it's a newsletter or alerts to promotions and sales.

Spam and scams are left to their screaming all-caps, looking like sore thumbs against the sophisticated interactive direct e-mails. They are annoying, but they are not likely to fool even the least seasoned Internet consumers. They won't go away completely any more than pyramid schemes have disappeared from direct mail, but as the months go by, this seamy side of Internet marketing will become a smaller and smaller percentage of online marketing communications.

THE WEB SITE EXPLOSION

Active e-commerce Web sites on the Internet now number in the millions. The great majority of these sites actually do very little e-commerce. Some are little more than private Web sites that have an affiliation link to Amazon.com. These sites may handle only a few transactions per year from the family and friends of the site owner. Still, there are thousands of legitimate, commercial sites actively engaged in e-commerce. Most of these are either niche sites or Web-based extensions of existing offline businesses. The plethora of sites has occurred as companies make it easy and inexpensive to create and sustain Web pages. Internet service providers offer their customers inexpensive ways to set up small Web stores and run their transactions through the server. Plus there are dozens of independent sites such as AOL and Yahoo! that offer inexpensive opportunities to create Web stores within a large mall of merchants.

Many Web merchants use a combination of locations, setting up an independent site and tying into services on the large malls with smaller portions of their sites. These independent site owners will often create their sites by using an off-the-shelf Web store package or by hiring a local Web design company or freelance designer to create the store. Over the course of a couple of years, a Web site may go through a number of incarnations with a variety of hosts and designers. At some points the site may be in-house, and at other times it mat be jobbed out. Web sites are almost always an evolutionary form of business.

Some Products Webify Better than Others

The success of Web sites varies wildly, but there are some patterns that are useful to note. For one, some product categories lend themselves better to Web stores than others. In a world of Amazon and CDNow, books and CDs are not strong product lines. Apparel is also a dicey prospect unless the business already has an established clientele willing to transfer offline shopping to the Internet. Services can also be difficult. A small travel agency, for instance, would have a very difficult time competing against the large sites like Travelocity or Expedia, no matter how loyal its audience. The larger sites can afford to offer customers better service. Not surprisingly, over 2,000 travel agencies failed in 1999 as the large travel sites grabbed larger and larger portions of the consumer travel pie.

The Web sites that have been the most successful are those that can afford major retail advertising, those that have an offline brand already established, and those that appeal to a very specialized group of consumers. Of the three, the model that stands the best chance for sustained profitability is the site that offers very specialized products and content. The model for mainstream sites such as Amazon.com, BlueLight (Kmart), or Wal-Mart is still up in the air. These sites may never reach the volume required to support the investment. Many niche sites, on the other hand, found profitability almost instantly on the Internet.

The Internet Loves Niches

A good example of a tough little niche site is PrairieFrontier.com. The site was launched by the owner of a company that sold wildflower and prairie grass seeds to local nurseries and landscapers in the Milwaukee, Wisconsin area. She became interested in the Internet and created a Web site to display some of the photos she had taken of her wildflowers. She hooked into a few search engines and was soon receiving traffic from enthusiasts who quizzed her on the availability of seeds. She mailed out catalogs on request and began receiving orders. She expanded her operation with a gift-card giveaway of her flower photos, which produced more inquiries and catalog requests.

She then turned to LinkExchange and LinkShare to gain more traffic through exchange affiliations. More traffic, more catalog requests, more orders. Then she added catalog pages to her Web site and a shopping cart program so her customers could order directly from the site instead of requesting a mail order catalog. This customer-convenience move increased her ratio of orders to traffic. Soon she was producing more sales online than she was with her offline business. Most recently, she forged a partnership with a gardening supply company to present her customers with a full line of gardening products and supplies.

This story has been repeated hundreds of times on the Internet. Enthusiasts and specialized audiences are willing to fight hard to find obscure sites that provide the products, services, and information about their interests. These niches can include fly fishing, Jamaican music, African drums, Beatles collectibles, or Civil War photography. The customers at these sites are very good at spreading the news of an excellent site to fellow enthusiasts, and they're very loyal, since they view the merchant as a fellow enthusiast. They are also very accepting of companies run as home mom-and-pop operations.

ONLINE BROKERAGE

Online brokerage was one of the first services to find an Internet consumer audience. Internet-based brokerage became so popular in 1998 and 1999, that by mid-1999 all of the older brokerage companies had succumbed to the need to offer it to their clients. The ability to buy, sell, and track stocks online has gained acceptance even with those who are not interested in the stocks of online companies. Generally it is the low cost-per-trade that makes online brokerage so popular. The other quality that encourages online trading is the wide accessibility of information on stocks and investments. Access to financial information on publicly traded companies at sites such as Hoover's is no longer the sole property of professional brokers.

A study by Zona Research shows that 75 percent of online traders are men in the age range of 25 to 54, which puts to rest the myth that the majority of those engaging in online brokerage are those within ten years of retirement. This indicates that the online trader is younger than the traditional individual investor. Another surprising result of the study showed that a full 24 percent of these traders earned less than $35,000 per year. This indicates that a good portion of the consumer trading market is in the lower end of the middle-income range. Only 16 percent of those using online brokerage services earn in excess of $100,000. A scant 9 percent of online traders were either retired or unemployed.

Who Cares for Brands?

Branding has not yet become a factor among online traders. The highest rating any online trading service reached in top-of-mind awareness was only 8 percent. This isn't surprising because online brokerage companies have found difficulty establishing brand awareness. In a survey of a broad selection of online consumers, only 54 percent were able to name an online brokerage firm despite intense media hype about the category. The traders themselves often do not select their trading firm by brand. Nearly one-third of traders used their search engines or online click-throughs to locate an online brokerage firm.

The growth in online brokerage follows the pattern of consumers becoming independent of experts as they gain a greater understanding of subjects they can research over the Internet. Just as many people go online to find prescription drugs or to buy insurance, individual investors are also gaining independence from the online brokers who provided an intermediary expert role between the consumer and the market. The Internet is also becoming a resource for those who are not quite ready to let go of expert advice. Now many of those who still want to work with an adviser use the Internet to communicate with the broker.

WIRELESS E-COMMERCE

Another trend shaping the future of e-commerce is the growing number of Internet-connected alternatives to PCs that are connected to telephone wires. Wireless Internet connectivity is getting faster, and more wireless devices are equipped for Internet usage. Internet retailers such as Amazon.com and eBay have been quick to make portions of their sites available on handheld devices. Likewise, service providers such as AOL and Yahoo! make it easy for their users to access e-mail and services over the airwaves. The changes are paving the way for laptops that can connect to services without wire.

A Forrester Research report indicates that mobile e-commerce will evolve as providers enhance their data capabilities and migrate from pure voice services to mobile information and, ultimately, mobile e-commerce. The study anticipates that smart carriers will partner with innovators to deliver compelling content to mobile users while unrestricted and open access to the Internet is ensured. These carriers will also pursue new partnerships and distribution channels to leverage the brand and reach of online content providers. Since carriers don't have the experience or competency to provide and support mobile Internet services on their own, they will partner with mobile data specialists for service bureau functions, customer support, and Web-based technologies.

Mobile E-commerce Is a Growth Industry

This will likely result in branded services from early players like Yahoo!, America Online, and Amazon.com. In addition to developing these new business partnerships, carriers will focus on usage and location-based services rather than content, which they'll leave to the branded content providers. Carriers will benefit from bundling new mobile data services with voice services, which means users will easily be able to use both screen and voice to retrieve and send communications and information. In order to support wireless service, carriers will charge customers and content providers usage fees. Business travelers are the early adopters of mobile data devices and services because they value mobile access to critical information. To attract and retain business travelers, carriers are co-marketing and distributing wireless phones and developing travel-focused content such as e-mail, flight updates, hotel scheduling, and driving instructions.

As the wireless market grows, more consumer e-commerce features will be added, including stock tracking and purchasing, auctioning access to sites like eBay, and consumer shopping. In addition, wireless devices may be the leading technology that finally makes e-book sales a reality. The surprisingly popular download of Stephen King's novella in early 2000 showed a willingness for consumers to accept the wireless screen for substantial content. In addition, wireless devices may be first to market with widespread, inexpensive high-speed connectivity, which could give wireless devices the edge on entertainment downloads of music and movies.

E-COMMERCE SECURITY ISSUES

One of the early barriers to e-commerce was concern about the security of consumers's financial information, in particular credit card theft. Online retailers fought this concern with logic, claiming that giving your credit card number to a Web site was no different than reading your card number to a catalog order-taker over the phone. They also argued that the Internet was probably safer than giving your card to a waiter who can easily copy the number from the store's receipt. The final argument is that most credit card issuers will only ask a card holder to be responsible for the first $50 of a theft incident. Beyond that, the card issuer takes responsibility. And many cards will waive their customers's liability for the $50. Yet consumers were still shy about typing in their card number and sending it into cyberspace. And it turns out they had good reason to be concerned.

The encryption software that was fashioned to produce secure communication between buyer and seller helped pave the way for direct e-commerce. In reality, the software used to create this private connection is flawed. It is not yet clear whether the flaws are in particular software packages, in the way the software is installed, or whether the entire concept of an entry-proof area within a publicly accessible Web site is suspect altogether. As hackers find ways to break into the databases of Internet merchants, the whole question of what constitutes credit card safety comes into question.

What, Consumers Worry?

Oddly, evidence of security weaknesses throughout the Internet didn't hit until a vast number of consumers had already overcome their credit card fears. News stories of engineers discovering security holes on major sites broke at the same time hackers were blocking major sites. Internet retailers braced for fallout, assuming they would lose a portion of their customer base. Nothing happened. Consumers went right on buying books, CDs, stocks, and used Barbies.

The database inside a merchant's site is filled with the credit card numbers of customers. Merchants retain these numbers after the sale so return customers get the convenience of being able to purchase again by simply agreeing to put the purchase on the same credit card used earlier. This is one of the customer-recognition devices that Internet consumers value in a service-oriented Web site. It's this database of stored numbers that is vulnerable to entry by hackers.

Vulnerabilities Will Persist

Problems with security around customer databases were discovered by engineers inadvertently, while they were working on other aspects of Web stores. Once they realized the weakness, they tested other sites with a variety of software solutions. The engineers found the weaknesses were widespread. They determined that only the largest sites could safely say their customers' information was safe. Yet during the time all this news was breaking, these large sites were getting battered by hackers who were jamming the sites into blackout.

Because security has always been an issue with Internet consumers, observers were surprised that Web retailers did not experience even a temporary setback in traffic and sales. Apparently the genie was out of the lamp. The eBay bidders and the Travelocity travel planners were not about to go back to the brick world. So far, security weaknesses have not resulted in widespread theft. Small sites remain particularly vulnerable to thieves, but hackers have been more interested in vandalism, such as jamming, than in outright theft. As for the future, security issues will not disappear quickly. But until security vulnerability turns into widespread stealing, it seems clear that consumers will not be discouraged from online shopping.

TOOLING THE GLOBE

Although the United States has dominated the development of e-commerce, it is spreading quickly around the globe. Forrester Research estimates that e-commerce will account for 8.6 percent of worldwide sales of goods and services in 2004. The expansion of global e-commerce is highly concentrated, with 12 countries representing nearly 85 percent of worldwide online sales. The United States will continue to lead e-commerce with online sales reaching $3.2 trillion in 2004. Western Europe will hit $1.5 trillion with stronger business-to-consumer sales than Asia. E-commerce in Latin America will hit $82 billion in spite of infrastructure problems and high connection fees. Eastern Europe, Africa, and the Middle East will contribute a combined $68.6 billion in 2004.

In Asian countries, e-commerce is strong in local economies. Consumers use the Internet to order from companies within their own cities. B2B Internet purchasing, however, is more international. This makes Asia an important player in the global Internet economy. Asia enjoys a number of advantages that will hurry its development as a major worldwide e-commerce player. A combination of pressure from global trading partners, falling trade barriers, and government enthusiasm for e-commerce will help push the region into the Internet economy.

Internet links to global e-marketplaces are accelerating Asian e-commerce as industry leaders pull their trading partners online. Eighty-six percent of Singapore's exports to the United States are sold in the computing and electronics industries, which leads online trade in Asia. National commitments to infrastructure development and economic growth will create new opportunities throughout the region. As with most countries, real e-commerce development is centered in B2B trade. More than $1.5 trillion of the region's total online sales move through B2B e-marketplaces.

E-commerce Follows the Strongest Economies

With Asia's varied levels of economic development, e-commerce has not developed evenly across the region. Strong online commerce needs public policy support, low trade barriers, stable currencies, and well-developed technology infrastructure. These factors are not equally present in the region's countries. In Hong Kong, low trade barriers support e-commerce, while India's heavy tariffs delayed its development. China's Internet economy is hindered by its weak infrastructure and its resistance to the entry of U.S. Internet companies. These disparities hold Asia back in its moves to Internet commerce. Consequently, Asia will be one of the last regions to reach full e-commerce maturity. According to Forrester, Japan will likely dominate the region with $880 billion in online sales in 2004. Australia, Korea, and Taiwan will each see more than 16 percent of their total sales conducted online.

Latin American e-commerce is expected to hit $82 billion in 2004. Latin America's Internet development has been hampered by its weak telecommunications infrastructure and limited Internet access. The region's Internet economy is dominated by B2B trade, which constitutes 93 percent of the region's e-commerce. E-commerce in Latin America faces significant challenges. Consumer connections in some countries run as high as $75 per month. Yet the combination of aggressive efforts to stabilize currencies combined with liberalized trade policies in countries like Brazil and Argentina are likely to bring about positive changes in consumer e-commerce.

In order for e-commerce to develop completely in Latin America, the countries will have to invest heavily in phone lines, PCs, Internet hosts, and cell phones. Latin America's current limited access to hosting and phone lines has stunted the region's e-commerce growth. Partnerships with U.S. corporations that are establishing corporate bases in Latin America will likely lead the growth to consumer online spending. E-commerce in Latin America will grow as governments roll back protectionist policies and develop mobile technology. Brazil is expected to lead this region by trading $64 billion online by 2004. Argentina will follow with more than $10 billion in online sales.

Europe Is Close on U.S. Heels

In Europe, e-commerce is set to grow more than 100 percent per year through 2003. This will bring Europe's e-commerce up to

$1.5 trillion in online sales in 2004, making Europe a major contributor to the global Internet economy. Europe and Asia both have comparable online sales totals, but Europe has a more balanced overall Internet economy that includes stronger growth in consumer e-commerce. E-commerce in Europe benefits from a number of inherent strengths: a coherent regional trading bloc, a strong technology infrastructure, and deep connections to global supply chains.

By 2004, Europe's online consumers are expected to turn from surfing to shopping, with sales of retail goods and services growing 140 percent annually. Forrester believes that one of the factors fueling this growth is improved online stores, which will inspire 100 million Europeans to shop online by 2004. As with many countries, the real driver behind Europe's e-commerce growth is online business trade, which accounts for nearly $1.4 trillion of Europe's expected online trade in 2004. These revenues come from the efforts of industry leaders to pull entire sectors online and the emergence of e-marketplaces that facilitate online business trade globally.

Online trade is expected to reach 6 percent of Europe's total sales in 2004. It has developed much more quickly in Northern Europe, with Germany and the United Kingdom leading the way. In Southern Europe, e-commerce has been hindered by weak infrastructure and cultural resistance to online trade. France represents the third-largest Internet economy in Europe. However, the emergence of new form factors, including WAP phones and interactive TV, is expected to help these countries overcome the hurdles to e-commerce acceptance. Europe will achieve e-commerce maturity very quickly, effectively closing the gap between it and the United States in the process. Despite some minor development hurdles, Europe's prospects as a global e-commerce leader look very good.

THE SLEEPY B2B GIANT

A few forward-looking giant companies took a look at the future in the mid-1990s and saw gold within easy reach. This easy gold was available because the procurement systems used by virtually every large corporation were woefully inefficient. After decades of information technology (IT) systems, industry had yet to take a meaningful productivity gain from the implementation of computers. Once the Internet offered widespread connectivity, all that changed. Companies such as GM, GE, and IBM created teams to move their companies to Internet procurement.

The first result was the simple savings a company could take on paperwork and endless meetings between buyers and sellers. These companies found little resistance from their suppliers and vendors. When GM tells a part manufacturer that it wants to buy its parts over the Internet, the parts vendor says, "What kind of system do I need to get so we're compatible?" GM, GE, and IBM alone dragged thousands of mid-size companies into the digital age in the late 1990s. Once GM was hooked into the parts manufacturer's Web site, a GM engineer could log onto the vendor's site and design the needed part on the vendor's CAD program.

Once finished, the engineer could click one icon to send the designed part to manufacturing with instructions on how many parts needed to appear in what factories by what date. The engineer then clicked on another icon to send a purchase order to the vendor's accounting system. In doing this little connectivity trick, GM could save from 3 to 6 percent on the purchase of the part. Not a giant percentage. But remember, this is savings, which means it goes straight to the bottom line. Whatever you don't spend is always yours. A 3 to 6 percent savings in procurement could deliver a 10 to 20 percent increase in profits if the savings was companywide.

Procurement Is the Low-Hanging Fruit

Online procurement brought instant savings to large corporations because of their inefficient purchasing systems, but it also provided savings for the vendors and suppliers. Suddenly the vendor could integrate its frontend sales process with backend fulfillment and make it all compatible with its customers. At any given time the vendor could track its sales, manufacturing, and delivery schedule on a system it shared with its customers. The vendor and the customer could view all stages of the order over a secure Web site. Even the purchase order and the invoice could be tracked online.

This automation gave the vendor the same efficiency gain its customer received. Given these direct benefits, vendors and suppliers offered little resistance as large corporations moved procurement to the Web.

Even back in 1998, analysts predicted that online business trade would find its way into all U.S. business supply chains by 2003. A number of research reports predicted that by 2003, most leading industries such as aerospace, petrochemicals, utilities, and motor vehicles would conduct some of their procurement on the Internet. Little did the analysts know this would take place by 2000. Researchers expected the switch from offline procurement to an online model to take 18 to 24 months to design, build, implement, and connect through the supply chain. This is the usual length of time it takes for a corporation to implement a completely revamped system.

Well, it might take 18 to 24 months if it were a normal improvement in corporate operation and efficiency. But when the savings are both ensured and dramatic, why wait? Motivated by the promise of major productivity gains, Fortune 1000 companies started moving at the speed of garage-based entrepreneurs. By late 1999, it became clear that the online business trade projected for 2003 was going to hit big in the year 2000, a full three years early.

Procurement Adoption Is the Big Easy

The dexterity of large corporate procurement departments has been one of the surprises of e-commerce. While dot-coms were making fun of traditional business for not "getting it," Fortune 1000 companies were quietly creating their own revolution. The rust companies are getting the last laugh. They're using the Internet to put new and unexpected earnings on their bottom lines, while most of the dot-coms continue to push their year of expected profitability further and further into the future.

Part of the reason for this dexterity is that brick companies have been in the process of revamping their buying systems and adopting new automation for 15 or 20 years. Moving to Internet procurement is not as much of a stretch for most corporations, especially after the pain and expense of installing EDI and enterprise software. Internet adoption is inexpensive, and the savings are almost immediate.

Though there are difficulties in integrating the Internet with a company's legacy systems, the expense is small compared with the benefits. Companies usually get their return on investment (ROI) within months. The shift also elevates the procurement managers, since the move to Internet purchasing delivers quick bottom-line benefits. So, with motivated managers and inexpensive technology, Web procurement developed swiftly across corporate America.

THE BIRTH OF E-MARKETPLACES

In 1999, news started to hit of a new Internet application making noise in the industrial chemical industry. The new killer apps were called e-marketplaces. Three of them were operating in the global chemical industry, converting chunks of chemical buying and selling to the Internet. All areas of chemicals were involved, from plastics and petrochemicals to the ingredients for fertilizers. E-marketplaces, such as eChemicals and CheMach, were letting buyers from all over the world post their wares, while global buyers could peruse the sites for the chemical they need. Buyers could also post their needs directly and wait for manufacturers to respond with availability and prices.

These e-marketplaces were sophisticated enough to allow negotiation in the process, so that factors such as quality, delivery prices, and turnaround could be factored into the buying and selling equation. The e-marketplaces were so successful that industry insiders began to predict that as much as 65 percent of the global industrial chemical market could move online over the next three or four years. Everyone in the system benefited from open trading. Buyers were able to reduce the internal costs of procurement and reduce their costs of goods by buying in a open market. The e-marketplaces were a benefit for sellers as well, because they could sell to a wider market and they could unload slow-moving inventory quickly.

E-marketplaces Spread like Weeds through Industry Sectors

Within a few weeks of the chemical industry's positive experience with large-scale e-marketplace commerce, other industries started trying the idea. Fortune 1000 companies quickly grasped that the principles that governed the chemical e-marketplaces could easily transfer to other industries including petroleum, forest products, electric energy, even seafood. All you needed to do was plug in the buyers and the sellers and make a few adjustments to accommodate the particulars of the individual industries. Companies such as VerticalNet started setting up e-marketplaces in dozens of industries. CheMach took its success in chemicals and created a parent company to go building e-marketplaces in other industries.

The savings to be taken on e-marketplaces are available to all involved. The corporate buyer gets the same increased procurement efficiencies that come with direct Internet procurement, only in an e-marketplace an outside company sets up the system and trains the buyers and sellers in its use. The corporate buyer also gets the benefit of being able to negotiate with a wider range of suppliers and vendors globally. The seller also benefits, since the e-marketplace makes the selling process more efficient. The seller may end up selling goods at a lower price, but it also reaches a wider global market, and in an open marketplace the seller can broker larger sales as well as unload excess inventory.

Big Players Enter the Market

The idea caught on full force in the spring of 2000. In a one-month period, during March of 2000, more than 55 major e-marketplaces were announced. These were not small efforts launched by service companies. Big players started to enter the market. The buyers themselves started setting up their own e-marketplaces, inviting their vendors and suppliers to participate. Some even invited their direct competition to get involved. When Ford and GM discovered they were each working on auto e-marketplaces, the rivals decided to join forces and invite DaimlerChrysler to participate.

Similar efforts were launched by other big players such as Sears and the European Carrefour. This was followed by ventures by Boeing, Chevron, Dow Chemical, and DuPont.

The e-marketplace launched by a procurement giant was a new model, but it made perfect sense. Why should the company that was bringing the weight of billions of dollars in procurement be a simple player in another company's enterprise? Many large corporations felt the e-marketplaces were just a new form of middleman. And they didn't want a new intermediary; they wanted to eliminate them. The large corporations typically launched an e-marketplace with a major software partner to take care of the technical aspects of the site. Companies such as Oracle partnered with Sears and the Big Three automakers. Commerce One was also a partner in the auto exchange. Other companies making the big e-marketplaces included Ariba, i2 Technologies, SAP, and Broadvision.

E-marketplaces Offer Multiple Revenue Streams

Even when they partnered with a large corporation, the software companies that built e-marketplaces found a number of lucrative revenue streams. First, the companies received an installation contract to set up the system. They also benefited from the licensing of their proprietary software and received consulting contracts to train users in both the buying companies and the selling businesses. The volume of consulting was so great most of the software companies outsourced the training to companies like PeopleSoft, KPMG, and Andersen. Software companies also took transaction fees for the commerce that moved across the e-marketplaces. Lastly, in some cases the software companies even took an equity position in these new ventures.

Prospects look very good for e-marketplaces, even though many industries are getting crowded with more ventures than they need. A number of research companies have reported that over 50 percent of B2B e-commerce will move through e-marketplaces by 2004. Corporations quickly embraced the advantages of open Internet markets, and when the big buyers went online, all their vendors and suppliers followed right along. This system of open bidding, auctions, and Internet negotiation is fast becoming the predominant way big companies buy from each other.

YOUR NET STRATEGY:

Given the wide range of business application on the Internet, your company will probably be involved in a number of Internet-based functions over the years. There is a very good chance you will turn to online purchasing of indirect materials such as office supplies, furniture, and equipment. The savings are great and systems developed by companies such as Staples, TotalMRO, and MarketMile offer ease of purchase, lower prices, and the ability to integrate your workflow controls to make sure all purchases are at the contracted rate and approved by the appropriate manager. These tools have become so ubiquitous and easy to use, they have become money-saving functions for small businesses as well as medium and large companies.

Over the coming years you will probably also utilize the following functions:

- Using auctions to buy and sell used equipment
- Using e-marketplaces to find new customers
- Using an internal e-mail system for communications
- Letting offsite employees hook into the e-mail system
- Outsourcing non-core functions such as accounting
- Communicating with customers
- Delivering sales presentations to customers and prospects
- Purchasing supplies
- Training employees
- Recruiting employees and conducting background checks

- Obtaining critical industry information
- Conducting market research
- Placing advertisements
- Educating your customers and prospects
- Storing company documents
- Printing and delivering proposals
- Entering global markets

The list will grow through the years. As you can see, there are few areas of business activity that are not touched directly by the Internet. The right strategy in the face of these sweeping new opportunities is to experiment with moving individual business functions to the Internet. It won't take much of a look to see whether the Internet offers savings or opportunities to your activities. Keep in mind, though, if the Net doesn't seem ready for a particular function today, check back in three to six months. Applications grow more sophisticated and easy to use by the day.

The best Net strategy is the one used by Jack Welch, CEO and Chairman at General Electric. He pushed his company to move functions to the Internet by becoming a cheerleader for getting GE wired. He emphasized that the Internet could positively affect each and every department. The strategy was successful. GE moved billions in procurement to the Internet and saved hundreds of millions in the process. There are two important things to remember as you get your company fully wired:

1. There are Net functions that can help every area of your company's activities, not just procurement and sales.

2. Experiment and keep searching for new applications. Outsourced logistics management or accounting may not look attractive right this moment, but in the near future, you may find you can save significantly by moving these functions to Web-based companies.

CHAPTER 4

E-TAILING

Three rules of thumb have emerged in Internet retailing.

1. The Internet loves niches.
2. Consumers love and trust their brick and mortar brands.
3. The Internet is a direct medium, and catalog companies understand direct sales.

If you keep these three thoughts in mind as you scan the e-tail landscape, a lot of the confusing data will make sense. Rule number one explains why fly fishing and chocolate sites do well. Rule two answers the baffling question about why Toys 'R' Us has consistently done well against eToys, even though its Net strategy has been a mess of shifting moves and abrupt changes in direction. And number three reinforces the notion that e-tailers have to sell in a direct manner while supporting sales with a strong fulfillment and customer service operation.

The biggest problem in e-tailing comes from dot-coms like Amazon.com that shun niche selling even though they don't have a strong offline retail system with a brand that ensures trust. If you just consider its books, Amazon.com is very successful, profitable even.

The company's fulfillment and customer service is the envy of the best catalog companies. Yet the Internet's largest retailer has suffered by trying to be everything to everyone. If you're Nordstrom, you can sell on your name. If you're L.L. Bean, you're an online extension of a successful catalog operation. If you're Emex custom car accessories <caraccessories.com>, you have a niche audience to serve.

If you do not excel in one of these three categories, you will have a difficult time in the e-tail world.

E-tailing: More Difficult Than It Looks

Why is it so hard to succeed as an online retailer? At a quick glance, it looks easy. You have millions of consumers scouring the Internet for products. Shopping bots proliferate, helping the hapless consumers to find the best place to buy quality products, your site. Banner ad trades and affiliations are everywhere, all designed to push a flood of consumers through your site. Stickiness is now a science, so once you receive a few visitors, you have devices at your fingertips to hold their attention and keep them coming back to buy.

E-tailing has to be easier than brick retailing. You don't have to pay hefty prices for mall leases and high tabs for advertising to a limited geographic market. On the Net you can reach your entire market from one moderately priced location. You can change your product mix in minutes. You don't have to sweat over inexperienced floor managers or teenagers who shoplift. Plus, your store is open 24 hours each day for the convenience of shoppers Down Under. How can you miss?

Easy. The shopping bots find products and deliver the list of sites in order of lowest price. You may have the lowest price today, but tomorrow, a competing site reduces its price on this one item and you've lost the sale. And stickiness only goes so far in keeping customers hanging around your site. You may have the best product information on the Internet, but if your customers know they can beat your prices at a stripped-down discounter, they'll peruse your information, then buy at the low-price site.

E-tail Customers Are Inconsistent

Affiliation programs come with their own trap doors. Trading banners with like sites may bring in new potential customers, but just as quickly, your customers can slip out of your site through the reciprocal banners on your site. Even if you keep your prices low, your service high, and your content excellent, you can be pushed right off the radar screen when a major offline retailer comes in to stake its claim with lower prices and a bigger brand name.

To make things even more difficult, more than half of Internet shoppers identify the products or services they need on the Internet, then log off and pick up the phone or drive to the mall to make their actual purchases. According to Jupiter Communications, this trend will grow through the years. Jupiter's study shows that 68 percent of Internet shoppers said they found products online, then purchased them at a physical store. Forty-seven percent of respondents said they bought by phone after researching online.

The same report projected that in 2005, more than $632 billion will be spent offline by consumers who used the Internet to shop for the product or service. This number dwarfs the projected $199 billion that consumers will spend on the Internet. This is great news for large offline retailers who also have a substantial Web presence, especially since many consumers are happy to shop at a Web site owned by an offline retailer or catalog, then log off and buy from that same company. But it's not very encouraging news for e-tailers without a widespread network of offline stores.

The Bricks Hold the E-tail Hammer

Given Jupiter's results, it's not surprising that analysts see an Internet future dominated by large offline retailers, niche sites, and a few major online companies such as Amazon.com who were able to establish a recognizable online brand before the bewildering onslaught of Net-only retailers. The research also explains why catalog companies are doing so well on the Internet. If 47 percent of your potential customers are going to log off and pick up a phone to make the order, it's handy if they're coming off your site and calling your 800 number. Companies such as Lands' End, L.L. Bean, and J. Crew have adapted to the back and forth between their Web sites and catalog operations in order to accommodate the customers desire to shop online and buy by phone.

Niche sites also weather this e-tailing challenge well. Most niche sites prosper by offering a combination of hard-to-find products and services as well as expert information. For niche sites, the customers don't have the option of logging off and driving to a discount store to buy the product. Plus, niche sites generally attract passionate enthusiasts who are fiercely loyal. These devoted consumers are usually grateful for the expert information and show their gratitude by purchasing. Niche sites that flourish on the Internet often become information centers for subjects such as hot sauces, fly fishing, wind surfing, or acoustic guitars.

Yet even with the challenges of consumers who want to shop on the Net and buy offline, the number of consumers who do buy online continues to grow. Some categories show more promise than others. This chapter takes a look at how the winners and losers are stacking up with online consumer sales. We will look at which categories are showing promise and which ones are floundering in their attempts to create a viable online market for their products.

CATEGORIES: THE E-TAIL WINNERS AND LOSERS

Not surprisingly, travel services is the number–one retail category. It beats the number-two category, computer hardware, and peripherals by more than twice the dollar figure. Research firms have estimated that over 2,000 offline travel agencies ceased business during 2000 because they had lost so much business to online travel services. One of the categories that still hasn't made it to the top ten is groceries. Although there was early excitement around online grocery ordering, so far consumers have been lukewarm on the category.

E-TAILING

Consumer E-commerce Revenue by Category
Q1 2000

Travel services	$ 2 billion
Computer hardware and peripherals	$852 million
Auction	$644
Clothing apparel	$619
Books	$461
Music/video	$340
Electronics	$287
Computer software	$257
Flowers/gifts/cards	$195
Health & Beauty	$153
Toys	$147
Home & Garden	$ 82
Fitness & Sports equipment	$ 69

Source: Harris Interactive e.commercePulse

Toys, clothing, and electronics produce sales all year, but they spike strongly during the holiday season, capturing the top three positions briefly between Thanksgiving and Christmas Eve. Some sites straddle a number of categories, which is taken into consideration in the rankings. For instance, eBay, is a top site for online electronics, toys, and flowers in addition to its auction. Amazon.com sells home and garden products as well as toys, and provides an auction in addition to its books and CDs.

The shifting patterns of consumer spending on the Internet affect the ranking of categories. Early on, the leading categories online were computers, books, music, and videos. While they continue to grow, these categories no longer dominate consumer spending on the Internet. For one thing, as categories, they are smaller than travel, apparel, or health and beauty products.

Tech Developments Affect Categories

Part of the reason for the shifts in categories is technical. The early travel sites didn't have the full range of choices that are common on travel sites now. The travel sector was weaker when consumers couldn't choose their seats or find a wide variety of hotel options. When travel sites were just emerging, travelers often used the services to choose their flights, then called the airlines to book directly. Travel surged to the top of the online retail chain when the travel sites became complete and easy to use.

Apparel had similar early problems. Without the ability to touch fabric, view high-resolution photos, or try on clothing, consumers were reluctant to buy over the Internet. The early apparel catalogs did little but post their catalog pages online. In time, visuals improved, giving consumers more confidence in the veracity of color and texture. Apparel catalogs produced Web sites that offered shoppers more than just their latest catalog. These developments coincided with an increase in the percentage of women shoppers online. All of these changes pushed apparel up the category ladder.

In Time, the Online Mix Will Mimic Offline Rankings

The category mix will likely shift a few more times before it stabilizes. Big ticket items will continue to increase, and eventually they will overtake apparel and books simply because of the price tags on the products. As consumers grow more accustomed to Internet shopping and learn to trust online merchants, furniture and appliances will rise in ranking. Clearly, there will come a day when automakers will rightfully take their place at the top of the online consumer mountain.

Over the next few years, the Internet category rankings will start to reflect the category rankings of offline retail sales. This gradual migration will come through a number of changes. Existing customers will become increasingly comfortable with online purchasing as Web sites improve their ease-of-use, security, and service back up. As the large offline brands like Sears, Kmart, and Wal-Mart expand their online presence, they'll bring consumer confidence to the marketplace. Demographics trends will help as well. Generation X and Generation Next are perfectly comfortable with online shopping. As they move into their high-earning years, they'll take their Internet shopping habits to the big-ticket retailers.

TROUBLE IN THE ONLINE MALL

The conventional wisdom about Internet retailing has swung from one extreme to another from the beginning. Initially, the Internet was considered unfit for mainstream consumer business. The World Wide Web was considered a marketplace for intense niche enthusiasts, business scams, and porn. As it began to prove itself a fertile ground for mainstream consumers, investors overreacted, pouring dollars into dot-coms with "irrational exuberance." Then gloom set in when the Nasdaq fell, and two year's worth of stock gain settled down to an increase that was merely two or three times the growth rate of the brick and mortar economy.

If we back away from the extremes, we can get a more realistic picture of Internet retailing. Yes, Internet retailing is a new channel for consumer sales that will gain a permanent place in retailing. Yes, every major retailer needs to stake a place on the Internet. No, it will not transform the entire global retail environment. Yes, the Internet channel works better for some products and services, such as travel and hard-to-find niche products. No, the Internet will not replace street browsing, that wonderful entertainment that began with village centers and evolved into the mall.

Content Is a Lure and an Anchor

Much of the retail environment on the Internet is like a commodities market surrounded by a plethora of free product information. Online consumers are very savvy. It doesn't take long online to learn a few tricks, especially if you are a regular consumer of a particular product such as CDs, books, electronics, or even office supplies. You can quickly find the sites that offer the best free information. Sites like Amazon.com and CDNow present excellent information about authors or music artists. Sites like BuyerZone.com offer tons of free management information for small business.

But do these sites offer the best prices on their products? Sometimes yes, sometimes no. The smart consumer can find the lowest-price outlet for CDs or office supplies with a couple of clicks, leaving the source of great information and heading for a source of great prices. If you're a retailer spending $60 to obtain a new customer, you may have a few problems with this new cyber customer. And the low-price shopping bots will only improve with time, further carving into the margins of the large, service-based e-tailers.

These competitive pressures will not go away. Web retailers are not only competing by offering up their products as commodities, they also compete on the shopping concepts offered to the online audience. A site like BulkBuy will aggregate consumers into buying groups that join together to purchase two or three hundred mobile phones or digital cameras at 40 percent off the retail price. Other companies present a price that declines as the company increases its number of items sold. All of these tricks are value-subtracted concepts that turn the Internet into a commodity market for consumer goods.

Content and Discounts Make a Tough Mix

This is great news for the consumer, who can get all needed information about consumer products and their use free from a value-added site, then turn to one of the super-discounters to make a purchase. Obviously something has to crack. Most of the value-added retailers are able to give away their high-content services because of the heavy investments they obtained while their stocks were valued beyond reason. If they cannot convert their investments in content and value into profitable sales, the great free information will go away.

Yet consumers are attracted to sites with high-value services, even if their loyalty doesn't compel them to pay higher prices for the privilege of free content. A new twist of the combination of heavily discounted items blended with superior content will eventually emerge to solve this fundamental problem facing Internet retailers. Amazon.com has solved the problem in its book division, which became profitable in the last quarter of 1999. After years of investing, they reached the critical volume that lets them deliver great content (reviews, powerful search capability), great service, and the online industry's best prices.

There's Little Room for Multiple Giants

Some argue only one or two of these giants will find room in each product category, because duplication offers no additional value to the consumer. In the offline world, geography was the reason for multiple companies offering similar goods. Borders Books can't be everywhere, which leaves room for Barnes and Noble stores. If geography were not a consideration, there would be no need for both a Borders Books and a Barnes and Noble, because their product selection and shopping environment are essentially the same. On the Internet, geography is not a consideration. This simple fact supports the argument that consumers don't need multiple companies presenting the same selection and shopping environment.

But the Internet is not simply a place for big retail operations to grab category dominance. There are still a few retail models that will come from the global connectivity of the Web. In the short run, a massive middleman in the center of a category may prove successful. In the long run, the Internet may bring about some distribution efficiencies that could bring manufacturers into play with direct-to-consumer retailing. In all areas of business, the middleman has the most to worry about regarding the connectivity of the Internet.

Most retailers are simply very sophisticated middlemen. They should keep looking over their shoulder at their manufacturers. Given the powerful connectivity of the Internet, at some point it may not make sense for your book to leave a printer in Michigan, go to a warehouse in New Jersey, then off to another warehouse in Nevada, before it ships to your home. One day a consortium of manufacturers may jointly own a Web service that sends the book to you directly from a warehouse adjacent to the printing facility.

TRAVEL AGENT IN A CAN

During the early days of the Internet, travel sites were a wonderful place to shop for flights and rates. Once you had obtained the needed information, you logged off and called the airlines directly to book the flight. Booking through the site itself was cumbersome, slow, and inefficient. Besides, booking online left you susceptible to a computer crash mid-booking that left you wondering whether your credit card had been charged before the site locked up.

As travel sites improved, it soon became more efficient just to let the site book the flight. The sites gained the ability to remember your seat preferences and frequent flyer numbers. The sites also became better at connecting travelers to related services, such as rental cars, hotels, event tickets, and restaurant reservations, all of which made travel sites timesavers.

Travel Consolidation Is Due

Jupiter Communications predicts that leisure travel and business travel that is booked online by individuals will reach $28 billion in 2005. In addition, Forrester Research predicts that $20.3 billion in business travel will be booked over the Internet by 2004. Forrester expects 70 percent of Fortune 1000 companies to adopt online booking services by 2002. Forrester also predicts that aggregators will target small businesses, buying up airline tickets in bulk and reselling them with incentives at a discount.

Most analysts anticipate a consolidation of Internet sites in the travel industry. The high-water mark of 1,000 travel sites will likely condense down to about 200, led by major sites such as Travelocity.com and Expedia. Niche sites with specialties such as cruises or international tours will also survive the contraction. With airlines finding their own ways to sell tickets online, Internet travel services will have to develop powerful service capabilities or niche expertise.

One of the difficulties facing the online travel market is its maturity. The triple-digit growth years are over, and unlike product-based sites, there is no significant international component to online travel sales. So unlike much of the Internet market, travel sites cannot rely on a larger future audience to bolster a weak model. As the travel market reaches maturity, mass-market sites will dominate with a wide array of services, including rental cars, hotel reservations, event and restaurant reservations, and tourism information.

The Travel Shopper Is Market Savvy

The online travel shopper is very cost-conscious. According to a report from the research firm PhoCusWright, 61 percent of online travel buyers cite price as the most important factor in buying an airline ticket. Only 15 percent listed getting the best connections as the top reason to buy tickets online. Another 15 percent chose a preferred airline.

The market for business travel booked by individuals behaves similarly to the consumer market. One difference is the greater emphasis business travelers place on getting the best connections. Business travelers who book their own travel arrangements cite price as their greatest concern, but not to the same extent as consumers. Only 48 percent of business travelers cite price as the top priority. A full 25 percent want the best connections.

The travel market battles of the future will be fought on price and service, with the heaviest emphasis on price. As with many Internet markets, there is some question about the role of the middleman. Will airlines sell directly to consumers over the Internet at a rate the travel agencies can't match? Will airlines band together to create a consumer site that offers the service mix consumers are accustomed to from their travel agents?

The Travel Agent Gets Disintermediated

Unlike the auto industry, which has close ties to its dealer network, the airlines have not been supportive of travel agencies over the past few years. In the late 1990s, airlines cut the discount they give to travel agencies, opening a rift in their relationship with agencies that continues. The airline industry was the first sector to see the service originator cavalierly enter into direct competition with its intermediary structure. In most industries, the originators and manufacturers struggled to maintain their dealer ties even as they toyed with direct-to-consumer sales. This is consistent with the way airlines have been treating travel agents for the past decade, chopping discounts to agents while selling direct to consumers and business travelers.

EBAY AND THE LAND OF RETAIL AUCTIONS

One of the reasons online auctions are so successful is that there are three times as many people bidding and buying as there are people selling. This means there is a strong market for the sellers in the Internet garage sale of online auctions. The sector delivered over $600 million in sales during 1999 and exceeded $1 billion in 2000, making it the third-largest online retail category after travel and computer hardware. That's not counting the business-to-business auction sites that are proliferating though the Internet.

As well as supporting the auction sites, this person-to-person e-commerce has spawned an army of garage entrepreneurs who buy low and sell high on the auction sites. A surprising 46 percent of Internet users have participated in an online auction, according to research firm Greenfield Online. These consumers are increasing the number of items they purchase per year as well.

eBay Is the Auction Gorilla

At the center of this retail action is early auction giant eBay. Research shows that more than 70 percent of online auction transactions take place on eBay. eBay retains its dominant competitive position even in the face of auction launches from Yahoo! and Amazon.com. eBay is even withstanding a competitive bid by a collective effort from a group that includes Microsoft, Dell, Lycos, and Excite@Home.

The collective effort intends to provide shared information that allows consumers to buy and sell across a number of auction sites. eBay has chosen to stay clear of cooperative efforts. The company routinely takes interlopers to court, successfully arguing that the postings and bids on its site are protected by copyright laws. Thus, eBay has remained independent with over four million auction listings.

eBay may control the center of the auction market, but niche sites are taking bites out of the giant's hide. Niche auction sites focus on specific areas, from antiques to collectibles such as stamps, coins, or movie memorabilia. You can find auction sites devoted to bottles (buckabottle.com) or even "statement" buttons (pinback.com).

Sell Niche, Buy Supermarket

The rule of thumb on niche auction sites is that the buyers are generally willing to pay more for the products listed at a niche site than they are for the same products sold at general auctions such as eBay. Many an entrepreneur (including my UPS driver), makes a good living by buying goods at eBay or other general auction sites, where sellers often have no idea of the real value of some of their attic items, then selling them at the niche sites where buyers are better versed in value.

The auction sites, particularly eBay, have been plagued with publicity over bizarre items put up for sale over its auction. These items have included a human kidney, cocaine, babies, even a human soul. Given the infrequency of these hoaxes, and given the overall volume of four million items, the auction sites are actually very clean and straightforward. The stories of the bizarre items, however, make good copy and get reported out of proportion to their actual occurrence.

The auction sites also have their share of unethical buyers and sellers, but most auction sites keep disreputable tactics to a minimum. eBay has a team that monitors auctions and takes action against offensive auction behavior. The company has a rating system that lets buyers and sellers quickly view the collective perception of their trading partner. eBay's SafeHarbor Investigations takes action against buyers and sellers who conduct illegal or unethical auction activity. eBay reports fraud and has the power to kick unethical buyers and sellers off the site permanently.

eBay has also been able to use its clout as an auction site to sell beyond its garage-sale roots. It now offers a business exchange for used office furniture and equipment, as well as holiday retail shopping, such as flowers on Mother's Day. The company has even taken its goodwill and launched an offline consumer magazine. Like all successful Internet retailers, eBay takes its goodwill and extends into numerous areas of consumer interest.

THE STICKY WICKET OF APPAREL

One of the futuristic devices that is supposed to come our way through the development of the Internet is the electronic clothes-shopping device. The device will be an electronic garment that fits us like a light jump suit. A cord will go from the jump suit to the computer so an apparel site can take our exact measurements electronically, thus matching us exactly with the appropriate clothing sizes.

Though I doubt this gadget will ever hang in more than a few closets, it does illustrate a solution to one of the Internet's greatest challenges in apparel, getting the size right. We all know that a size 32 waist in Gap jeans is not the same as a size 32 waist in Levi's jeans. The other problems in apparel, of course, is that you can't see yourself in the mirror, and you don't find out of the sweater is itchy by looking at a computer screen.

Apparel is one of the most difficult retail categories on the Internet. Until 1999, apparel was barely on the online radar. Poor graphics made it difficult to present clothing attractively. Yet the category is beginning to show promise with a ranking of fourth among retail products, just behind auctions. Apparel is expected to reach $7 billion in online retail sales by 2003, according to Jupiter Communications. Though that number may keep apparel in the top 5 of online categories, it represents only 4 percent of projected apparel spending.

Clothing sites launched by the major offline retailers present an additional problem for dot-com apparel retailers. In order of total sales, the leading clothing sites are:

- JCPenney.com
- Gap.com
- EddieBauer.com
- Landsend.com
- JCrew.com
- Walmart.com

These sites are all well-branded brick-and-clicks. Many industry experts believe these sites rank highest because they are best equipped to overcome the difficulties in selling clothing over the Internet. You can trust these companies to deliver. You can trust these companies to make returns relatively easy. And chances are you already know how their clothes feel and fit on you.

Research shows that price is the most important quality in seeking an online apparel site. Over 66 percent of clothing shoppers rate price as extremely important. Curiously, Greenfield found that brand names had very little influence over online apparel shopper's decisions, surprising considering that all of the top-ranking clothing sites are powerful brands. Other reasons consumers gave for buying apparel over the Internet include: a desire to avoid crowds (58 percent) and the time-savings of Internet purchasing (57 percent).

Many Shoppers Will Never Buy Clothing Online

There is one large group of consumers who would never consider buying clothing over the Internet. The apparel E-commerce Report conducted by NPD Group suggests that online consumers can be divided into two camps: those who are willing to buy clothing online, and those who say they will never purchase apparel over the Internet. Even when the respondent group was restricted to veteran Internet users with several years of experience buying online, 40 percent still said they would never buy clothes. Reasons consumers gave for their reluctance to shop online include the inability to touch items (73 percent), shipping charges (63 percent), and difficulty in returning unwanted items (57 percent).

Age is a significant factor in the apparel market, according to the NPD Group. The 35 to 44 year-old demographic is the biggest slice of the online clothing market with 41 percent of buyers. Next is the 25 to 34 group with 24 percent of the apparel market. All other age groups are in single digits. Income is another major factor. Those with an income over $70,000 constitute 61 percent of apparel buyers. Offline, their share of the market is only 38 percent.

The long-term prospects for apparel shopping look positive, with double-digit growth predicted for years to come. Yet online sales are expected to remain a small portion of overall apparel spending, remaining in single digits for the foreseeable future. The big winners in online clothing are expected to continue to be known catalog companies and large department stores. Online consumers want to buy from companies they know and understand. As one analyst explained, online shoppers are willing to buy jeans from Gap because they know how Gap jeans fit.

VIRTUAL HEALTH CARE

Are worldwide consumers ready to buy prescription drugs, health insurance, and doctor's advice over the Internet? To a small degree, yes. One of the big-demand items in the consumer pharmaceutical category is Viagra. The popularity of this prescription can be attributed to the anonymity of Internet purchasing. Many people are embarrassed to purchase face-to-face a drug that combats impotence.

For the most part, though, consumer purchases of health-related products over the Internet will constitute a small percentage of the overall consumer health market. On the business-to-business side, however, sales will be considerably more robust. Various research estimates show the healthcare industry reaching from $300 to $400 billion in online transactions by 2004. The bulk of the activity will come from business-to-business trade. The retail side will constitute $22 billion by 2004, which constitutes 8 percent of overall retail health sales. Business-to-business health trade will move more eagerly to the Internet, with a full 17 percent of the industry migrating online.

Health Care Is Popular on the Internet

More than 45 percent of Internet users access health information online. A smaller percentage, 32 percent, shop for health products over the Internet. Online health consumers fall into two groups, according to drkoop.com: those who are interested in wellness and health and those who have been diagnosed with a medical condition. Most retail health sites provide information for both groups. Prescription drug sales dominate retail health, with predictions of $15 billion in sales for 2004. Nutraceuticals (nutrition and vitamin products) are expected to generate $3.3 billion. Next come over-the-counter drugs and beauty aids at $1.9 billion.

The largest online healthcare market is women and children, but because mothers buy for children, women constitute the largest market. Seventy-five percent of all pharmaceuticals on PlanetRx are prescribed for women or children. Consequently, most of the advertising for healthcare products is placed on women's sites such as the women's network iVillage. Another big market for health care is health maintenance organizations (HMOs). Pharmacy sites such as PlanetRx make service available to members of HMOs.

Internet Health Care Will Consolidate

As with the apparel market, there is a portion of online consumers that is reluctant to buy health products over the Internet. Jupiter Communications finds that 49 percent of respondents state that they don't buy health products online because they feel it is more convenient to pick up health items while doing other shopping. Consumers also cited difficulty in returning items to an online merchant and slow product delivery as significant deterrents.

Industry analysts suggest that the way the healthcare industry will bring in consumers is by creating collaborations between health sites to give customers all of the health care services they need in one site. The idea is to create a resilient fabric of interdependent healthcare players linked in real time over the Internet. This would include doctors, medical labs, pharmacies, nutraceutical manufacturers, and insurance companies. Presently, health care over the Internet is fragmented and difficult for users to navigate.

Many analysts predict a shakeout among Internet healthcare players because of the glut of players, the small percentage of consumer dollars flowing to the Net from the retail healthcare market, and the fact that advertising on healthcare sites isn't enough to cover the costs of health content. Advertising on healthcare sites is only expected to reach $700 million in 2004. The shakeout, according to analysts, will occur through mergers and acquisitions. It will result in sites that are more comprehensive and easier for consumers to use.

FINANCIAL SERVICES: THE MOUSE AS ATM

Financial services online are overwhelmingly dominated by Internet stock trading. But the financial services market online also includes banking, credit and lending, online insurance, and bill-paying services. According to research firm eMarketer's eFinancial report, 16.9 million individuals used the Internet to research investment opportunities or manage investments during 1999. This number is expected to reach 33.4 million by 2002. As many as 3.6 million of these investors actively traded 70 percent or more of their investments over the Internet. The assets of these investors will reach $1.2 trillion in 2002.

Analysts expect online investments to total $3 trillion by 2003. This number is a bit misleading, as it represents the total invested dollars. The income from processing trades is a very small percentage of this number. The online brokerage sector also lags behind other Internet retailers in customer service. The study found only 39 percent of financial services sites responded to customers inquiries within one day, a percentage deemed inadequate for a service-intensive business. Researchers expect that more than 20 million individuals will trade online by 2003.

Online Financial Services Will Continue Growth

Online trading has already become widely accepted by U.S. consumers. A full 41 percent of U.S. households that hold stock will have online trading accounts by 2003. Jupiter Communications expects that online brokerage revenues from interest, fees, and non-transaction services will increase to represent 80 percent of total online brokerage revenues by 2003, up from 36 percent of the total in 1998.

Jupiter's report also cites fast increases in other financial services online. By 2003, 30 percent of U.S. households will manage their bank accounts online. The 4 million online banking consumers of 1998 will expand to 26 million in 2003. Revenues derived from online banking will grow at a slower rate as competitive pressures keep costs low.

The future looks bright on the mortgage side of financial services as well. Jupiter expects online-originated mortgages to increase to 1.1 million in 2003. The total value will hit $155 billion. This will represent 16 percent of all U.S. mortgages in 2003, up from the $4 billion in online mortgages generated in 1998.

Traditional Financial Companies Will Go Net Savvy

Offline financial institutions will need to change their business culture and move service online to keep up with Net-savvy consumers. A growing number of Internet consumers do not value the traditional service provided by financial firms. Financial organizations need to undercut their productive channels, products, and organizations in order to meet the expectations of consumers on the Internet.

Financial services are ground-zero for Internet commerce. The companies that survive the rush to the Internet will be those that can aggressively change their culture to adapt to the demands of Internet consumers. Financial institutions that are unable to change their culture quickly will be wise to invest in or acquire Net financial players that are able to deliver the services demanded by an online customer base.

Even Insurance Companies Get It

Insurance is another area of financial services being transformed by the Internet. Andersen Consulting predicts that the Internet will influence every aspect of the insurance industry, including distribution channels, customer servicing, and pricing. By 2005, the consulting company expects that more than 17 percent of insurance products will be sold online. This includes everything from life insurance to asset accumulation products, retirement accounts, and health-related insurance. Within the insurance industry, 66 percent of executives believe insurance products sold over the Internet will be less expensive than the products sold through traditional channels. The majority of insurance executives also believe the Internet will improve the efficiency of the traditional agent.

All of this adds up to a financial services sector primed for major shifts to Internet sales and service. Unlike most retail trade, the Internet provides all of the benefits consumers seek: ease-of-use, time-savings, convenience, and cost savings. Consumers can buy pharmaceuticals at their grocery store. They are happy to shop for clothes at the mall. But when it comes to buying insurance, paying bills, or trading stocks, there is no offline system that beats the computer.

SECURITY ISSUES

One of the persistent challenges facing online retailing is the problem of security. Millions of Web sites, from entrepreneurial niche sites to major retailers, believed they had safe sites only to find out their systems had holes left by software manufacturers such as Microsoft. One security company found that even the largest sites can be penetrated. Hacker attacks that shut down major sites foster the impression that Internet sites are vulnerable to penetration.

This is a concern to consumers for two major reasons. It compromises their financial information, and it invades their privacy. Even though the consumer carries only $50 liability for most credit card fraud, and even though most credit card companies waive even this exposure, Internet consumers still worry. The vulnerability of card numbers likely triggers a greater worry that personal financial information can be easily examined on the Internet.

Sites Can Do More for Security

Web sites could solve part of this problem by refraining from storing card numbers on the Web site, but this solution would hamper one of the strongest loyalty devices on the Internet, a site's ability to prefill purchasing forms with their customers's card numbers and names. Obtaining purchase and shipping information is the most time-consuming portion of an online purchase, so most customers appreciate the convenience of pre-filled forms at sites they frequent. This practice leaves their card numbers vulnerable to hackers.

A study by research firm Deloitte & Touche and The Information Systems Audit and Control Association looked at e-commerce security around the world. The results revealed that Web sites generally use several overlapping security measures to fight virus attacks and prevent intrusions. Most sites use security firewalls and encryption software to protect customer information.

Online Shoppers Are Wary

Consumers remain unconvinced of the Internet's ability to provide transaction security and privacy. According to a recent survey by research firm @dplan, nearly eight out of ten consumers are concerned about online security. The number one concern is the unauthorized use of personal credit cards by hackers. A full 79 percent of consumers do not feel security is high enough to protect their card numbers. Seventy-eight percent of consumers are also concerned about access to credit card information.

Sixty-three percent of online consumers are also concerned about hackers obtaining access to their passwords online. Sixty-two percent worry that hackers will be able to obtain their name and address. Fifty-eight percent are concerned that their online activity can be monitored. Forty-five percent have anxiety about receiving unsolicited e-mail, and 36 percent revealed concerns about others being able to find out what they buy online.

Most Web site owners believe their sites are safer than they actually are. This is partly because Web site producers were under the impression the software they were using was safe. The study also revealed that Web retailers are far more concerned with ways to develop revenue than they are with providing security for their customers.

Though Internet retailers continually stress the overall safety of the Internet, high-profile security violations undermine the sense that the Internet provides a safe and private environment for shopping and obtaining information. To make life even more difficult for Internet retailers, many of the security infractions come to sites that have added security measures to ensure the protection of their customers.

THE FUTURE OF INTERNET RETAILING

In the short term, Internet retailing will experience consolidation. Total retail sales will continue their upward trend, but the number of shoppers in the United States will level off at about 50 million. According to Forrester Research, online spending per household will grow from $1,167 in 1999 to $3,738 in 2004. Consumers will switch from convenience and researched items to replenishment purchases such as groceries, an area of Internet retailing that will not produce large sales growth. This means the double- and sometimes triple-digit growth in retail sales during the late 1990s will likely drop to low double-digit or even single-digit growth during the early years of this decade. The next surge in retail e-commerce is expected to come in the next decade as Gen Y consumers start to enter their prime earning years.

The challenge for retailers will be to find the right balance between product categories offered and customer segments served. General merchants like Macy's and Wal-Mart will need to identify their most profitable customers and narrow their product offerings to capture these consumers. One-sector superstores, such as PETsMART and Linens 'n Things, will either have to expand their product offerings or partner with other Internet retailers that can deliver their customer base. Small specialty niche sites will likely continue to flourish in an environment of expert information.

The More Things Change . . .

In the long term, Internet retailing may see some more significant changes. For all of the talk about new models of retailing exploding onto the Internet scene, the models look remarkably like a blend of traditional retail stores and catalogs. Online retailing is still based on creating a middleman between the manufacturer and the consumer. Like stores and catalogs, the Web retailers purchase inventory from a large number of manufacturers and sell these products to shoppers. The Internet has remarkable powers of connectivity, allowing an Australian consumer to browse the same storefront as the New Jersey shopper, but most online retailers have yet to take full advantage of the Internet's true connectivity. The model still supports a fat middleman company that tries to build efficiencies by growing fatter and fatter in its product mix.

A few retailers are using the unique powers of the Internet. Shopping bots that seek products across hundreds of sites are a new tool that takes the Internet retail environment beyond catalog pages. Web sites that pool buyers in order to gain lower prices through quantity purchasing certainly utilize the special powers of the Internet. Online auctions also take garage sales into a global territory that would be impossible without the Internet. Yet all these sites add up to a small portion of the entire retail mix on the Internet.

The Biggest Changes Are Yet to Come

In its present from, Internet retailing is very limited. Even the most optimistic forecasts envision Internet retailing as a small player on the retail scene. In 5 years, Internet sales may reach 10 percent of all U.S. retail sales. In business-to-business e-commerce, on the other hand, some corporations such as Intel expect to move 100 percent of purchasing to the Internet. Is Internet retailing doomed to be an also-ran in the consumer buying world? Not likely. Eventually it will become clear that the Internet offers the possibility of radically changing the relationships between manufacturer, distributor, wholesaler, and retailer.

Given the powerful connectivity of the Internet, there is no need for a hefty middleman. As powerful as companies like Kmart and Wal-Mart may be, they are essentially just huge middlemen between the producers and buyers of consumer products. They exist to collect goods in one place for offline shoppers. In this regard they are critical for mass distribution. Manufacturers are well aware of their importance and work hard to preserve their relationship to retailers.

The Future Belongs to Those Who Add Value

On the Internet, the role of retailers is less crucial. Just ask the traditional travel agents. Since travel agents are less critical to the sale of airline tickets, rental cars, and hotel reservations, the travel industry was willing to turn its back on these retailers when the Internet provided a more efficient way to deliver travel products to consumers and businesses. The consumer product manufacturers are not going to be so quick to offend their retailers. Just ask the auto makers as they try to figure out how to sell cars directly to customers without destroying their cozy relationship with their dealers.

The opportunity to gain efficiencies through direct sales to consumers over the Internet exists for manufacturers; it just hasn't yet been developed. A new model could replicate the developments in business-to-business where the intermediary is getting squeezed out unless value can be added to the product. Internet retailers that do not add value to the products in the form of expert information or other enhancements will lose out to manufacturers, who will eventually start selling direct to consumers online.

YOUR NET STRATEGY:

Your response to the world of Internet retailing will depend on where you find yourself as you ponder Web sales. There is one appropriate strategy for a brick company that plans to extend its business to the Internet, and there is quite another for a start-up that wants to launch a Web-only enterprise. The plan, the goals, and the expected results will vary greatly depending on your starting point.

One thing to keep in mind no matter what your starting point is that the Internet, though young, is actually quite developed now. Models for success have emerged, and models for failure have become crystal clear. The sector-by-sector look in this chapter shows that retailers have explored online sales with significant depth. There is still plenty of room for success, but in all likelihood, success will come to those who have already established a brand, those who can carve a deep niche with high subject expertise, and those who can dream up innovative, customer-oriented systems that are superior to our current Internet retailing.

Here are some strategy suggestions for a number of different launching points:

- *Established offline brands with existing Web presence.* Many established offline brands, such as Toys 'R' Us and Wal-Mart, failed in their initial Web initiative. Many of these companies found they couldn't simply evolve their sites. In order to revamp their strategy and improve their results, they started from scratch, rethinking their goals. The mistaken early attempts were often little more than online catalogs of store inventory. The revamped sites usually offer greater integration of customer service between stores and Web sites, as well as the development of a Web-oriented product mix.

- *Offline brands entering the Web.* Customers love and trust their brands, which gives the well-established offline brand a jump-start on the Net. However, you get a black eye if your site doesn't also include state-of-the-art Web panache. You can't afford to look like you don't get it when a savvy Net consumer visits. Make sure you appear in your market with a powerful search engine, fast-clicking pages, smart graphics, nifty maneuvering, easy purchasing technology, and great customer service. Also plan to monitor your site for opportunities to create a product mix tailored to your Net customers.

- *Local companies extending reach.* Over 60 percent of small retailers ignore international orders because they don't know how to serve these customers. Local companies can benefit greatly from the Internet, but they have to be prepared to meet the sales style of the medium. Part of that style is the global nature of the Internet. Prepare your Web business for the demands of your Web customers. This includes giving your customers a selection of delivery solutions, both global and national.

- *Pure-play start-ups.* The rule-of-thumb for the new Net-only company is to offer customers something they can't get anywhere else on the Internet. This can take the form of greater expertise within a given niche or a deeper cut off an existing corner of the Web. There is no room on the Internet for me-too companies. If you cannot offer customers something new, something different, or something more, you don't stand much chance of success.

CHAPTER 5

NET CONSUMERS
Brands and Loyalty

Ultimately, brands and loyalty will win on the Internet just as they win offline. The biggest difference, though, will be the methods used to create brands and encourage loyalty. This ground is well-traveled for offline consumer marketing. In the offline world, advertising and promotional efforts can be measured for results and refined over time. On the Internet, e-tailers are still trying to figure out the most efficient strategies for capturing and holding customers. It will still be some time before the measurement tools are fully in place.

Obviously, e-tailers will have to develop marketing programs before the questions of effectiveness have been adequately answered. Moreover, Net consumers are a moving target. Their purchasing behaviors are changing as the Internet presents an increasing array of product choices and purchasing tricks, such as shopping bots and aggregated buying groups. Yet a retailer can't put off its marketing until the landscape begins to make sense. So e-tailers work from sketch pads, altering their strategies week-by-week.

One strategy for finding some semistability in this ever-changing consumer market is to follow the smart money. Watch the marketing moves of the sector leaders, especially those e-tailers that are succeeding as they go. Be skeptical of companies that are growing their market share without an immediate need to grow their revenues and profits. Highly capitalized companies and big brick corporations willing to lose countless millions in development mask inefficiencies with their massive budgets. Instead, watch the large niche sites and the mid-size catalogers. These companies cannot afford inefficient marketing strategies. If they're pushing hard into opt-in email, it's probably because their tests are proving it successful.

The Internet Rewards Targeting

What do Internet consumers really want? What makes a shopper come to your site and click the buy button? Novelty? Convenience? A holiday shopping deadline? Cheap prices? A chance to win in a drawing? A sense of loyalty to an enthusiast site? Perhaps your customer is a Gen Y consumer who is accustomed to buying online. Maybe your customer is a retiree buying toys for his grandchildren (25 percent of all toys are purchased by consumers over 60).

Now that U.S. online consumers are reaching saturation, there are enough Internet consumers for sites to focus on very targeted sections of the online population. Niche sites can reach their customers based on the unique content and product mix of a specialty market. Mass market sites have to target their customers by demographic group.

But wait. The Internet is not about demographic groups. The Internet is the anti–Proctor & Gamble. The Internet is about highly precise targeting to consumers who know pretty much exactly what they want before they log on. Or do they? Is there window shopping on the Internet? Is there a place for impulse purchasing? Does the Internet hold a place for the marketing lessons learned by Coke and McDonald's?

Customer Retention Is Paramount

Sometimes you have to throw the baby out with the bath water because it becomes impossible to distinguish what's baby and what's bath water. It may very well be that the only marketing strategy that can be borrowed from the brick world and successfully transported to the Internet is McDonald's famous, "Would you like fries with your order?"

Oddly, though, few Web sites have utilized this technique, even though they are uniquely qualified to make it effective. It can appear in an e-mail like this: "Last time you visited our site, you bought a Bob Dylan CD. Are you aware he just released a new album this week? It's getting great reviews. (Click below for review links.) Because you recently purchased from us, you can take a 10 percent discount on this new CD. Also, Bob Dylan is touring to support the new CD. Click below to see the tour itinerary. If you purchase a concert ticket through our link to Ticketmaster, we can give you an additional 10 percent discount. P.S., you agreed to receive e-mails like this when you purchased your last CD."

The old Music Blvd did a pretty good job of this type of marketing until it got purchased by CDNow. CDNow can't quite hit the mark with me the way Music Blvd did, and thus I've returned to buying my CDs at the local Hastings. Meanwhile, Hickory Farms, of all places, keeps reminding me of my mother's birthday (I was in a dreadful hurry one year). I have to give them credit. And I've repeated my purchase there. (Yes, they have non-sausage gifts, such as fruit, for Mom.)

The Long-Term Net Users Are the Best Consumers

The market for Internet consumers is improving, even if the Net companies are often the last to figure out how to develop a relationship with them. According to ActivMedia, the longer shoppers have been online, the more they spend. Those who have been online five years spend twice the amount of recent arrivals. Among shoppers who expect to increase their online spending, on average they expect to increase it by 43 percent. The report also noted that the time between a consumer's first Net connectivity and first online purchase has dropped significantly. Four years ago it used to take 22 months. Now it happens in an average of 4 quick months.

Given the high costs of obtaining an online retail customer, $60 on average, Internet retailers need to create a base of repeat buyers in order to survive. Yet consumers are fickle online by the very nature of the Internet, which allows quick travel from site to site. All it takes is a slow-loading page and your customers are off down the road, even if they were in mid-purchase. To obtain retail success on the Internet, merchants need to build a recognizable brand and create an effective loyalty program to keep customers returning again and again.

Sounds easy, but the Internet is filled with trap doors and twisted turns on its own conventional wisdom. For every report that explains the tools of loyalty programs, there's a report that shows the loyalty programs are woefully disappointing. For every disappointed apparel site, there is a jubilant travel site. For every encouraging statistic about rising Net purchasing, there's a study that shows that Internet consumer spending represents less than 5 percent of total retail spending. Yet even with all the confusion and overblown hopes, there are millions of hefty-income consumers poking around online, and they are getting freer and freer with their credit card numbers.

THE INTERNET FAMILY

With the majority of American households now on the Internet, e-commerce has become mainstream. Time spent online is beginning to change most family routines, from TV viewership to time spent writing letters. A study of consumer Internet usage by Greenfield Online's NetStyles revealed that one-third of Internet users expect to spend more time online in the future. A full 71 percent of adults with Internet access log on to check e-mail as soon as they get home from work, and a fourth stay online all evening.

This change in routine doesn't necessarily change the amount of time the television is on. Fifty-two percent say they keep the TV on while they're online. The study also found that people are relying on the Internet for news as much or more than newspapers or radio. In order to illustrate the ways a typical Net-connected family interacts with media, Greenfield created a composite digital family, the Greenfields.

Dad: News and Niches

The imaginary dad, Greg Greenfield, is a 46-year-old manager in an information-based business. Greg goes online from home every day, a pattern that goes back three years. He spends less time with the newspaper because the Internet gives him most of the news that he needs. This includes local, regional, and national news. He finds the Internet news more useful than the newspaper because he has more control over the amount of information he receives from each online news source.

One of Greg's favorite categories for shopping on the Internet is model trains. The selection of supplies in town for his hobby is very limited. On the Internet, the selection is virtually unlimited. As well as finding a wide selection of supplies, he can also find expertise and fellow hobbyists on the Internet. He corresponds regularly with other hobbyists about suppliers and model train history. Greg also secretly plays games online, like 84 percent of real Net users.

Mom: Health and Education

Greg's wife, Georgette, is 45 and a kindergarten teacher. She has decided the Internet is more important to her than TV, a view she shares with 19 percent of Internet users. Like 81 percent of people in the NetStyles study, Georgette uses e-mail to keep in touch with more people and she writes fewer traditional letters. She feels this is a good thing, since her e-mail is less formal and more intimate than her letter writing. She feels e-mail correspondence connects better than letters, since it is more immediate.

When Georgette is online, she is drawn to banner ads that invite her to join contests. She also uses the Internet to do research on some of the projects for her students. Georgette views the Internet as time well-used. Like 89 percent of Net users, Georgette believes the Internet saves her time, taking some of the pressure off running a home and teaching.

Kids: Entertain Us

Greg and Georgette have a 17-year-old son who spends 20 hours of unsupervised time on the Internet each week. His 11-year-old sister, Gretchen, is also granted unsupervised access to the Internet by her parents. The study found that 75 percent of children in on-line families have Web access by age 11. Fifty-five percent of online families let their kids go online whenever they want. Twenty-five percent of online kids are also permitted to make purchases online.

When Gerry shops online, he usually buys CDs, which he can afford easily since he has a part-time job. Gretchen likes to go to kids-oriented sites such as gurl.com, but she doesn't purchase very often. With limited free money from her allowance, Gretchen spends most of her money at brick malls with her friends. Sometimes, though, friends come over and they shop together on the Internet. Both Gerry and Gretchen use the Internet for school projects at least one each week, like most kids in the NetStyles study.

Greg and Georgette are well aware of parental control devices that can help limit kid's exposure to the less seemly territory of the Internet. But like 63 percent of parents in the study, they don't utilize these devices. They believe their kids have good enough judgement to stay away from inappropriate sites. The study doesn't reveal whether they are correct about their kids' judgement.

The New Mainstream Nelsons

The remarkable aspect of the Greenfield family is how overwhelmingly mainstream they are. The Internet is no longer a secret territory for those with specialized knowledge. The Internet has become thoroughly usual. It is not quite as ubiquitous as a mall. Connectivity still requires an investment of both time and learning. But the entry to Internet competence is a much shorter journey than in the early days. Most people are quickly trained at work or in school.

Connectivity is easier than ever. Decent computers continue to come down in price, but many connected families don't have to invest much to get up and going online. Many families use computers that are on loan from work for after-hours research. Other families use equipment passed down from friends or relatives. Since the market for used computer equipment is weak, most consumers give away old computers when they upgrade every two or three years.

All this means that the online audience is no longer made up of those who are intensely interested in the subjects they search. The new Internet consumer is very casual, just as interested in playing an online game as going to a special-interest site. Enthusiast sites continue to attract strong traffic, but these research-oriented consumers no longer dominate the Internet. The Net is now crawling with former television viewers.

THE INTERNET GENERATIONS

The NetStyles survey captures the flavor of the new Internet consumers, but it doesn't show the whole picture. You can break down Internet consumers into distinct generational groups, each with its own relationship to the Internet. The following shows each generation's relationship to retail e-commerce:

- *Seniors (born before 1945).* This is the "greatest generation," having saved the free world during WWII. They then came home and built the interstate highway system, not to mention rebuilding Europe and Japan. The seniors are the most surprising group on the Internet. This group of Internet shoppers buys 25 percent of all toys sold online, presumably for grandchildren. This group is the least inclined to be Net savvy, but they have other qualities in their favor, time on their hands and discretionary income. A good number of seniors are using retirement time to poke around the Internet.

- *Boomers (born between 1945 and 1964).* This is actually two generations, the sixties and the post-sixties, but for the purposes of Internet spending, they are very much alike. The baby boom generation is online at work. Like the Greenfields, they also come home and log on to the Internet. This generation is also deep into its prime earning years. But this is a busy, stressed-out lot. Boomers have kids in college and aging parents. They also have to worry about retirement. They don't trust Social Security, so they're desperately trying to make investments pay off before they leave the workforce. This is the online stock trading crowd, and they get it about online banking, but they're not much on frivolous online spending. Their impulse buys still go to the malls.

- *Xers (born between 1965 and 1974).* Generation Xers are the slackers who grew up and went to work at dot-coms. They're anything but slackers these days. A 60-hour week is light duty for an Xer in Silicon Valley. Like all young generations, they shocked their elders by growing up and changing the world. Generation X rolled up its sleeves and built the Internet economy with long hours and a knack for the wired world. They really get it because they built it. When they hit their high earning years, they will move a big portion of their retail spending online.

- *Generation Next (born between 1975 and 1990).* "You mean there was a time when people didn't go online?" This is the generation that assumes the Internet. Not only do they get it, they talk it and base their sense of hipness on where they go on it. There's just one big problem with Next: they don't have much money. In about ten years, they will begin to swing a heavy wallet, but right now they poke around hip sites that sell inexpensive clothing, CDs, make-up, and lifestyle accessories.

These thumbnails on the generations offer a rough guide to the buying habits of each generation. Forrester Research has done some additional exploration on the buying proclivities of Generation Next. Forrester sees this group as very sophisticated in online purchasing. More than one-third of Nexters now buy online. Their total online spending is $4.5 billion annually, which is 10 percent of their disposable income. They buy convenience items. Low-cost, low-risk purchases dominate, such as CDs, books, and clothes. Twenty-five percent buy computer hardware. Few buy replenishment goods (moderate-cost items such as health products, cosmetics, and groceries) over the Net.

Because most of their purchasing occurs offline, Nexters expect cross-channel synchronization. A positive experience in a retailer's offline store encourages them to try its online branch, and vice versa. These customers also expect to be able to pick up or return online purchases in physical stores, as well as to be able to order out-of-stock items online. Nexters also use coupons freely both online and offline.

Seniors are also becoming more Net-savvy. Keeping in touch with friends and family through e-mail is this group's largest interest in the Internet, but they are also willing to buy online, and many make large purchases such as travel packages and computer hardware. A SeniorNet survey finds that seniors also research stocks and investments and buy books and drugstore items. Seniors also use the Internet for gift-giving purchases.

Matching Age with Product Sectors

Generations show different Internet buying styles as well. Young people buy more CDs and videos online, according to an Ernst & Young study. Seventy percent of people under 29 bought CDs online versus 60 percent of 30- to 49-year-olds and 52 percent of those 50 and over. When it comes to unplanned purchases, seniors are the least likely to show spontaneity. Eighty-eight percent of people under 25 have made an unplanned purchase versus 60 percent of seniors. Seniors tend to stick to a few favorite sites, while young consumers make their purchase decisions from a wide selection of sites.

Gartner Group argues that there are more similarities among the generations than there are differences. Gartner found that brand loyalty matters as much to the Nexters as to older consumers. Though research shows that Nexters prefer online ordering to phone ordering, they actually place proportionally nearly the same number of phone orders as older consumers. Gartner suggests Internet marketers should avoid any assumptions that Nexters are somehow different when they go online. The research shows that Nexters are careful shoppers and need just as much reassurance from a site as any other online shoppers.

INTERNET SHOPPING BY GENDER AND INCOME

The number of women shopping online continues to grow. In late 1999, the percentage of women connected to the Internet rose to parity with men. Women, however, shop at different sites and buy different products. Research from Ernst & Young shows differences in Internet shopping by gender, age, and income level. According to the research, both men and women list books and CDs as their top choices for buying products online. After these, the differences appeared in both the types of sites visited and the types of products purchased.

When it comes to Internet sites, men favor sites that feature electronics, entertainment, and home/office supplies, while women turn to sites that feature health, beauty products, apparel, and e-greetings. When asked to name their favorite online product categories, both men and women selected computers, books, and CDs first. After these categories, the sexes diverged on Internet product selection. Men chose small consumer electronics, videos, and air travel, while women preferred health, beauty products, toys, and apparel.

Women Are the Care-Giving Consumers

As well as buying more health and beauty products and clothing online, women also buy more for kids on the Internet. Thirty one percent of women versus 18 percent of men bought children's clothing online, while 41 percent of women versus 29 percent of men have purchased toys. Men are apparently taking care of the travel needs for the family. Thirty-four percent of men versus 24 percent of women made airline reservations, and 26 percent of men versus 18 percent of women made hotel reservations. For car rentals, it was 18 percent of the men and 10 percent of the women.

Of the retail sites that receive a majority of women visitors, the top two sites were Toysrus.com and eToys.com. After that came the major portals that focus on women, iVillage.com and Women.com. The other sites in the top ten for female traffic supported the Ernst & Young research showing women's interest in kids, greetings, and health. Kbkids.com, egreetings.com and onhealth.com were all in the top ten.

Watch the Household Income Numbers

The total amount of dollars consumers spend online was directly related to their household income. No surprise: as income rises, so does the frequency of online purchases. Sixty-one percent of Internet-connected people with an annual household income over $100,000 made 10 or more purchases in 1999, while only 32 percent of those with household income under $30,000 made 10 or more purchases.

The dollar amount of online purchases rises with income as well. Eighty percent of online consumers with household income of $100,000 or more are considered "heavy Internet buyers," spending over $500 online during the previous 12 months, versus only 20 percent of those with household incomes $30,000 or below.

The categories of products purchased are also affected by the income level of the buyers. The favorite categories of people with household incomes of $100,000 or more included computers (73 percent), books (67 percent), air travel (55 percent), and small consumer electronics (47 percent). Favorite categories for those with household incomes under $30,000 were computers (65 percent), CDs (59 percent), books (51 percent), videos (21 percent), and toys (29 percent).

BRANDING ON THE INTERNET

Branding is critical to retailing success in the offline world, especially in mass merchandise products. Branding is just as important to online sites and products. But what the heck is a brand, and does it behave differently online than it does offline? David Ogilvy, often viewed as the founder of modern advertising, believed a brand was an image consumers have of a product. By image, he meant personality, which is the packaging, price, style of advertising, and above all, the nature of the product itself.

In the textbook, *Marketing Management,* author Philip Kotler described brand as a name, term, symbol, or design intended to signify and differentiate it from its competitors. Stuart Agres of the ad agency Young & Rubicam said, "A brand is a set of differentiation promises that link a product or a service to its customers."

In the book *Digital Darwinism,* author Evan Schwartz traces brands back to the livestock markings that began in ancient Egypt and continued to the American West. In television advertising, Evan sees commercial products branded in very emotional terms. He argues that the Internet is an information-based medium and thus requires branding with rational appeal rather than emotional appeal, especially since an Internet brand includes interactivity.

The Shifting World of Branding

On the Internet, the leading brand in early 2000 was America Online (AOL). By that time, AOL had surpassed America's major TV networks, NBC, ABC, CBS, and Fox. Analysts agree that AOL has reached the point where its brand is so strong, it can take its brand into the offline world. Some online companies have already taken this step. Both Yahoo! and eBay have launched print magazines. Analysts also noted that as the Internet becomes increasingly crowded, brand equity becomes a new form of currency.

The Internet world is shaking up a lot of the traditional brands. More than 40 percent of adult Internet users have changed their view of specific brands due to information they received online, according to Cyber Dialogue's American Internet User Survey. Among product categories, auto brands were the most likely to be reevaluated (21 percent of users changed their impression of the brand), followed by airlines (20 percent), investments (13 percent), and household items (12 percent). The effects of reevaluation were mixed between positive and negative.

Can You Build a Net Brand?

The users whose views were changed were most likely to be persuaded by visits to manufacturers's sites or comparison shopping sites. Seventy percent cited manufacturers's sites as the source of brand-changing information, while 60 percent cited comparison sites as the source of the perception-changing information. Only 26 percent of shoppers were influenced by banner advertising.

Many in the advertising industry claim you can't build a brand online. Yet it's clear that the Internet can deliver a brand's promises and give it the exposure it needs to blossom. Although the Internet may still be in its infancy, a significant number of consumers log on each day. Given an audience in the scores of millions, the Internet can fit right in alongside television, print, billboards, and other media to build brands. The Internet can be especially effective because it allows customers to interact more intimately with brands than other media.

Learning the Big Blue Lesson

IBM is a company that has used the Internet heavily to promote its existing services, as well as its Web-based services. In 1999, the company developed an "e-culture" campaign across all media to present IBM as a Net-savvy company. The company used media to introduce the problems of IBM customers along with the company's solutions. The goal was to establish IBM as an online brand.

IBM used rich media banners to rise above the clutter. The full story and message were delivered through the ads so users would not have to go to IBM's site to get the concept. The approach was designed to deliver a strong brand message regardless of the user's action. The result was above-average click rates, increased user interaction rates, and increased time spent within the site, not to mention favorable buzz in the Internet community.

Using Brand to Differentiate

As well as using the Internet to build an existing brand, Web-only businesses need to build brands to differentiate themselves from the clutter of dot-coms. Chipshot.com aimed to create an online brand that could be the leader in the Internet golf category. One of the company's strategies toward that goal was branded golf clubs that were produced through mass customization. Customers send in their height, skill level, and price range, and Chipshot.com builds the clubs. Now, half of the company's $6 million in revenues come from sales of the branded clubs.

Just the fact that Chipshot.com chose to create its own line of products differentiates the company from other Net players. Almost all retail companies on the Internet resell the products of other companies. Chipshot.com also benefits from a competitive environment that doesn't have giants stomping around. An athletic shoe site would have a difficult time branding a line of shoes and going up against Nike.

Most Internet retailers only have the option of branding the level of their service. Amazon.com has committed all of its commercial energy into giving its customers an excellent and inexpensive online shopping experience. The company's "second to none in service" is paying off for the Internet's top retailer, all without any branded products. Thus, Amazon.com's brand shares similarities with an offline company like Wal-Mart, which also lacks unique branded products. The essential retail nature of most Internet companies forces them into differentiating themselves only by product mix and retail service.

LOYALTY STRATEGIES

With the high cost of obtaining an Internet customer, retention is critical for retail success. That means you need to create loyal customers, those wonderful consumers who come back again and again, often telling their friends about your business. Building loyalty online is not quite the same as creating loyalty in a store. You don't have the advantage of being the geographically closest store to your customers, and you don't have the option of pouring on the charm when the customer walks in the door. The Internet presents retailers with a whole new set of problems on how to create customer loyalty.

Jupiter Communications finds that 75 percent of Internet consumers participate in some form of loyalty program, but most online consumers are quite lukewarm about the programs. The most common loyalty programs on the Internet are points-based. These initiatives offer customers the chance to collect points, much like frequent-flyer miles, that can be redeemed for merchandise. The problem is, Internet consumers are not impressed with point-based reward programs. Some analysts suggest that retailers must go beyond giving out points and should reward loyalty with improved service such as priority service, personalized offers, or e-mail updates.

That's not very helpful, since these items are part of the normal mix of Internet marketing and should be in place whether the consumer is a first-time customer or a repeat consumer. Some sites see the role of service as paramount, whether it is the customer's first purchase or 51st purchase. Amazon.com is an example of an Internet retailer that believes excellent service is one of the few real tools of differentiation in a crowded market.

Service Is the Heart of Loyalty

Customer loyalty can't be bought through points. If a customer has an unimpressive visit to a site, they won't come back to build on a few points given during an initial uninspired purchase. You receive loyalty from customers when you have given them a good reason to come back. Those reasons are usually built on more than points. They come from delivering the product on time. They come from one-to-one interaction. They come from the courtesy the site offers its customers by asking permission before marketing to them. The reasons come from providing the customers with content that goes to the heart of why the customer came to the site in the first place.

Online loyalty comes from the following features:

- Content that communicates expertise
- Offers customized to the customer's interest
- Reward programs tied to visitor interest
- A customer-friendly site
- Complete service backup if anything goes awry

Internet retailing can create essentially two types of loyalty. One is a great shopping experience that builds customer trust. The other is high domain expertise. Some Internet consumers go to the Internet to find the best price and appropriate service. They usually have a good idea what they're looking for, and they simply want to find the best combination of price and service. If they get points, that's fine, but the points will not weigh in as high as price and service.

Serving the Enthusiasts

The other Net user is an enthusiast. He wants to find the site that has the very best content about the subject. This may be a fly fisherman looking for a new reel or a blues lover looking to find a rare

Muddy Waters recording. These Net users will be persuaded by the knowledge and helpfulness of the site. With enthusiasts, points programs help, but only by relating to the content of the customers's enthusiasm. But even with a points system, these customers are much more attuned to the quality of the site's content or expertise than they are to rewards points.

Most Internet shoppers fall into both groups, depending on the item they're out to purchase. The same Muddy Waters fan may stop by Amazon.com to buy toys for a child's birthday. The same music enthusiast who is devoted to the site that sells rare recordings suddenly is looking only at price and service when it comes to buying the toys that need to arrive next Tuesday.

Match Loyalty to Customer Behavior

Loyalty programs will work if the retailer knows what group his customer is in when shopping on the individual site. When a first-time customer buys, you should know whether to smother that customer with content or deliver service and price. One or the other will ring the bells that will encourage the customer to sign up to receive e-mail promotions and put the site into the favorites folder.

Do your customers view you as the Wal-Mart that gives great service and price with no knowledge of the products? Or do your customers see you as that special gardening shop where all of the personnel know exactly when to plant bulbs or seeds? Once you know the answer to this question, it becomes easy to decide what type of loyalty program to implement.

Loyalty programs do not necessarily need to be created from scratch. Companies such as MyPoints.com, clickRewards.com, and FreeRide.com are available to merchants on an outsourced basis. These programs let merchants give away points that can be redeemed at Internet sites throughout the Web, even for frequent flyer miles. One service, Stario, creates custom-branded loyalty programs on an outsourced basis. Outsourced loyalty systems are a less expensive alternative for small sites that don't have the resources to develop a full-blown customer rewards program.

BUILDING LOYALTY WITH SERVICE

Service is no small tool for holding customers close. A whopping 90 percent of online shoppers consider good customer service to be critical when choosing a Web site. Customer service is not just a system to help customers with returns after the sale and delivery of products. To Web users, service is an experience that begins when the customer enters the site and continues through the return process. A full 37 percent of Web purchasers in the last year used customer service while shopping online. Forty-two percent of those purchasers use customer service online more than they do in offline shopping and would stop shopping at a Web merchant if they were unhappy with the service.

Net shoppers rely on online customer service because it is easy, not because the Web buying experience requires more hand-holding. One-third of shoppers who use customer service on the Internet do so more than in offline stores because on the Net, it's easier to use the services. Web buyers also approve of the service level they receive from most Web sites. Forty-seven percent of consumers who have requested service from a Web site say the service exceeded their expectations.

There are a number of points at which a customer employs service from a Web merchant. A breakdown showing where customers most often ask for assistance identifies areas of particular customer service need. Here are the percentages of online shoppers who have needed customer service for various moments in the shopping experience:

Product search	19%
Product information	10%
Billing	21%
Checkout	14%
Order status	58%
Shipping	22%
Post delivery	19%

These figures break the common perception that customer service is primarily called in when a customer has trouble with a product after it arrives. The dominant area of need is in the tracking of order status and shipping. This concern isn't restricted to retail operations. In industries that depend on the delivery of parts or materials for production, the period between order and delivery is considered the most sensitive in the process of obtaining parts or materials. Excellent service in the trade of industrial products and parts always includes the ability to track every moment in the shipping and delivery process.

Blending Your Points of Contact

There are a number of ways that consumers obtain their customer service. E-mail is both the most common form of customer service communication, and it is also the one most preferred by customers. Second in use and preference is telephone communication. Over 90 percent of online customers prefer e-mail or telephone to all other forms of service communication. Another service option is a FAQ section (list of answers to frequently asked questions), which customers use even though they do not prefer it. Other forms of service that are infrequently utilized are online chats, U.S. mail, faxes, and in-store visits.

Great service can actually drive future sales. It is not simply a way to keep customers satisfied through the buying process. Exceptional customer service can lead to repeat visits and positive word-of-mouth advertising. Over 90 percent of satisfied customers report that they are likely to visit a site again, while only 9 percent of unsatisfied shoppers will do so. The statistics are similar with word-of-mouth promotion. Eight-seven percent of satisfied shoppers will recommend a site to friends and family, while only 5 percent of unsatisfied customers will spread the word.

Defining Service Strategies

There are two styles of service delivered by Web sites: reactive service and proactive service. Reactive customer service is simply the act of responding to customer requests, from search or product questions to inquiries about shipping and order status. One of the strongest components of reactive customer service is a no-hassle return process. Good sites include return shipping labels with all products. Easy order tracking is another area of service of high importance to customers.

Proactive customer service is the act of going beyond customer expectations by offering smart, unexpected touches that assist shoppers throughout the purchase process. Retailers who satisfy their customers can expect 34 percent to return, while those retailers that exceed their customers's expectations can expect a 90 percent return. Outpost.com offers free overnight shipping to make anxious customers happy. eToys adds stickers for the kids in each package.

Service as Competitive Edge

Other examples of proactive customer service include sites that offer detailed product information. Amazon pioneered this strategy by adding editorial and customer reviews to books. Other sites utilize gift shopping recommendations and product reviews from experts to enhance the shopper's experience. On the after-purchase service side, some sites are coordinating their customer service with that of manufacturers, so the online shopper isn't simply shipped off to the manufacturer when a product malfunctions.

A site with excellent service should use it as a point of competitive advantage. Strong proactive customer service can be stated as a promise to customers to make sure they have a satisfying buying experience. Companies that advertise their call center and their service touches can expect to increase the likelihood of attracting shoppers, since service is one of the highest concerns among Internet consumers.

There is, however, another side to the service question. Because an excellent service program is a deep investment for any Internet company, there are some Net retailers that go counter-trend. They set up bargain bottom sites that offer very little service. Many manufacturers are reluctant to sell their prime retail merchandise through these sites and instead sell their excess inventory at these warehouse sites.

THE POWER OF CONTENT

The Internet has always been about obtaining information. Whether to get the latest papers on physics, or information on the best trout streams in Montana, people go to the Internet for information. Even the large sites like Amazon.com, which seek to be all things to all consumers, use information as a big part of the lure to the site. Amazon.com originally gained its reputation for excellence by delivering great information about books. With its powerful search engine, Amazon.com also made it easy to obtain that information. This information is now called content, and it is universally recognized as a critical part of Internet retailing. The need to present strong content has launched a small industry of content providers. You can now go to conferences on how to buy content.

The model of attracting customers with content is the heart of most media. Newspapers, magazines, radio, and television are all built around the concept that if you give consumers strong content, they will be willing to view your clients's advertisements. The biggest difference between the old media and the new media is that on the Internet, consumers don't just view advertising, they actually buy the merchandise.

Surround Yourself with Experts

Mass merchandisers have learned that content needs to play a central role in their customers's buying experience on the Internet. On the Kmart site, you can get expert information on fashion and home decorating. Lands' End has presented Jim Fowler, former chief wildlife guide for *Wild Kingdom,* to tell tales to viewers. CDNow, the top music retailer, hired *Rolling Stone*'s Anthony Decurtis to be the executive editor of its content.

Even large industry is using content to bring buyers and sellers to the large e-marketplaces at the center of each business sector. Farmers can go to any of a number of agriculture sites to check the weather, which can be personalized to their locality. They can also check the prices of crops and livestock. One site will even send a message to a farmer's beeper when a particular crop hits a specific price, which lets the farmer rush to market at the point of highest return. This example shows how crucial content can become in the battle for online customers.

Content Is the Lure

Content can attract customers in a variety of ways, from e-mail newsletters to statistical information about an industry or about consumer products that is posted at the site. Many sites use content as a marketing tool to keep the customers close. The e-mail newsletter has evolved into a daily stream of news going out to customers who want a continual update on what is occuring in their business or hobby. I receive some newsletters that are produced three times each weekday.

Content helps to attract customers, and it also works to build credibility and confidence in the site. Whether it is a business site or a consumer site, the online business will be judged by the quality of its content. If you go to a site on June 1 and you see that the latest news item posted on the home page is dated March 13, you are naturally going to wonder if the staleness of the content reflects the quality of the site's products and services. Likewise, if you go to a site that has three news stories that have broken in the past two or three hours, you'll get the impression that this site is at the absolute heart of its market.

Borrowing Content

You don't have to launch an internal news service in order to provide quality information to your audience, but you may need to partner with a top news source. Though most sites provide at least a portion of their own online content, it is becoming increasingly common to see Web sites partner with news and media organizations to deliver excellent content to visitors. Content has become a competitive tool that can be as important as price or service, so Internet companies are turning to services to provide the best possible information for their customers.

Most sites that focus on content as a draw will create a custom blend of content that includes news, how-to articles, statistics, product or service information, and some version of customer support or help. Many sites also provide space for customers to interact with each other. The custom blend of content is critical for niche sites that attract customers by taking the role of the expert in the subject. This expertise is also important for industry-based e-marketplaces.

Content as a Give-Away

The use of content to attract Web customers is eating into the paid content market. If major sites utilize content to attract customers, it's hard to sell similar content. Adult content accounts for 69 percent of the market of paid content on the Internet. This market is not likely to be threatened by giveaway content, but other paid content markets may face competition from sites that give it away in order to reach preferred customers.

I recently saw a plan for a Net company that intends to create procedure templates for the health care industry. The templates would provide a hospital or medical practice a range of options, ranked by effectiveness, for each diagnosis. This template would allow a doctor to see quickly all the potential treatments for a diagnosis and how each fared in practice. The template would also provide a procedure recommendation based on the patient's individual condition.

The company behind the templates expected to derive revenue by selling the package to hospitals. Its templates would be updated continually, so hospitals would need to subscribe to the template program, thus providing the template producer with a continuous stream of revenue. Not knowing much about the medical field, the concept seemed to have merit, since the founders were well-schooled in the medical industry. The idea would be especially effective if it could be determined that hospitals would improve their treatment results by using the templates as an aide in determining how a patient should be treated.

Content Needs Perceived Value

There was one huge hole in the concept, though. Paid content has become a dicey matter. All you need is for a business-to-business marketplace to take the template concept and give it away to hospitals in order to attract them to a site that sells surgical supplies and medical equipment. If the template idea has the ability to win the confidence of medical practitioners, it will also have the power to bring them to an e-marketplace where it can be obtained at no charge.

Any company involved in producing expert content that is clearly valuable to professionals, industry, or consumers may find that the ultimate market for the content is not with the end users but with the Web sites that need to sell to the end users. My suggestion to the medical template company was to attempt to forge an agreement to sell the content to players in medical supplies and equipment. These companies may be very interested in a program that can attract and hold their customers.

YOUR NET STRATEGY:

At the heart of all successful business is the effort to create and sustain a brand. Whether you're marketing a magazine, cleaning products, a restaurant, or a Web site, your ability to create a brand is critical to success. AOL and Yahoo! have become leading Internet brands because they were able to establish brand identity. In both cases, the companies offered nontechnical consumers the ability to maneuver the Internet without knowing anything about the inner workings of computers. Also, both companies managed to create a user experience that is helpful and consistent. These are two of the most recognized brands on the Internet. Indeed, they have become two of the most highly recognized brands across the consumer brands universe. Both companies are also profitable, which is not a coincidence.

Stay aware at all times that as you move onto the Internet, you are creating a new brand or extending an existing brand. It doesn't matter whether you are developing a consumer-based enterprise or a business-to-business operation. Brand names such as IBM, Oracle, and Cisco are just as important to their companies as Sears, Wal-Mart, and Ford are to their business models.

The qualities of brand awareness are created by simply putting a name before customers again and again, though promotion is certainly important. The qualities that build a brand include strong customer service, quality products, high perceived value, and personality. Wal-Mart builds personality with store greeters and the well-communicated image of founder Sam Walton driving store-to-store in his pickup. With AOL, the personality comes from the ubiquitous "You've Got Mail," which became a symbol of the widespread use of e-mail, as well as the style of the site itself.

At the center of most Internet branding is content. The early Internet brands were built largely through the use and development of content. This was true of AOL with its chat and subject areas. Yahoo!'s reputation is based almost entirely on its use of content. Even Amazon.com is known as much for the content surrounding its products as it is for its stellar fulfillment and customer service operation.

The Internet also offers a rich opportunity to create personality, since the user experience is very intimate. When your customers interact directly and regularly with your product and service, it's relatively easy to introduce style to the experience. Ask Jeeves stands out not simply because of its quality service, but also for its identification with the highly personable character. Likewise, sites such as Monster.com and eBay deliver personality even without a character, using bright graphics and top ease-of-use.

Another aspect of branding that is essential to Web success is the focus on core competency. All successful Web ventures clearly identify the one or two elements of their service that are of greatest importance to their customers. With Priceline.com, it's the name-your-own-price model. With Amazon.com, it's comprehensive selection and product content. With Yahoo!, it's widespread content. If you cannot quickly name the core competency of the business, it probably has a weak brand. Make sure as you build your Web brand that your message is always tied to your greatest strength.

CHAPTER 6

ENTERTAINMENT

Entertainment on the Internet won't come into full bloom until high-speed connectivity is widespread among consumers. Until then, entertainment companies will use the Internet to support their offline products. Disney offers a number of sites created to help their customers learn about their entertainment programs or plan vacations at the Disney theme parks. Game platforms, such as Sega and Sony, present sites that enhance and extend the games on their video platforms. There are some original content sites in development, but they anticipate small audiences until connectivity expands.

Once broadband becomes widely available, the Internet experience for consumers will change quickly and completely. It's one thing to shop for a Mother's Day present at 1-800-FLOWERS. It's quite another thing to click onto an Internet channel on your television set and rent a movie from a selection that includes every movie ever made. Broadband will make the Internet truly user friendly. It will also open the doors to increases in picture clarity that will at first rival cable television, then equal it. Just as cable has diluted the network brands of ABC, CBS, and NBC, Internet entertainment will obliterate the television brands we know now, unless they work aggressively to keep up with the changes.

Net Entertainment Is Just around the Corner

Entertainment will explode on the Internet when high-speed broadband is widespread in the homes of American consumers. That's a given. But when it actually arrives, it may not look much like the Internet. A rush to user friendliness will open the doors to experimentation in presentation, graphics, and content itself. Broadband will blend television with the Internet in a way that will allow inexpensive upstart channels to build niche audiences.

The type of general programming that has dominated network television for 50 years may finally pass altogether as niche programming wins favor with viewers. This happened in the magazine industry in the 1980s as *Life, Look,* and the *Saturday Evening Post* lost their ability to hold the attention of a homogenous culture with general interest content. In the magazine industry, as magazine printing costs came down, it became increasingly possible for a magazine to succeed by serving small portions of the magazine-reading audience, ending the reign of big magazine. We can look for the same thing to happen once high-speed Net access gives us a million choices in television programming.

Cable television opened up the possibility of niche-branded television, but the costs to develop programming still necessitated large audiences. So even though cable opened a new spectrum of channels, the ante to get into the television game still required the kind of programming that could attract a mass audience, and programs that can attract large viewership mean high production costs. Broadband Internet access will end television's reign as a medium of mass viewership and turn the set into a great platform for inexpensive niche programming, much like Net radio has done for music.

The Web Will Make TV Interactive

Once you can turn on your television and watch any Web site on the Internet, the revenue model for television will change as well as the programming. Television began life as a vehicle for advertising sales. With cable it morphed into the magazine model with its combination of advertising revenue and subscription fees. When broadband becomes widespread, portions of the television market will take on the Internet revenue market, which involves using content (in this case programming) to attract an audience for advertising and product sales.

Just as Internet radio programming allows listeners to purchase CDs while they are listening to the music, television programs and advertising will encourage on-the-spot product buys. Another revenue model that will likely proliferate through broadband Internet is on-demand rental of movies and television shows. Rather than subscription-based pricing, the costs for on-demand viewing will probably be discounted through competitive commercial channels owned by companies such as Blockbuster. Since the rentals will come through the Internet rather than the monopolistic cable company, prices on rentals will likely be billed at a small fraction of the current pay-per-view provided by cable companies.

CHEAP CHANNELS MEAN CONTENT WINS

The real winners of the switch to Internet delivery of entertainment will be the content makers. The movie, television, music, and sports industries have been controlled by channel providers rather than content providers for as long as a mass audience for entertainment has existed. Network television companies, record companies, and movie distribution corporations have held the strings of entertainment because they owned the means to deliver the programming to a mass audience. Broadband Internet access will change this landscape completely.

The actual content providers will be able to deliver their product directly to their customers. Disney may wake up one day and wonder why it ever bothered to purchase ABC, especially when it can rent its products directly to its audience, complete with product promotions. Sports teams will be able to send their programming directly to fans through team-owned Internet channels, also with product promotions. Original television programming will be able to go out directly to audiences without striking a deal with a major network. Instead of selling program ideas to channels, production companies will be able to sell programs directly to viewers.

Quality Content Will Still Rule Entertainment

There is only one thing that won't change in entertainment programming, the necessity of excellence in programming. But the size of the audience needed to support that excellence will change. Just as Net radio has supported niche programming such as 24-hour blues, bluegrass, folk, and Celtic, forms of music that have no home in commercial radio, broadband will allow niche programming to move to the television screen.

The networks that survive this evolution will be those that help viewers organize and navigate an entertainment world with a bewildering number of options. When provided with too many choices, viewers will gravitate to entertainment browsers that can present the endless options in a comprehensible manner that guides the viewer to quality content without sacrificing choice. The AOL Time Warner corporation will certainly have the wherewithal to deliver an entertainment browser to a mass audience, especially if they lean more heavily on the AOL model rather than the Time Warner model. AOL found success by making the Internet comprehensible to newcomers, so their model shows they understand how to present an incomprehensible world to a mass audience.

The TV Will Morph into a Yahoo!-like Platform

Yahoo! may also have a shot at becoming an entryway into an expanded world of entertainment choices. Right now, Yahoo! is more prepared for the new world of millions of television channels than the television networks or cable companies. Unless they change their basic services, the major networks may be marginalized by the changes broadband produces. In response to these changes, networks may choose to become production companies that deliver content such as sitcoms or news programs to a wide array of channels, or they may attempt to assume the role of content navigators. They will probably have to choose one or the other.

The branded content providers such as Disney and Warner Brothers will be the biggest of all winners. The world loves its entertainment brands however they are delivered. Both Disney and Warner Brothers have been able to survive through all the media

ENTERTAINMENT

changes by connecting directly with an audience and establishing characters that endure through cultural and technological changes. Mickey Mouse and Bugs Bunny may reach new commercial highs as their programming and products reach new viewers through high-speed interactive Internet distribution.

Entertainment Content Will Thrive in Brands

Ultimately, we may look back at Michael Eisner's tenure at Disney and applaud it not for acquisitions such as ABC, but for the revival of full-length animation that launched new characters such as Aladdin, Belle, Simba, and Woody. Disney has a rare ability to create new characters, and a talent for taking popular literary characters such as Pooh Bear, and commercializing them. In a world where everyone has access to channels, recognizable, branded programming will dominate entertainment. The Yankees, Mickey Mouse, and Bugs Bunny will handily win the war set off by broadband's explosion of entertainment options.

News bureaus also stand a chance to weather the storm that will come with widespread broadband. Networks have already gone a long way toward branding their news programming and building their hosts into celebrities. Viewers will quickly forget the ABC logo, but they will not easily let go of personalities such as Regis Filbin, Sam Donaldson, and Ted Koppel. Likewise with the morning show personalities. The networks will likely hold on to their branded news and personality programming even as the network structures break down.

They will meet new competition, though, as new Net programming will turn inevitably to promoting a younger generation of personalities as hosts of news and entertainment shows. The bankable stars currently on the original shows presented by the networks, from *Nightline* to *60 Minutes,* are aging. The next generation of these hosts may come from Net-based programming rather than from the networks. It may already be too late for the networks to introduce, promote, and establish a younger crew who can ride out the switch from cable and broadcast to broadband. Mickey Mouse will make the transition in fine shape; the present news stars probably won't.

THE BROADBAND AUDIENCE IS ALREADY WAITING

Once high-speed Internet access becomes available, consumers won't take long to jump aboard. There is pent-up demand for residential broadband connectivity. By 2004, there will be more than 25 million high-speed households in the United States, up from 1.9 million consumers with broadband in 1999. The rapid increase is expected to drive service revenues from $580 million in 1999 to $7.67 billion in 2004. Broadband access will come in the form of cable modem (through television cable lines), digital subscriber line (DSL), direct broadcast satellite, or wireless broadband.

Cable television is considered the first-to-market, with DSL gaining steadily. Cable and DSL are expected to capture almost 90 percent of the market by 2004. Confusion over availability and cost are seen as constraints in the market's growth. Strategists estimate that 75 percent of Internet users do not know whether high-speed access services are provided in their areas. Another two-thirds say they know little or nothing about cable modems. More than 80 percent say the same thing about DSL.

AOL Is Poised for the Broadband Breakthrough

America Online subscribers hope the merger with Time Warner will bring answers to some of these questions. More than other Internet users, the 22 million AOL subscribers expect the merger to usher in a "wonder world" of media convergence for entertainment and media, according to research from Greenfield Online and Myers Group. Ninety percent of AOL subscribers expect the merger to hasten the availability of high-speed access. Half of AOL's market also expects Internet telephone service to become available as well. Almost half of AOL subscribers also anticipate the merger will lead to easy downloading of music and Internet access through the TV. Interest in these services was strongest among those 35 and younger. The study also found the more affluent the subscriber, the higher the expectations.

One survey reported that AOL customers so eagerly expect AOL to lead them to high-speed access, that AOL as a company may be

ENTERTAINMENT

in jeopardy if it doesn't address the need for broadband access for its customers. The survey from The Phillips Group shows that AOL customers expect the company to aggressively seek out new deals that develop its broadband relationship with DSL and wireless services as well as with cable, even though its merger with Time Warner may give the company more access to cable connectivity.

The survey also confirmed that broadband will come most readily through the cable system. Because of this, The Phillips Group expects U.S. consumers to be up and going on broadband far more quickly than their European counterparts, because the United States is more universally wired for cable. Europe is ahead in wireless Internet connectivity because it cannot rely on a cable system to bring widespread high-speed connectivity. The United States tends to be behind on high-speed wireless, partly because telecommunication companies don't want to make the investment in the new technology until they have a better perception of the amount of demand there will be for the service.

The Phillips Group sees broadband connectivity through satellite access as having a longer-term potential. But since service providers don't have a two-way system in place, the time-lag prevents satellite from being an immediate threat to cable-based broadband in the residential market. Even as cable is likely to win the access war for connecting consumers, DSL is expected to continue to dominate the business market.

THE WEB STIMULATES TRADITIONAL ENTERTAINMENT

In a pre-broadband world, the Internet is not competing with offline entertainment, even though young people are spending 10 to 20 hours per week online. For young consumers, movie theaters, CD players, and stadiums remain the favorites for experiencing entertainment. The Internet has become a vehicle to help young consumers choose their entertainment options. Chats and Web sites hold greater sway over entertainment choices than TV ads and movie previews, supporting the argument for integrated offline and online promotional campaigns.

According to Forrester Research, the Web often stimulates offline entertainment, rather than depressing it. A quarter of young online consumers report they are spending more on CDs, concert tickets, videos/DVDs, and computer games since going online. Almost 60 percent of wired 16- to 22-year olds research entertainment choices over the Internet. An even greater number visit sites dedicated to movies or recording artists without specifically intending to do research. Seventy percent of young consumers who visit sites with entertainment information admit the research directly influences their choices in CDs.

Word-of-Mouse Promotion Thrives

Web sites and e-mail promotions are as effective as offline promotion in magazine ads, billboards, and theater previews. Word-of-mouth earns the highest value in offline promotion, while tips gathered in chat rooms and instant messages lead online promotion. In comparing offline entertainment promotion to online efforts, Web promotion surpasses television for its effectiveness with young consumers.

MTV.com, MPS.com, Disney.com, and Uproar.com are favorite sites among young consumers. Between one-third and one-half of young Internet users have visited these sites and rated them highly. These sites provide young consumers with information that is in-depth, up-to-date, easy to access, and unique to the Web, all of which are high priorities for young consumers. These users find sites through word-of-mouth, search engines, TV ads, hyperlinks, banners, print and radio ads, and e-mail marketing. Forrester also noted that these consumers spend $26.9 billion per year on movies, CDs, and video games.

MUSIC: A WORLD OF DOWNLOADS

To say the Internet is going to change the music business is like saying it might rain in Seattle. The real question is whether a music business will be left after the Internet cuts its tornado-like raze through the heart of the music industry. At first glance, the Internet seems to be providing a new channel for music distribution that will grow incrementally over the next few years. Internet sales represent 3.8 percent of the revenues of the music industry. This will grow to 14 percent in 2003. These revenues will come through CD sales and music downloads.

Downloading music and video products, though, brings up problems with securing the downloads so they cannot be copied and shared. The entertainment industry has yet to create a safe way to send their products over the Internet. Some music industry watchers see opportunity at the center of this problem. The Web will allow record labels to market their artists in new ways while also using the Internet to deliver big savings from the production of CDs, to the marketing of new releases. Labels have the opportunity to become Internet music networks with control of their content (their artists) through new channels of distribution, such as Web sites and Net broadcasting. This will allow labels to create new revenue streams through advertising and artist-based, product sales on everything from concert tickets to artist-based, private-label clothing.

Music Labels Will Add Value to Survive

The labels, if they choose to become entrepreneurial, can take the role of the information center for their artists. Why shouldn't labels muscle into the territory of memorabilia auctions, streaming Web videos, bonus songs, alternate takes, concert footage, interview postings, live set lists and reviews, live chats with the artists, and chats for fans? Labels have not taken this initiative, instead choosing to protect their CD turf against copyright infringement through downloads. History may prove this defensiveness kept labels from participating in more aggressive marketing and promotion opportunities that exist for their artists.

Some artists are pointing the way. The release by Matchbox Twenty, *Mad Season,* came with custom versions of AOL's Winamp downloading software and its Spinner.com streaming-media service. This allows the owners of the CD to get access to a bonus video of a Matchbox Twenty performance in Australia and a radio channel programmed by the band. With the merger of AOL and Time Warner, this type of promotion can be an easy piece of work and an effective way to promote an artist. It wouldn't be difficult to take this concept a touch further, incorporating cross promotions with other label artists.

Downloads Will Dominate Distribution

The actual distribution of music will change as downloading becomes the fans's preferred way of obtaining music. Universal and Sony are beginning to see the light. The two companies are developing a joint subscription service for audio and video music. Companies are also looking at reviving the single, offering a single song downloaded at consumer-friendly prices such as $.75 or $.99 apiece.

The implications of a change in the distribution of music are global. If labels jump online and make their music available at a reduced price, they may even recapture part of the international market that has long been lost to piracy, which is estimated at over 30 percent of overall sales on an artist's CD. Labels are not going to be able to put the lid on digital downloads any more than they were able to control cassette taping of music or the expanding CD replication of music. With all music in digital form, it is simply too easy to make perfect copies.

Relationships between Audience, Artist, and Label Will Change Completely

To survive this radical change in the distribution of music, labels will need to develop new relationships with artists and new relationships with fans. Some predict that music will ultimately be given away to promote live shows. This is The Grateful Dead model. The band freely encouraged audience members to record its concerts and share them. The band believed this giveaway promoted its live shows. Because the band spent its last decade in the top five of gross concert revenues, even without hit records, they may have been on to something.

If record labels lose control of their finished recorded product, they will be wise to take some control over other aspects of their artists's careers, such as concerts and product sales. Ultimately, recorded music may become a loss leader to build concert attendance. With the genie of free downloading out of the box, the smart record companies may look toward developing new revenue streams rather than trying to pressure the government to help them coax the genie back into the CD.

MOVIES: PROMOTION ON THE NET

Just as Internet promotions work to influence young Net users to buy CDs, online movie promotions can encourage movie goers in their selections. A report from Cyber Dialogue's Cybercitizen shows that online promotions affect which movies Internet users choose to see. The report finds that 28 percent of general movie goers report their choice of movies changed as a result of visiting movie-related Web sites. Among intensive movie fans, 42 percent reported changing attitudes about entertainment brands. Movie sites are drawing over 18 million movie-going consumers.

The Internet already has one phenomenal success story in movie promotion to act as a guide to using the Internet effectively in encouraging movie attendance. *The Blair Witch Project* was the sleeper hit of the summer of 1999. The movie cost only $35,000 to make, but it grossed $140 million, making it one of the most profitable movies in film history. One of the secrets behind the movie's success was the use of the Internet in promoting attendance at the movie.

The Web Site Extends the Story

The creative team responsible for promoting the film didn't spend millions of dollars on movie trailers, television commercials, full-page newspaper spreads, and other pricey avenues to the consumer. Many of the film's early fans were first turned on to the movie by its Web site. *The Blair Witch Project* Web site cost $15,000 to launch. In its first week it received 75 million hits and helped create a fan base so strong, some theaters ran out of tickets on opening night.

The movie is a mock documentary about three students who are making a film about the Blair Witch, a mythical witch in Maryland who supposedly caused the murder of seven children in the woods outside a small town. The movie captures the increasing hysteria of the filmmakers as they become lost in the woods while making their film. Though *The Blair Witch Project* was inexpensive to produce, it was very effective at creating the impression that the filmmakers were truly in trouble.

The Web site succeeds by extending the story of the three filmmakers. Further details are contained at the site, and during the movie's run in theaters, the site was updated regularly with new information concerning the characters. All of this is presented in the style of the movie's documentary, which furthers the impression of reality. Instead of presenting stills from the movie or interviews with the stars, the site allows viewers to go deeper into the mystery of the story.

Because the site extended the drama of the movie, it had the effect of sending viewers back to the theater for second viewings. So moviegoers would see the movie, visit the site, then go back and see the movie again. As the film neared the end of its theatrical release, the site started to promote the video release, complete with additional footage that added more to the story, including interviews with the family members of the filmmakers.

The Web Site Also Becomes a Revenue Source

The movie's Web site also hawks ancillary products related to the movie. Though there is no music on the film, you can purchase Josh's Blair Witch soundtrack, which is the replication of a tape supposedly found in the car of one of the characters. You can also purchase a wanted poster for the missing filmmakers, also not in the movie. The site also sells various key chains, magnets, and pins depicting scenes from the film.

The success of the Web promotion has spawned a number of additional Web sites related to the story. You can go to a Web site devoted to the mythical town of Burkittsville, Maryland, a small town of 200 where *The Blair Witch Project* was filmed. On the site, residents provide facts about the town, which includes 75 old Victorian homes, one post office, and a church. This ancillary site drew a half a million visits per day during the film's theatrical run.

The Movie's Story Determines the Site's Marketing Potential

Not all movies lend themselves to this type of Web promotion. It takes inventive and creative effort more than financial muscle to make it work. In order for this type of promotion to take hold, it needs to be matched to a story that is compelling enough to grip an audience that wants to investigate the story further. There are other movies, though, that have an engaging depth of subject that could be extended for the viewer. Web sites for movies such as *The Perfect Storm,* a movie based on real events, could be used to give the movie fan more depth into the background of the story.

Though the movie industry didn't immediately jump to story-based sites in the aftermath of the *Blair Witch* success, we can expect this type of promotion to begin to seep into movie promotion as others do it successfully. Even though the movie industry may now view *Blair Witch* as a fluke rather than a trend, given the willingness of viewers to visit a story-based site and respond to its merchandising as well as its repeat-viewing capabilities, other movie promotion teams will certainly experiment with Internet promotions that go beyond clips and star shots, especially since the cost of Web promotion is tallied in creativity and inventiveness rather than in dollars.

SPORTS: THE TEAMS GO ELECTRONIC

The sports world has discovered the Internet. Consumers are expected to spend approximately $3 billion in sporting goods, apparel, footwear, and event tickets online in 2003, according to Jupiter Communications. And unlike other industries that have seen the

Web cannibalize sales from traditional revenues, sports content on the Internet actually presents an additional business opportunity for the sports industry.

Online sports consumption is one of the Internet's most important segments for consumers. Sports content is ranked as one of the top five favorite activities for online consumers. In its dial-up stage, sports content online is complimentary to offline sports presentations. This will change when broadband becomes widely available to Internet consumers, but in the meantime, sports leagues and organizations can benefit by adding the Internet as a channel for the sales of sporting event tickets and team-related merchandise.

Branded Teams Will Benefit Most from Web Sports

In the long run, though, as consumers adopt broadband delivery of Internet programming, the sports industry will be dramatically affected by online channels. In early 2000, according to Forrester Research, 22 percent of North American households actively followed sports on the Web, a total audience of close to 10 million. As broadband connectivity begins to proliferate, the sports industry will be changed in the same dramatic manner that online trading changed the brokerage industry.

New Web technologies will allow professional sports leagues to create and deliver innovative broadband sports programming directly to fans, effectively shifting power away from the networks and redefining the model behind the business of sports entertainment. Presently networks control the delivery of sports programming at the national level. The networks are at the center of the exchange between professional or college leagues, marketers, and sports fans.

Team Sites Will Become a Revenue Source

As broadband becomes widespread, a power shift will move the professional and college leagues to the center of a world that has been controlled by broadcasters since the proliferation of radio. As consumers turn to high-speed connectivity, league sites, team sites, and the sites of Web partners will provide a non-network distribution alternative, not only for the presentation of events, but also for the sale of merchandise and tickets.

This will begin to take place by 2004, as the sports power shift starts to dictate new roles for the major players in the sports marketplace. For professional leagues like the National Football League or associations like the Professional Golf Association, the Internet will become more than just another distribution channel. It will become an opportunity to exploit whole new revenue streams.

Broadband Will Further Team-centric Programming

By 2003, more than 27 million households will have broadband access that will give consumers high-quality video streaming. In this world of Web delivery alternatives, leagues will no longer license exclusive distribution rights for an event to a single network. Instead, several entities will share the task, offering their own unique experiences on television, the Web, or wireless devices. As the viewership fragments, the leagues will find themselves at the center of a market with wide choices.

This is similar to the scenario spelled out for entertainment, where content providers gain control of the distribution once there are multiple channels and the conduit to consumers becomes inexpensive. By 2004, advertising on sports-related Web sites will reach $2.4 billion, with sports-related e-commerce climbing to $7 billion. For a typical league like the NBA, online revenue is predicted to contribute as much as 15 percent of total revenues in 2004.

Web Sports Will Deepen Sponsor Relationships

The presentation of sports on the Internet ushers in a world where brand advertisers abandon the one-size-fits-all mass-market advertising model in favor of cross-media targeted campaigns. Sponsorship packages will include a prominent presence on sports-related sites, and on-air advertisements will point audiences to archival highlight footage, promotions, and e-commerce opportunities on the Web.

Many teams are currently generating modest amounts of revenue through online ad sales, ticketing, and merchandising, and by offering paid subscriptions for premium content. The median team site revenue is now $100,000, dominated by online advertising. Teams expect that site revenues will grow tenfold to $1 million by 2004. But the real change will come when leagues and teams gain more control over their distribution. When that begins to happen, leagues and teams will see their Web-based revenues increase more dramatically.

GLOBAL GAMING

Another area of the sports world comes in the form of online sports betting, although there is no current Net gambling legislation. Net gambling is considered illegal under the Interstate Wire Act of 1961, which prohibits interstate wagering via phone or telegraph wire. Some enterprises have tried to jump this hurdle by opening offshore operations in places like Antigua where gambling is legal, then making the service available in the United States.

The offshore approach didn't protect World Sports Exchange from an FBI sting in 1998. In that year, 21 individuals from 9 offshore gambling Web sites were indicted by the U.S. government for allowing a resident of New York (a state where gambling is illegal) to place sports bets. So far, only one of those indicted has returned to the United States to face charges. He argued that the United States has no jurisdiction over a company fully licensed by the government of Antigua.

He lost his argument, and the jury decision calls into question the future of Internet gaming. Some experts suggest that the case only had merit because the defendant was a U.S. citizen. That leaves the question, would the U.S. courts be able to prosecute a citizen of Antigua for taking a wager from a New York resident? There are a number of international ramifications to the question of whether a government can prosecute the native of another country for breaking the laws of his or her own country. If so, U.S. pornographers could face charges in countries that outlaw porn.

The High Rollers Bet Offline

In the meantime, online gambling faces an uncertain future, both legally and in regards to its audience. So far, online gambling sites have not attracted the high rollers of the gaming world. According to Greenfield Online's study, "What's the Odds?", 81 percent of online gamblers play only for free. Of those who do play for money, 66 percent are only willing to spend $10 per visit.

By comparison, the study found that when respondents gamble in a casino, most are willing to risk an average of $300 per visit. The results indicate that online gambling does not measure up to the entertainment value of casino gambling. Almost a quarter of the respondents stated that casino gambling is more exciting or more fun than online gambling. Nearly 17 percent enjoy the social interaction of casinos, while only 2 percent state that online gambling was fun.

Even though online gamblers do not give gaming sites high marks, online gambling sites are visited an average of three times more often than casinos annually. Among 40 sites included in the study, here are the most popular online gambling destinations:

Site	Percent of Online Gamblers Who Visited
Golden Palace	24
Caesar's Gold	15
Gold Nugget Online	9
Casino on Net	7
Caribbean Cyber Casino	6

TELEVISION: BRACING FOR THE CHANGES

The delivery of broadcast radio over the Internet has proved to be successful. But delivering broadcast television online may be a more difficult proposition, especially when it comes to the legal questions involved. So far, lawmakers are saying no to Internet companies that want to deliver broadcast television programming online.

The question first came up in 1999 when Congress extended the local TV license to satellite firms. Congress has given cable television services permission to retransmit broadcast TV channels under a compulsory license, but those rights limit the retransmissions to a specific geographic territory to prevent broadcasts from one city bleeding into the audience from another city. When Congress picked up the question of satellite TV services, TV programming creators attempted to insert a provision clearly denying Internet companies from retransmitting TV programs. A lobbying battle ensued and the legislation was postponed.

Meanwhile, a Canadian Web site, icraveTV.com, began retransmitting programs from numerous U.S. TV stations over the Internet, arguing the practice was allowed under Canadian law. The site blocked non-Canadians by asking Web viewers to give their telephone area code. A U.S. federal court did not find the security adequate to protect U.S. television stations and ordered the Web site to shut down.

Ultimately, the Viewer Will Win with More Choices

These moments in time will not fully answer the questions about the use of retransmitted television programming over the Internet. Ultimately the questions will reach a high level of concern when widespread broadband connectivity extends the reach of Net TV to 25 to 40 million U.S. households sometime in 2004 or 2005. At that time, networks will likely attempt to deliver their own solutions to territorial coverage with the support of lawmakers.

If the distribution of Internet television programming breaks down in Congress, alternatives will arrive to give consumers more choices than they currently have with broadcast, cable, or satellite television distribution. With a mass audience that is eager for greater choices in Web-based entertainment, movies, sports, news, and games, content providers will eagerly find ways to deliver to its hungry market. As the audience grows, congressional representatives will become increasingly sensitive to the voice of the TV consumers who are also voters.

ENTERTAINMENT

YOUR NET STRATEGY:

The appropriate Net strategy for entertainment companies is very much up in the air. Companies that sell music, movies, television programming, and sports have not yet forged a productive Internet model. Disney faltered in it attempts to create a horizontal entertainment portal, even though its Go.com was one of the most popular destinations on the Internet. Instead, Disney wisely turned its horizontal effort into a vertical portal to focus on the company's core products.

With the question of how to sell digitized music and movies over the Internet, Net solutions for entertainment producers present a cloudy picture. Widespread consumer access to high-speed Web connectivity will make the uncertainties even more pronounced. It will become far easier to deliver entertainment to consumers, but the revenue sources are not certain. Will entertainment companies be able to control the products they own as consumers buy them through downloads? Disney leader, Michael Eisner, brought the problem to the U.S. Congress in 2000, asking for protection of entertainment products in the face of free downloads of music. He argued that Disney's greatest treasures, from *Snow White* to *The Lion King,* were in jeopardy of falling into the clutches of a technology that can distribute these corporate assets for free.

The entertainment industry may find an encryption technology that prevents copyright infringement, but an unbreakable security device doesn't currently exist, and many security experts doubt it will ever exist. These uncertainties have rocked the industry to its foundations. Given this environment, many in the entertainment industry are not optimistic about the changes the Internet will bring. The strategy most entertainment companies are adopting is a cautious, even defensive, wait-and-see wariness.

Some aspects of the industry are finding ways to make the Internet useful even though the big picture is foggy. Movie production companies are obtaining efficiencies by using the Internet to manage schedules and budgets. Marketing departments in Hollywood are using the Internet to turn fans into communities. But overall, the entertainment industry has not discovered a widespread model for gathering audiences and creating revenue streams. It will likely take many years before the entertainment industry finds its sea legs in the dangerous waters of the Internet.

Yet the opportunities to reach out to a worldwide Web audience are irresistible. The current environment is much like the early days of television. The smart radio leaders swiftly moved their strongest products and entertainers to the new medium, while at the same time they began to experiment with live shows that could take advantage of the visual elements of television.

New Web programming is already emerging even without a mass audience. Smart TV executives can take a lesson from the brick-and-mortar companies that invested in the business-to-business Internet upstarts entering their sectors. Invest in the upstarts, and compete against the upstarts at the same time. This "portfolio" approach is an effective strategy to make sure your sails catch the wind, whichever way it shifts. For entertainment companies, this means preparing aggressively for the inevitable transition to Internet distribution.

Gerald Levin was smart to let Time Warner get snatched by AOL. If the quality of your Net strategy will ultimately determine your position in a Webified entertainment world, it's wise to get cozy with the leading Net brand. At this point, Disney should probably start investing in some of the production companies that are launching Web programming. The company would also be wise to follow Paul McCartney and begin investing in encryption technology to protect the treasures in the company vault.

CHAPTER 7

E-MAIL AND CLICK THROUGHS

E-mail is the most successful tool on the Internet thus far. It has eliminated a good portion of traditional white mail (personalized business correspondence), and it has almost completely eliminated the need for fax machines. For many professionals, it has also reduced the volume of phone calls. E-mail provides the immediacy of a phone message without the phone's intrusiveness. As a personal communications tool, it has served to bring millions of geographically distant family and friends back into regular communication.

As a marketing tool, e-mail is still in its infancy. A number of firms have developed e-mail programs to help companies with customer service support and marketing efforts. Some are already sophisticated enough to identify the nature of customer requests and route the messages automatically to the appropriate department or person. These companies are also developing opt-in marketing programs that help companies reach consumers and retain existing customers by delivering content with perceived value.

The success of banner advertising is less certain. When was the last time you clicked through on a banner ad? Can you recall the last time you responded positively to spam e-mail? If you're like most Internet users, the answer is either "Never," or "During my first three days on the Internet." On the other hand, when was the last time you welcomed an e-mail from a site that covers a favorite topic such as Bob Dylan or hot sauces? When was the last time you popped into a niche site just to see what's new in both their information and the products, after receiving a simple e-mail that did little more than remind you the site still exists?

The Internet Is a Measurable Medium

The do's and don't's of Internet marketing are getting clearer by the day. Internet promotion shares the simple beauty of direct marketing: you can measure it. And because you can measure it, it evolves quickly as marketers discover almost instantly what works and what fails. You don't have to be a genius to get good at Internet marketing; you just have to do some measuring, or copy those big-budget marketers who are taking precise measurements.

Using the Internet as a tool for marketing is like playing with a Swiss army knife for the first time. You know that it can be used for dozens of tasks, but when you first hold it, you're not even sure you can figure out how to use it as a knife. To use a more convoluted metaphor, the Internet is like an elephant to a group of blind marketing pros. One marketer grabs e-mail and says, "The Internet is direct marketing." Another marketer uses a banner ad on a travel site and claims, "A Web site is a magazine." A third tries a rich media ad and declares the Internet is a television. A public relations professional uses a Webcast for a news briefing and exclaims, "The Web is a press conference!"

Net Marketing Offers Direct Personalization

At first, marketers tried to move their traditional marketing concepts directly to the Internet, just as retailers tried to make Web sites into storefronts. These attempts were less than fruitful. Just as magazine ads are ineffective as direct mail pieces and television commercials bomb in movie theaters, offline marketing concepts fail on the Internet. Online advertising works best when it takes advantage of the Internet's powers of interconnectivity and personalization.

On the Internet, you can tap into a consumer's niche interests and create a direct link to products and services related to the niche subject. There is no equivalent to this in the offline world. You can also create a stream of information that flows to your customers, at your customers's request in the form of e-mails. And if you surround your marketing message with quality content, the customer will actually anticipate your e-mails, viewing them as positive communication. You can even personalize to the point where your customer is choosing the content and frequency of the messages.

Mass One-to-One Marketing

Permission marketing, or opt in, is the tag given to this form of marketing. In the past it was often called relationship marketing. Small retail stores have been doing it for hundreds of years. The difference with the Internet, however, is that you can develop a one-to-one relationship with your customers on a mass level. This one-to-one marketing has the same effect online as in mom-and-pop retail stores; it promotes loyalty and allows the merchant to present specials, sales, and new product introductions to a market that is eager to listen.

Advertising on the Web is coming of age. Gone are the days when advertisers mistook e-mail for a cheap direct mail alternative. Another myth that has recently hit the garbage heap is the belief that banner advertising can be effective without the support of a whole program of Web promotion efforts. If you want to create an effective marketing mix on the Internet, be prepared to put together a coordinated effort to give your customer high-value content related directly to your products or services.

INTERNET ADVERTISING IS A GROWTH INDUSTRY

Although Internet advertising has yet to produce predictable models for success, online advertising clearly is a growth industry. Forrester Research estimates that global spending for Internet advertising will reach $33 billion by 2004. Of this, one third will be spent outside the United States. The increase will come from several sources, including the shift of dollars away from traditional media.

So far, traditional media has prospered from the growth of the Internet. In 2000, more than 40 percent of the venture capital flowing into dot-com retailers was allocated for media spending. Most of these media dollars moved into newspapers, magazines, and television. Traditional media has experienced a boom from the rush to e-commerce. By 2004, this tide will have changed.

U.S. online advertising will grow to $22 billion by 2004, according to Forrester Research. This figure constitutes 8.1 percent of projected expenditures for all media. This will put the Internet ahead of traditional media such as magazines, yellow pages, and radio. The compound growth rate of online advertising growth is expected to reach 51 percent over the five-year period from 2000 to 2004.

Web Ad Prices Are on a Long-Term Downward Trend

During this period, higher consumer Internet usage will create excess ad inventory, which will lower the cost-per-thousand (CPM) rates, which will make Web advertising more cost-effective and accessible to small marketers. The excess inventory of Web advertising will increase during this period because the growth rate of new Web pages will outpace the growth in Web ad dollars.

These developments are good news for Web marketers. As the cost of Internet advertising moves downward, the value of online advertising will increase. New audience-tracking tools and return on investment measurements will become part of the competitive landscape, which will benefit online advertisers. Fifty-three percent of online ad spending will be based on performance.

After an Initial Boost, Traditional Advertising Will Take a Hit

The shift of ad dollars to the Internet will put a dent in traditional media in two ways. They will lose ad dollars that move directly from the budget for traditional media to the budget for online ad spending. They will also lose through downward pressure on rates that will come as Internet ad spending grows. While this trend will affect all forms of traditional media, newspapers and direct mail will take the hardest hit, losing as much as 18 percent of their expected revenues in 2004.

Outside the United States, traditional media will take a harder hit as Internet advertising captures 33 percent of global ad spending. The worldwide markets will grow at a faster pace because they are starting from a smaller base. European online ad spending will reach $5.5 billion in 2004, while the Asia/Pacific nations will hit $3.3 billion that same year. Latin America will place $1.6 billion in online ad spending.

Large Sites Will Increase Their Ad Sales

Large portals, such as AOL, Yahoo!, and MSN, will compete for ad dollars instead of focusing on audience growth. Vertical portals, such as CBS Sportsline, CNNfn, Garden.com, and CNET, are gathering ad dollars because their targeted audience appeals to advertisers. The portals that are most vulnerable to the shift in ad spending to vertical sites are the mid-tier broad-based portals, such as GO.com (Disney), Excite, and Lycos. Their ad share will decline from 5 percent in 1999 to less than 1 percent in 2004.

Vertical portals will see their ad share rise from 20 percent in 1999 to 24 percent in 2004. Given this forecast, it isn't surprising that Disney has decided to shift the focus of GO.com from a broad-based portal to a vertically targeted portal that will draw on the company's strength in entertainment. The other winner in the sea change will be niche Web sites. They will see their share of 11 percent of Internet ad dollars in 1999 rise to 25 percent in 2004.

Ads Will Follow the Content

The increased usage of measurement and tracking is expected to support the shift from broad-based portals to vertical portals and niche Web sites. Much as the magazine industry experienced a shift in ad dollars to niche titles in the 1990s, the Internet will experience this shift as advertisers move their message close to the content related to their products. Niche sites are traditionally more expensive than broad-based sites on a cost-per-thousand basis, but tracking mechanisms are expected to show that this additional cost results in a more efficient advertising buy.

WEB ADVERTISING: FROM BANNERS TO WEBCASTS

A wide range of advertising forms exist on the Internet, and new forms will crop up as more users get access to broadband connectivity. At the present moment, Web advertising includes forms such as banner ads, sponsorships, e-mail, pop-up windows, buttons, and Webcasts. With the growth of high-speed connectivity, new forms of television-like advertising will probably appear. Technology, though, will allow the audience to interact with the ad, perhaps in the form of television advertising with click-through capabilities.

The breakdown in advertising spending categories favors the consumer sector. Consumer-related advertising in 1999 was 30 percent of the advertising pie, according to the Internet Advertising Bureau. After consumer advertising, computing and financial services tied for second place with 19 percent each. Other categories included business services at 7 percent and Internet services at 6 percent. Of the different forms of advertising, banner ads took the lion's share of advertising placement at 56 percent. Sponsorships constitute 27 percent of online advertising, and e-mail racks up a tiny 2 percent. The balance of placements fell below 1 percent.

The bureau's report showing e-mail advertising at 2 percent of the advertising buy doesn't reflect the full force of e-mail promotions on the Internet. The 2 percent represents actual ads that are placed in e-mail newsletters or other e-mail correspondence, as opposed to the use of e-mail as a marketing tool to bring customers back to a site again and again.

Use of Webcasts Will Increase

A growing form of advertising, webcasts, presents live-action advertising similar to television but with greatly reduced visual quality. According to Arbitron Internet Information Services, 77 percent of ad agencies bought online advertising during 2000. Of these agencies, 20 percent have placed webcast ads. Arbitron expects webcasts to increase in popularity as quality improves.

Most ad executives in Arbitron's survey of webcast usage agree that webcasts will become more attractive as quality improves, since webcasts are more effective than banner ads. Of the agencies using webcasts, only 15 percent are spending more than 10 percent of their budgets on the Internet. Sixty-two percent spend less than 5 percent of their budgets on webcasts.

Yet for those agencies using webcasts, most expect to continue buying this new form of Internet advertising. Sixty-nine percent of agencies using webcasts plan to use more in the next year. Ninety-six percent will spend at least as much or more than in the previous year. Fifty-six percent of agencies not using webcasts plan to begin using them in the coming year. Eighty-one percent of advertising executives agree that webcasts will grow significantly in the beginning of the new millennium.

VIRAL MARKETING

Viral marketing is the equivalent of word-of-mouth advertising on the Internet. When your customers spread the word about your site like a virus to their friends, you benefit from viral marketing. The biggest difference between offline word-of-mouth and online viral marketing is that you can more easily encourage the viral effect online than you can encourage word-of-mouth offline. Online marketers have developed techniques that foster the spread of Web addresses through viral means.

E-commerce consultant Ralph F. Wilson has created a list of six viral marketing techniques, which together form a viral marketing strategy.

1. *Give away valuable products or services.* Everyone likes to get something of value for free. Free services can include information, e-mail, software, or anything related to the interest of the site's visitors. Viral often works with those with a shared interest. Content related to that interest can suffice as a free service that will encourage viral marketing.

2. *Provide for effortless transfer to others.* Make it easy for your visitors or customers to send the word to others. A simple "e-mail this to a friend" device, which allows the visitor to click a couple of buttons, will encourage the virus.

3. *Make it scale easily from small to very large.* Make sure you can absorb the level of popularity your virus may create. Make sure you can gear up quickly if your program is successful.

4. *Make it exploit common motivations and behaviors.* Design a program that uses the common motivations people have to be popular, loved, well-regarded, and accepted. If the spread of your giveaway helps people further these motivations, you increase your likelihood of success.

5. *Utilize existing communications networks.* Place your message in the center of the places where your customers gather. Don't rely entirely on those who visit your site. Place a viral starter in newsgroups and message boards where potential customers visit.

6. *Take advantage of the others's resources.* Use the resources of other sites to get your word to potential customers. Use affiliation programs to place your viral starter on other Web sites.

The online article from which these guidelines were taken, "The Six Simple Principles of Viral Marketing," was itself used as a viral marketing tool to get readers to spread the work about Ralph Wilson's site, wilsonweb.com. The article was distributed freely to Web marketing e-zines with a button in the article stating, "Recommend It," so readers could quickly e-mail it to a friend.

Banner Advertising

Banner advertising was the first useful form of Internet promotion. With the ability to click right through to the advertiser's site, banner ads bragged about their interactivity and measurability. Banners promised to be the promotion vehicle that would make Web sites like magazines. Early Web ventures were convinced that if you gave away excellent content, the banners would make your site profitable. A lot of visitors have flowed past banners since they first arrived, and disappointing click-through results have tarnished the image of banners.

The early results of banner advertising were disappointing mostly because Internet marketers brought unreasonable expectations to the table. These expectations were fueled by high click-through rates during the Web's early days, when banner ads were a novelty. After a positive early start, research consistently downgraded the effectiveness of banner ads. Click-through rates have fallen steadily, and relatively large shares of Internet users have reported ignoring banners altogether.

Banners Work with Experienced Net Shoppers

A study by Andersen Consulting buffed up the image of banner ads as a useful advertising medium, when it found that banner ads were actually rating higher than newspapers, magazines, or television at driving experienced Internet users to shopping. Experienced Internet users are less likely than the general population to respond to offline advertising and more likely to respond to banners. The study also found that this group is the most likely shop regularly online as well as to spend the most online.

One of the surprises of the study was that while most Web site banner ads are price-oriented, less than half of the users cited price as the primary factor driving their Web purchases. Consumers ranked convenience, time savings, and site security as the most meaningful factors in deciding where to do their online shopping. The study cautioned merchants to promote their services holistically, incorporating their full range of services and security.

Banners Need to Be Fresh and Strong

Not all banner ads work the same. Some marketing professionals claim that weak banner click-through reflects nothing more than the proliferation of poor banner designs combined with poor banner placement selection. Just as with any advertising, it takes a well-designed banner ad to earn click-through traffic. The general rule is that if a banner does not catch the viewer's attention within three seconds, it never will. This fact calls for strong ads that can appeal immediately to a viewer's interest, as well as motivate the viewer to click. Banner ads also wear out quickly. On average, banners lose their drawing power in about 30 days. After that, the click rates fall quickly.

If the results of the study hold over time, the response rates to banners will probably begin to increase as a larger and larger portion of Internet shoppers grow into the experienced group. Banner advertisers that test and re-test their messages against click-throughs and purchases will improve their banner advertising results over time. Given these trends, banner advertising may regain its respectability.

BANNER EXCHANGES

The Internet with its powerful connectivity offers alternatives to the traditional way of buying banners by selecting sites by interest or demographics. Free banner exchange programs have appeared that allow sites to trade their banners with those from other Web sites. Most trading is done on a two-for-one basis, though some are on a three-to-one basis. This means you trade one of your ads for one month on a site, and you are obligated to place an ad on your site for two months, or two ads for one month.

With the banner exchanges, you get free advertising, but you also have to give up space on your site, and frequently the placement of the banner on your site is precious space. Most exchanges specify that the trade ad appears "above the fold," which means it's on the first screen display. For a low-traffic site, giving up this space may not be meaningful, but if you already have substantial traffic, you may lose more by giving up the space than you gain from the free ad on the other end of cyberspace.

Pay-as-You-Go Emerges as an Ad Payment Option

As an alternative to free exchanges, you can pay to have your banners on the sites of others without giving up space on your site. In this case, sites will charge for advertising in two ways. One is by page views. This method counts the number of impressions your ad gets to visitors of the site posting your banner. Usually page views are counted in the thousands and cost-per-thousand (CPM) rates are quoted to advertisers. The other method is to set rates by the number of clicks on the banner. Click-through pricing is more expensive for the obvious reason that it's more closely tied to potential response.

There is a great advantage to click-through pricing; you are paying only for those contacts that are well enough targeted to actually click into your Web site. Even if the click-through rate is considerably higher than the CPM rate, it is very likely to be less expensive when you calculate the return on investment (ROI) of your advertising expenditures.

Whatever program you choose for your banner advertising, make sure you get the statistics on your efforts. The beauty of Internet advertising is that you can measure the traffic and purchase of every banner. Track this information and use the results to improve your advertising design and placement. If you do, you will be ahead of the curve, since most Internet advertisers don't bother to gather and utilize their measurement data.

AFFILIATION MARKETING

On the Internet, you don't have to create a totally autonomous business. One of the beauties of the online business landscape is the availability of shared resources. You can enter buying pools to reduce your procurement costs, and you can join hands with other marketers when you go hunting for new customers. Affiliation marketing has emerged as a new way for Internet companies to share noncompeting markets at a fraction of the cost of developing markets on a solo basis.

Marketing through affiliation programs is one of the most powerful ways to harness the power of the Internet to promote your business. Affiliation is simply a way for Internet retailers to partner to share traffic, content, merchandising, and revenue. Done right, affiliation programs benefit all of the parties involved. The banner exchanges mentioned earlier constitute one example of an affiliation program. The most successful affiliation programs are developed one-on-one rather than through a third-party exchange.

Amazon.com Is the Master of Affiliation

Affiliation marketing gained initial popularity through Amazon.com's program that allowed virtually anyone to put Amazon.com's search engine on a Web site. If you have a hot sauce site, you can post related books on your site, and your customers will click through to Amazon to make the purchase. For recommended books, you receive a 15 percent commission from Amazon.com. If one of your visitors buys anything else on Amazon.com after clicking through from your site, you receive a five percent commission. You can set up the affiliation in a matter of minutes by simply clicking through the instructions on Amazon.com's site. The company has accumulated more than 400,000 affiliates over the past few years.

The affiliation model has exploded across the Internet since the early days of Amazon.com's efforts. Affiliation programs and outbound e-mail campaigns score the highest in effectively driving visitors to a site. Once you have the affiliation in place with another Web site, it is very inexpensive, since most of these relationships are priced on performance. If you receive a customer through an affiliation, you pay a commission on the purchase. If there is no purchase, you pay nothing.

Affiliation Management Is Labor Intensive

The biggest problem with affiliation programs is that they are most successful when they are developed one-on-one, a managerial nightmare because the process is very time-consuming. Forrester Research reports that 64 percent of Web merchants have two or fewer employees to manage their burgeoning affiliate programs. The affiliation programs will survive because of their instant profitability. Though they take time to form, they are relatively easy to manage once they're in place.

By 2003, 21 percent of Internet retail sales will come from affiliation programs. Even the largest sites engage freely in affiliations. Any search on Yahoo! produces a flag suggesting a book on the subject through Amazon.com. Because most affiliations work on a pure commission basis, any site that generates more than $10 per month in incremental revenue covers the processing costs and spreads the site's brand name. Any site delivering more than $10 per month in sales delivers real profit.

A number of automated affiliation programs work similarly to banner exchanges. These programs are often successful at creating a plethora of links and sizable traffic, but they usually bring visitors who are not well-targeted. Most retailers find that the most successful affiliations come when an employee searches through the Internet for appropriate partners, then approaches the potential partner directly. The automated programs will improve in their ability to match partners over the next few years.

Affiliation Programs Will Evolve into Vast Networks

In the future, the affiliation model will evolve into "elastic" retailing in which several sites network together to serve a customer's needs. A fly fishing site, for instance, may offer connections from its site to fishing permits in every state, as well as links to travel services, guides, and accommodations listings for each great location. The site may also hook up to apparel sites. The goal for the fly fishing site is to offer the customer any possible related need that the site's own inventory or services cannot serve directly.

This type of affiliation networking will becoming easier as XML technology makes it simpler for sites to communicate with each other. Tracking technology will also simplify the process of identifying which sales belong to which affiliate. And lastly, technical progress will make it easier for sites to find each other and band together to present customers with a full range of products and services related to a subject interest.

PERMISSION MARKETING

One of the major buzzwords to come from the growth of Internet marketing is *permission marketing*. The word has been associated with the book, *Permission Marketing,* by Internet marketing consultant and CEO of Yoyodyne, Seth Godin. In describing permission marketing, Godin describes two different methods of finding a spouse.

In the first method, you go to a tailor and spend a lot of money for a custom-designed suit that makes you look very attractive, even appealing. You then meet with a demographer who identifies a ZIP code that is likely to include the home of an appropriate spouse. From there, you go to a singles bar in that ZIP code and ask the first person to marry you. Once you've been rejected, you move to the second person and ask again. If you ask everyone in the bar and end up with nothing but rejection, you fire the tailor and demographer and start over.

In the second method, you try dating. You start with some small talk, which leads to a cup of coffee and a more intimate level of talking. If both of you find this enjoyable, you move to the next stage of dating, going to movies and getting to know each other better. After many months, maybe even a year or two, the two of you decide to get married.

Which of these two methods is likely to be successful?

Spam versus Permission Marketing

According to Godin, the first method is like spam, while the second method is like permission marketing. The first method is quick and easy, but its results are poor at best. The second method takes time and investment, but it lets you develop long-term relationships with customers that can last a lifetime. Done right, the expense of permission marketing is rewarded with high returns.

Godin claims that if permission marketing is done right, it can result in a response rate of 36 percent, as opposed to the traditional direct mail rate of 2 percent, or even lower returns for spam campaigns. Permission marketing campaigns are based on opt-in e-mail. When customers visit a site, they are given the option of receiving e-mail messages from the site. To make the opt-in program attractive, the e-mails are usually based on content from the site. So if you're visiting CDNow, you can opt to receive information on your favorite artists. This can include interviews, tour updates, and notices of new releases.

Godin equates the effectiveness of an opt-in program with its ability to deliver content of value to the customer. Once you get the attention of customers through this permission marketing, develop-

E-MAIL AND CLICK THROUGHS 149

ing the relationship requires the ongoing delivery of content that the customer values. Godin uses the analogy of Muhammad Ali's rise to become champ. He didn't win by hitting 20 different people one time. He won by hitting one person 20 times. Frequency is the key to a permission program.

Godin sets out five golden rules of permission marketing.

1. It takes time and money. Short cuts, such as spam, don't work and will usually backfire.
2. Permission cannot be transferred. You cannot rent the goodwill developed by another company. You have to build your own.
3. Successful permission marketing programs do not happen by accident. They have to be carefully conceived and implemented.
4. The permission relationship must be cultivated.
5. Permission marketing is based on the self-interest of the customer. If you put your interests before your customers's interests, the program will fail.

Permission marketing programs work best with companies that have content of value to customers. For a fly fisherman, it might be a fly fishing site with expert information on techniques or specific streams and lakes. For the farmer, it might be an agribusiness that offers daily weather updates by location and posts fluctuations in the price of crops and livestock. Content-rich e-mails, which are delivered to customers who have chosen both the content and the frequency of delivery, can be powerful tools for customer relationship development.

THE STATISTICS ON PERMISSION PROGRAMS

So what is the real story on permission marketing? The theory makes sense on paper, but not all planes designed on paper are actually capable of flying. Research firm, IMT Strategies, conducted a study on permission marketing, and the results show that permission e-mail marketing is 5 times more cost effective than direct mail and 20 times more effective than Web banners. The study also found that permission e-mail is a form of advertising that consumers actually like.

In keeping with the general definition of permission e-mail, for the purposes of the study, it was defined as e-mail that consumers had selected to receive. Consumers in the study were easily able to distinguish between permission e-mail and unsolicited commercial e-mail (spam). The consumers not only welcomed the permission e-mail, they greeted it with response rates that far exceeded other targeted vehicles such as banners, direct mail, or spam.

Consumers Welcome Permission Efforts

According to the research results, more than half of e-mail users feel positively about permission e-mail, and nearly three quarters of users respond to permission e-mail with some frequency. By contrast, the findings show that spam can hurt the brand image of companies that use it. Sixty-seven percent of customers had "very negative" reactions to receiving spam.

Surprisingly, it was marketers who had a hard time telling the difference between spam and permission e-mail. Because of the misperception on the part of e-mail marketers, many inexperienced practitioners have acquired e-mail addresses through questionable means, only to have their e-mail equated with pornography, pyramid schemes, and con artists in the minds of consumers.

Permission Marketing Is Comparatively Inexpensive

The research also shows that permission e-mail programs are not all that expensive. According to a cross-section of leading Fortune 500 companies and e-commerce marketers, including Xerox, Hilton, GTE, Federal Express, Beyond.com, Deja.com, eFax, and Match.com, the cost-effectiveness of permission e-mail, relative to other marketing vehicles like banners and direct mail, makes it their number one priority for driving Internet business over the next 12 months.

The study predicts that the positive results of permission marketing will drive a "race for permission" over the next two years.

IMT Strategies also believes consumers will be willing to accept permission programs for a limited time before they become so plentiful that they lose their appeal. The study forecasts total permission e-mail spending will reach $1 billion by 2001. Additional findings include:

- Almost half of e-mail users with more than two years's experience feel they get "too much" e-mail.
- Less than one third of customers have responded to spam more than once, while more than 70 percent have responded to permission e-mail offers more than once.
- Loyalty and response through permission e-mail strategies improve over time. Users with over two years of experience view permission more favorably, and spam more negatively, than new users.
- Seventy percent of marketers do not measure the performance of their e-mail marketing campaigns, despite the availability of measurement tools.

THE GROWTH OF E-MAIL MARKETING

Affiliation programs are great for gaining new customers, but when it comes to boosting customer retention and increasing sales, the number one form of marketing is e-mail. According to Forrester Research, Internet marketers will send more than 200 billion e-mails in 2004, surpassing the number of direct mail pieces sent to consumers. To maintain visibility, companies will outsource strategic and technical elements of their e-mail marketing initiatives, which will create a $4.8 billion e-mail marketing industry by 2004.

Internet marketers are like hunters. First they follow the tracks of consumers, scattering promotional bait to lure elusive dollars out of hiding places. E-mail marketing turns these marketers into herders. Once they trap consumers, they need to learn how to tame and cultivate them as ongoing sources of nourishment. E-mail becomes the primary tool in the process of taming consumers into repeat customers.

E-mail promotions should not be equated with direct mail, however. Three distinct differences between e-mail and direct mail should be noted by marketers:

1. Instead of broadcasting to customers, begin a dialogue on a one-to-one basis.
2. Offer value in the form of service and ease-of-use instead of simply pushing products.
3. Measure the depth and breadth of the relationships with customers by the amount of information shared rather than the traditional measurements of timing and frequency.

Merchants who utilize the expertise of e-mail service bureaus achieve purchase rates four times higher than those who keep their e-mail operations in-house. Because of this, demand for e-mail marketing services will accelerate to create a $3.2 billion pie in 2004, which will go to e-mail service companies helping merchants retain existing customers. Another $1.6 billion will be spent by merchants who use e-mail service companies to acquire new customers.

A study by eMarketer.com shows even greater levels of e-mail marketing, projecting a total of 240 billion e-mail messages by 2003 in the opt-in category alone. EMarketer.com also expects the total average cost of e-mail to range from $.01 to $.25 per piece. By contrast, direct mail ranges from $1 to $2 per piece. The findings also estimate that only 20 percent of all U.S. e-mail is now commercial, and that these e-mail messages are evenly split between the spam and permission types.

E-mail Will Replace Much of Direct Mail

The growth of e-mail marketing will certainly cut into direct mail expenditures. A study from Jupiter Communications finds that by 2005, e-mail marketing will capture 13 percent of the dollars that are currently going to direct mail. The Jupiter report echoes Seth Godin's concern that increased use of commercial e-mail will begin to erode its effectiveness as the volume of messages grows forty-fold from 2000 to 2005. The report warns e-mail marketers to get very good at incorporating feedback in their programs, as well as improving targeting methods, or risk an increase in opt-out rates.

The growth in e-mail messages over the next few years is enough to give any marketer pause. In 1999, the average online consumer received 40 commercial e-mails. By 2005, that number will hit 1,600. Non-commercial e-mail messages will also grow steeply during the same period, from 1,750 in 1999, to almost 4,000 in 2005. Jupiter suggests that merchants need to keep their e-mail messages packed with relevant, quality information in order to retain their customers's attention as the volume of e-mail skyrockets.

SUCCESSFUL E-MAIL MARKETING TECHNIQUES

What are the techniques that marketers can use to cut through the coming e-mail clutter? Forrester outlines a number of imperatives in its report "The E-mail Marketing Dialog." The strategy outlined in these points is designed to help turn marketers from hunters into effective herders.

Engage in a Dialog with Your Customers

E-mail messages allow you to send your message to customers, and they allow your customers to send messages back to you. Marketers need to craft a strategy that makes the dialog personal and responsive. Your communication needs to go beyond criteria such as gender or interests and reflect a deeper level of knowledge. When e-mail service company, Digital Impact, put together a program for Tower Records, they based the individual e-mail on customers's past purchases and response profiles. The resulting e-mails were personalized to the point that only three or four customers out of tens of thousands saw the same combination of products and offers.

HTML technology gives marketers response cues from customers by reporting on the percentage of e-mails opened. If the rate declines, the service company, Bigfoot Interactive, recommends reducing e-mail frequency to avoid alienating the consumer with unwanted communications. E-mail programs should evolve to customers's needs as well. Service company, FloNetwork, presents customers with a page that allows them to change the frequency and narrow the topics.

Offer Value in Your Messages

Online retailers continually need to give customers a reason to buy from them. Forrester Research points out that if you do nothing more than send product offers to your customers, you are like the friend who become an Amway salesperson. You avoid her because she always asks how your detergent is holding out. Online, service becomes your message. 3Com's InSync program provides tips and links to non-3Com shareware that improves the customers's Palm experience.

Ease-of-use is another prized value on the Internet. RadicalMail's technology lets the consumer buy a featured item within the e-mail rather than clicking through to the site and navigating the site's order process. It also helps to appeal to your customers's sense of humor. Peet's Coffee e-mailed a *New Yorker* cartoon along with a reminder to replenish the caffeine stockpile, generating a 32 percent click-through rate, as well as hundreds of appreciative comments from customers.

Grow Your Customer Relationship over a Lifetime

A successful e-mail program will allow the relationship with the customer to grow over time. It is presumptuous to ask for a customer's e-mail address without offering a benefit and assuring the customer of privacy. Make sure you are explicit about privacy matters. When a site says, "From time to time, we will send along announcements about similar products," customers take this to mean that the offers will come from the same site. Some marketers, however, take this to mean they can sell the e-mail address to a third party, which most customers find offensive.

In building an e-mail relationship, avoid coming across as Big Brother intruding into their private behavior. If you find a leftover item in a customer's shopping cart, you risk alienating that customer if you e-mail a reminder. You may see it as being helpful, but your customer is likely to see it as snooping. Some marketers preserve trust by discreetly including the product in a future e-mail with no mention of the shopping cart.

Choose the Right E-mail Outsourcer

Since e-mail service firms are four times more effective than in-house e-mail programs, most merchants find it is cost effective to hire professionals to design and implement their e-mail retention programs. But outsourcing is only effective if you find the right service company. There are two basic types of service companies, those that provide a full program of data analysis and customer management skills, and those that simply provide the technical applications to segment and send e-mails.

If you are a direct marketing company or a sophisticated catalog operation, you have the data analysis and customer relationship knowledge in-house, so you probably need little more than an application service provider such as Responsys to provide the technology to manage your program. If you're a traditional retailer, it makes more sense to work with an agency such as Post Communications to create strategy, develop content, and provide the technology to deliver, track, and analyze your program.

Use All Forms of Customer Contact to Promote Your Relationship

In order to reach their customers in every possible manner, merchants should include requests for e-mail addresses in all of their contact information. In all of these cases, though, make sure you offer a benefit with this request and assure your customers that their privacy will be protected. Once you have the e-mail address, the initial contact should focus on the customer's interest, not yours. Instead of blasting your new e-mail addressee with a one-size-fits-all sales message, use the initial contact to ask about the individual's interests and preferences for frequency of contact.

Bolster Your Customer Service Mix

A successful e-mail retention program needs to be well-integrated into an overall customer service program. The two cannot be separated in the customer's experience. It doesn't matter how well you relate personally to your customers through e-mail if you are unable to respond quickly to their service needs. You should expect customers to use your e-mail response channel to address service concerns. Your customers will assume your operation is fully integrated. Just as a supermarket customer will ask the checkout clerk where the pickles are and expect the correct answer, even though the clerk never ventures into the pickle aisle, your customers will use your marketing channel to reach out for service help. Make sure your e-mail system is equipped to satisfy this need effortlessly and seamlessly.

THE FUTURE OF INTERNET MARKETING

How will Internet companies market to consumers in the future? We already know e-mail programs will have to improve continually in order to stand out amidst the coming deluge of commercial e-mails, and we also know that affiliation programs will become more sophisticated in automation and targeting. We know that widespread broadband connectivity will lead to new ways for companies to promote their goods and services directly to customers. Broadband will allow customers to click directly into a Web site from a commercial that looks like a television spot, all while pausing the program that contains the commercial.

But the advantages of Internet marketing are ultimately more conceptual than technical. Consumers quickly adapt to technical advances in advertising. A new video device will be an eye-catching novelty for a very short period. The real power of Internet advertising lies in its ability to foster an ongoing personal relationship with customers. Fast and powerful databases can be utilized to keep customer information at the merchant's fingertips. As long as the merchant maintains strict privacy boundaries, this technology will allow the merchant to anticipate customer needs even before those needs occur to the customer.

Consumer Behavior Can Be Mapped and Mined

Anyone who buys a car seat today will need a tricycle shortly. It doesn't matter if the customer is mom or granddad. Anyone who has high frequent-flyer mileage with Delta may want to be reminded when choosing between American and Delta flights. Anyone who attended a Britney Spears concert in 2000 may want to know that she's coming to town again and that past concert attendees get a two-day jump on ticket sales. These are just tiny customer conveniences that are available through Internet connectivity when it's matched with database technology.

I tried one of those movie selector programs that anticipates which movies you might like based on your ranking of a selection of movies it presents to you. Once you've ranked a couple of dozen previously-viewed moves such as *Titanic* or *Leaving Las Vegas* on a one-to-ten scale, the program can anticipate how much you will enjoy, or hate, *Toy Story 2*. After I entered the rankings, I asked about other movies I'd seen just to test the accuracy of the system. Like every other human being, I assumed my taste in movies was so eclectic and individual, the program would fail to anticipate my preferences. I was humbled to discover the program was accurate to about 95 percent. This is the same software that sites utilize to help people choose gifts for distant grandchildren.

As this type of behavior analysis mixes with a large storage pool of past purchasing, merchants will be able to present us with products as our needs arise. If there is a future impulse purchase component to Internet sales, it will likely come from marketers who use consumer behavior analysis to anticipate customers's needs before they arise in the consciousness of the customer. Marketers will have to handle this type of marketing carefully to make sure it is not intrusive. If consumers get the feeling the computer is pretending to be able to read their minds, they'll shut down the relationship.

Privacy Will Continue to Clash with Effective Data Mining

Privacy will continue to be a major issue with consumers. Any marketer that uses a customer's data in a manner not explicitly stated at the time of the data's capture will find themselves on the outs with the customer, and possibly on the outs with the legal system, which will develop new protections for consumers over the coming years. Marketers who are direct and helpful with their customers will find that the Internet is an amazing tool to develop relationships and deliver customized messages directly to the heart of their interests.

YOUR NET STRATEGY:

There is a period in any new technology when advertising opportunities appear in abrupt and awkward fits and starts. Early radio ads were essentially newspaper ads that were read aloud to an audience accustomed to reading. Within a few years, these clunky spots were replaced with ads that were better tailored to the medium and more effective at promoting products. Likewise, during the early days of television, the ad spots were very similar to radio spots, sophisticated in aural engagement but humorously devoid of captivating graphics. The Internet is in that place now.

The early advertisers on radio and television measured their levels of effectiveness even as the new media struggled to find a new voice. Most companies will be well-served by testing the Internet waters in all their variety, from e-mail to graphic-rich banners. Because the Internet is essentially a direct medium, testing a variety of approaches will generate measurable results that can be tweaked and tweaked again until the successful strategies become apparent.

It's the direct, measurable quality of Internet advertising that makes online advertising so enticing. You don't have to wait long to discover which messages deliver visits and which approaches lead to sales. As with any direct form of advertising, from cataloging to direct mail, message and delivery can be tested and tested until you can balance investment and results to create a profitable campaign. And if a company cannot produce success, it comes away with a solid argument for changing or even withdrawing from its Internet ad program.

The most powerful quality of Internet marketing is its capacity to connect to customers and prospects on a one-to-one basis. The Internet offers the chance for companies to switch from mass marketing to personal marketing. If a company can identify specific interests from consumers, it can address those needs with product mix and message. This remains an undeveloped territory of Net advertising, though its prospects are very appealing. One-to-one marketing will be particularly productive in marketing high-ticket items such as autos. Whether it can be utilized effectively with inexpensive goods is still unclear.

In the meantime, there are some rules of thumb that have emerged in Internet marketing that can guide you through your Net-based marketing programs.

- Turn to the e-mail ad vendors for their expertise in developing effective and measurable programs for obtaining new customers and retaining your existing base.

- Use banners that are clear and strong, and change the banner message frequently. Keep your banners close to appropriate content.

- Invest in developing an affiliation network. Also, remember that effective affiliation marketing requires labor-intensive tweaking, so budget for a long-term program.

- Use the hottest techniques in permission marketing and personalization. Make sure you stay on the cutting edge of these trends.

- The Internet is a direct medium, so measure, measure, measure. Set up tools to track the effectiveness of all your programs, from customer acquisition to retention and customer service.

CHAPTER 8

B2B
The Nimble Giant

What's in your portfolio of Internet options? Partial ownership in your sector's most promising e-marketplace? A role in your industry's exchange formed by a consortium of brick-and-mortar leaders? Traditional companies know they need to get their Net strategy right, so many are launching a number of initiatives in the belief they will be on the winning road if they invest in every potential road. Since B2B is vast in its potential avenues, companies may find that more than one of their portfolio efforts bears fruit.

The menu of B2B options includes online auctions, content portals, exchanges, e-marketplaces, and private trading networks. These operations help companies buy excess inventory: large used machines, direct materials, and indirect products such as office supplies and janitorial products. Internet trading sites allow companies to collaborate on design, production, logistics, and scheduling with their closest vendors. They can also provide a view into an industry's supply chain, allowing companies to maintain lower levels of inventory without risk of shortages. Some of these trade platforms are owned and run by third-party vendors that operate much like distributors, while others are installed directly inside a large corporation.

Most large companies are opting to enter into all of these new forms of trade. Their vendors are jumping aboard more tentatively, concerned that Internet trading may encourage their customers to shop globally for products they used to purchase across town. But so far, Internet trading has worked to create closer relationships between companies and their vendors. In these early days of B2B trading, vendors have more to gain through trading efficiencies than they have to lose through increased competition.

Even if vendors and their corporate customers remain mostly in place, the Internet is transforming the way trading is conducted between companies. If you're a mid-level salesperson in a large chemical company, I suggest you take advantage of your company's education benefit and begin work toward a master's in engineering. Much of the sales glad-handing is gone and with it the time-consuming order tracking. Your customers are not faxing you their Requests For Quotes (RFQs) any longer. Instead, they go straight from your customer's procurement to your production group. Your future role will be technical in nature, working with your customers in collaborative design and production.

Even Greenspan Gets It

Most vendors knew their customers would move procurement to the Internet, but never expected it to happen so quickly. The chemical salesperson was convinced it would take Fortune 500 clients decades to move procurement onto the Internet. Meanwhile, Alan Greenspan, chairman of the Federal Reserve, attempts to explain how an economy can grow at the rate of 4, 5, even 7 percent without showing any signs of inflation. Previously, if the economy rose above the level of 3 percent, inflation would come in and spoil the growth party. "It's the computers," says the stone-faced chairman. "After 40 years of investment in computers, they are finally delivering increased productivity."

Oddly, computers did not help companies become more efficient until the Internet showed up. The addition of IT departments to corporations tended to create new bureaucracies that needed care and feeding. Internet communication with its simple and ubiquitous connectivity suddenly allowed companies to overcome the endless stream of faxes, phone calls, and sales meetings that have been part of corporate procurement since the dawn of the Industrial Age. Now, suddenly, the engineer who needs a part can log onto the Internet and go directly into the customer's CAD program to design it. Who needs all the hassles with the buyers and salespeople?

The Big Companies Took to the Net Eagerly

Even before the emergence of e-marketplaces and online auctions, big companies, such as GE, GM, and IBM, had figured out they could reach some very impressive savings by communicating with their vendors online, leaving behind their internal operations that were hopelessly inefficient. Some analysts say the corporations were delighted to shift their buying online because it finally brought their renegade buyers into a system of measurable accountability. GE alone expects to save $500 million on its procurement costs in 2002 simply by moving to Internet buying. These are just the internal savings. This doesn't count what happens if the company can also reduce the prices it pays vendors by moving some buying to auctions.

There is something very special about savings taken on the procurement side. Unlike revenues derived through new sales or new markets, savings go directly to the bottom line, undiluted. A dollar saved on procurement is an extra dollar on the bottom line. If you can save millions on procurement, it's worth changing the culture of your organization. The salesperson and the wholesale jobber mentioned above shouldn't be surprised at the rapidity of change. When it comes to saving millions, why wait a second longer than necessary?

The Bricks Are the Biggest Winners

There is a little secret about e-commerce that is rarely discussed. The big winners will not be the online retailers or entertainment companies. The ultimate big winners may not even be AOL and Yahoo!, though they have claimed positions that would be hard to shake. The true winners of Internet trade will have familiar names like Dow, Ford, U.S. Steel, and GE. Their efforts to move purchasing to the Internet will be profitable from day one, and they will require very little investment.

For years, the promise of B2B e-commerce bubbled below the surface of the Internet. The projections from research firms have always showed it on the horizon, slowly moving to overshadow Internet retailing. The numbers are very impressive. Forrester Research forecasts the following for retailing and B2B e-commerce during the five years from 2000 to 2004. This is U.S. e-commerce alone:

Year	Retail E-commerce	B2B E-commerce
2000	$ 40 billion	$480 billion
2001	$ 61 billion	$600 billion
2002	$100 billion	$1.1 trillion
2003	$141 billion	$1.8 trillion
2004	$181 billion	$2.7 trillion

The surprising aspect of these numbers is that of all the research produced on e-commerce, these figures are some of the most conservative. Over the next five to ten years, Internet retailing is expected to capture up to 10 percent of all U.S. retailing. The percentage of B2B ecommerce moving to the Internet will more than double that percentage by 2005. Worldwide, the Gartner Group predicts B2B e-commerce will exceed $7.2 trillion.

Pretty Soon We're Talking Real Money

The savings that companies take by pushing their procurement online range from 3 to 6 percent. These percentages may not seem great, but when companies take savings in the 3 to 6 percent range, they usually increase the company's overall income by 10 to 20 percent. And the greater a company's internal inefficiencies, the greater the savings. These figures do not take into consideration any reduction on the cost of goods. All of these savings come by making the internal procurement process more efficient, which makes the overall corporation more productive. These are the savings Greenspan was referring to when he said the computer was finally making business more productive.

Tons of controversy surrounds e-marketplaces and whether they will prove productive in helping corporations take even greater savings. Many suppliers view e-marketplaces and particularly online auctions as devices that corporations use to put greater price squeezes on their vendors and suppliers. But many top executives say they don't expect their vendors and suppliers to cut prices unnecessarily. They say they're after the internal savings that are there for the taking, savings that will move swiftly to the corporation's bottom line.

THE INTERNET MAKES PROCUREMENT EFFICIENT

When you think of saving on procurement by moving a company's purchasing to the Internet, the image that comes to mind quickest is the elimination of tedious paperwork. The Internet will certainly accomplish this necessary feat, but process automation is just one piece of the internal savings that come through B2B e-commerce. The savings categories below don't even take into account lower prices for goods that come through intensified competition among suppliers, which is the most controversial aspect of B2B e-commerce. These savings come simply from taking some of the inefficient processes out of everyday procurement.

- *The cost of purchase orders goes down.* Savings from automating the purchase process are the most immediate savings in online procurement. They can be considerable. The average purchase order at GM takes $250 to create and process. Some online procurement specialists claim the cost of a purchase order will go down to an average of $25 per purchase order. When you take a $225 savings 10 or 20 thousand times each month, pretty soon you're talking about real money.

    The savings on purchase orders is what the fuss is all about. When people talk about the profound savings that come by streamlining the internal procurement process, they are usually talking about reducing the cost to produce a purchase order. All of the additional savings listed below are usually an afterthought, but all of these afterthoughts can add up to even greater savings than those taken by automating purchase-order generation.

- *The cost of sales goes down.* There are inefficiencies in both the front end and the back end of our corporations. So the seller can take savings just as quickly as the buyer. But since all corporations are both buyers and sellers, every company gets to automate their buying and selling operations. U.S. Steel expects to take considerable internal savings by moving their procurement to FreeMarkets.com, but the company anticipates taking additional savings by selling its steel over the Internet to the automakers and appliance manufacturers. Like the savings in procurement processes, the savings taken from an Internet sales transaction go straight to the company's bottom line.

- *Inefficient anomalies are eliminated.* Most companies have renegade buyers who are difficult to control. Some corporations have renegade departments that have slipped out of control. Internet procurement allows the company to create hard standards through which all procurement must pass. This can eliminate inefficient anomalies without setting off costly Internet turf battles. Some analysts claim that these kinds of internal problems are rampant in American corporations and that executives are relieved that the Internet finally presents a solution to this nagging problem.

- *Everyone can watch the company's internal mechanisms.* As companies move their procurement and selling to the Internet, their internal processes become visible throughout the company. Managers can watch raw materials enter the corporation, move through production, and become finished goods that are sold and shipped. Businesses fund enormous inefficiencies when they tackle complex collaborative processes manually. Getting the right information to the right department at the right time is a challenge in a large organization. The Internet not only automates many of the processes, it also makes the processes visible throughout the organization, ending a good chunk of endemic corporate inefficiencies.

- *The Internet reduces market fragmentation.* Most industries are fragmented geographically. The Internet brings the whole world to the desktop. Buyers learn about suppliers with better products or more available inventory. Sellers discover buyers they previously had not considered. Some industries are so fragmented, the move to online procurement is motivated by the need to be able to reach the entire market rather than a need to streamline the process of creating purchase orders.

- *The Internet makes the market transparent.* Many shrewd middlemen have long profited by the lack of information within an industry. A shortage here is fulfilled by a glut here. The middleman buys at surplus prices and sells at a super premium. The Internet makes the industry transparent. Suddenly the whole industry can see what until now only the middleman could see, and prices fall accordingly. The analysts Charles Phillips and Mary Meeker of Morgan Stanley Dean Witter liken B2B e-commerce to the building of the Erie Canal, another B2B network. When the canal opened in 1825, shipping costs between Chicago and New York instantly dropped by 85 percent.

  In a world of transparency, artificially high prices and unusually low quality get isolated quickly as competitive alternatives become apparent. Hidden information in a market provides cover for manipulators. When you shine a bright light on these shenanigans, the bugs scurry away. Some suppliers complain that the main goal of buyers is to get a peek at real prices. Well, so? If you were the buyer, wouldn't you want to know what the real price is, especially if you suspect you've been paying an amount that is unreasonably higher than the real price?

- *Inventories can be kept at a lower level.* High inventory level is the quiet-but-deadly dragon that every company would love to slay. When you ask most economists why we have recessions, they usually begin the answer with an unintelligible sentence that begins with "high inventory levels." A company needs to stay ahead of customers by maintaining enough inventory to avoid shortages. But how much is necessary? Who knows when you're blind? So demand goes down and you're stuck with too much inventory, which is a lousy place to hold your assets in hard times, especially since you leveraged your liquid assets to build that overly high inventory.

Internet procurement allows companies to maintain lower levels of inventory without risking shortages. I started to see this happen just as Greenspan was talking about the computer delivering unusually high productivity levels. Hmmm. So I asked a number of economists whether the reduced inventory levels made possible by Internet-based procurement could end the cycle of boom and recession. The answer I received, of course, was, "maybe," which seemed exuberantly positive coming from economists. Since then, I've learned that the same thoughts about the end of the boom-and-bust cycle occurred to market watchers in the 1920s.

When you add up all of the savings that can possibly come from B2B Internet trade, the potential benefits are staggering. The hype that flows from these possibilities is understandable. If only a couple of these potential benefits materialize, they will have a profound effect on corporate profits. Internet retailing looks like a novelty when compared with the potential proceeds from B2B trade. The real business revolution on the Internet lives and breathes in the transactions between companies. As these efficiencies spread across the globe, and into government as well, the economic benefits will be widespread and long lasting.

THE BIGGER THEY COME, THE BETTER THEY GET IT

There used to be a distinction between those companies that "got it" about the Internet and those that "didn't get it." That distinction has blurred now that everybody "gets it," but there was an evolutionary process in corporate America's transition to the Internet. The first stage occurred in the mid-1990s, when IT managers knocked on the doors of the CEO, saying, "We've got to get on the Internet. The whole business world is passing us by!"

That plea was followed a couple years later by CEOs knocking on the doors of their IT managers, saying, "We've got to get on the Internet. The whole business world is passing us by!" Corporate CEOs were late to "get it" on the marketing possibilities of the Internet. But when it came to direct online trade, the CEOs were out in front of the pack like cheerleaders screaming for the managers to "get it, get it, get it." Jack Welch at GE pushed his whole corporation online. Jacques Nasser at Ford Motor Company sent 325,000 PCs home with employees so they would be sure to "get it." Why? Because they discovered the power of the Internet to deliver efficiencies, and they knew those efficiencies lead directly to profits.

In interviews with top executives of traditional economy companies, it's surprising just how strongly they embrace the Internet and its possibilities. Even the brickest of the bricks, U.S. Steel, has invested in e-Steel, a metals e-marketplace that U.S. Steel sells through. The company is also moving portions of its procurement onto FreeMarkets.com. Both Ford and GM have aggressively moved to online purchasing. Well before the companies joined hands to launch the trading exchange, Covisint, they were already buying from their suppliers individually over the Internet. All of the automakers are also working hard to figure out ways to sell cars directly to consumers over the Internet without jeopardizing relationships with their dealers.

No matter how far from Silicon Valley some of these companies may be, they have become fervent followers of e-commerce. There now seems to be a direct relationship between the size of the company and its commitment to moving its purchasing operations online. This is based, I'm sure, on simple mathematics. The bigger the company, the greater its inefficiencies, and the greater its inefficiencies, the more the company is likely to save through e-procurement. And finally, the more a company stands to gain from Internet purchasing, the more evangelical its CEO.

What's Your Net Strategy?

In a study of corporations with revenues over $5 billion, PricewaterhouseCoopers found that two-thirds have strategic plans in place for Internet initiatives. More than 47 percent have full-time units dedicated to e-business strategy. The survey also showed that executives see the Internet's importance beyond the branding and cost-saving side of e-business; 88 percent of these large corporations already have plans to link with suppliers and partners.

The final convincing evidence that large corporations understand the importance of B2B e-commerce is their willingness to launch their own e-marketplaces. Many large corporations have gone to the trouble of creating consortia exchanges in partnership with direct competitors in order to create a trading hub that services the entire industry. In sectors such as the auto industry, the cooperation is unprecedented, leading some analysts to doubt whether the grouping is truly feasible. Whether the consortium hubs will succeed or not is unknown, but the effort is certainly evidence that the traditional brick giants take e-commerce seriously.

Few industries have been left untouched by giants that are either forming e-marketplaces like the automakers's exchange, Covisint, or investing in the neutral exchanges. The list of participating corporations reads like a who's who of the Fortune 100, including Dow, DuPont, Ford, GM, Compaq, Hewlett Packard, Sears, and Kmart. The technology partners in these efforts are equally stellar, with companies such as Oracle, IBM, and Microsoft participating. With these companies leading the charge into Internet B2B trade, it's certainly clear the brick executives "get it."

ONLINE PROCUREMENT HEATS UP

American corporations are not waiting for the e-marketplaces to get up and running before they begin clicking to buy over the Internet. Research shows that companies are already moving portions of their procurement online. A study by Zona Research found that 70 percent of companies are currently buying, or plan to buy within the next 12 months, office-related products through Web-based procurement. The research also found that 52 percent of American companies currently buy or plan to buy travel-related products over the Internet. Office products alone constitute a buying total of more than $250 billion.

Since travel is the leading sector in Internet retailing, it's not surprising that the business travel market is rushing to the Internet. There are now a number of solutions companies one can turn to for booking travel, from airline-based sites to the sophisticated Sabre applications, which can plug into the corporate purchasing systems. Also, a number of travel sites, such as BizTravel.com, have designed their services to accommodate corporate travel planning.

You can even book charter flights over the Internet. The retail travel sites such as Travelocity still expect to pick up a good portion of the travel bookings for small business and independent professionals. All of these services combined are expected to take more than two thirds of business travel to the Internet by 2003.

Commodities and Spot Purchases Lead the Charge

In the heavy industries, the first items to move strong to e-procurement have been the items that are basic and easy to quantify. Chemicals, metals, and energy are all strong because they are not as complex as, say, machinery. Online purchasing systems are being prepared for the trading of complex items, but there is no wait for goods that can be treated like commodities. Thus, spot purchases of chemicals or oil move easily through online exchanges.

The oil company, BP Amoco, expects to save at least $200 million per year by moving business onto the Web. Royal Dutch/Shell expects to move $29 billion of spending to the Internet through the e-marketplace it formed with Commerce One, Norway's state-run Statoil, and Europe's software giant SAP. Shell expects the procurement total to reach $40 billion once it brings in its joint ventures. Statoil will bring another $4 billion of procurement into the e-marketplace. These oil companies are very bullish on Net procurement. Analysts expect they'll take a savings of 5 to 15 percent on the purchasing they do over the Internet. When you begin to add these figures up, you have to wonder who the true Internet companies will really be over the long run. Those who sell music downloads, or those who sell mundane items such as oil, chemicals, and steel?

A B2B SMORGASBORD

Not all companies buy from each other in the same manner. Some purchases are direct raw goods that go into the finished product the company produces, while other items are for maintenance, repair, and operating equipment (MRO). Some companies buy finished goods from manufacturers and resell them to a network of retailers. Other companies sell services, from consulting to accounting and financial legal, and fulfillment services. Internet procurement systems are developing to accommodate each and every one of these purchasing needs.

Likewise with selling. Companies use the Internet to hook their back-end systems directly into the front-end systems of their customers. A whole new flock of integration companies have appeared to make these connections seamless enough to deliver streamlined communication between the two companies. These integrators have learned how to tie together wildly divergent systems. The great equalizer, of course, is the Internet itself. Since the Internet can accommodate a wide spectrum of complex information, once the integration is in place on both the buyer's and seller's side, commerce can begin in earnest.

As well as being procured for different purposes, various goods and services are purchased in differing manners. Some raw materials, like grain or livestock, are purchased at auction. More complex goods are purchased by request-for-quote (RFQ). A good portion of a company's procurement is goods or services that are purchased on a recurring basis, while other purchases are "spot" purchases that occur on an irregular basis. Some companies identify a small handful of potential vendors, while others find there is only one source for some of the goods or services they need.

First You Automate Your Existing Procurement . . .

When Internet procurement first arrived with some force in the late 1990s, B2B Internet commerce came in two forms. One was direct procurement by a buyer who already had an ongoing relationship with the vendor or supplier. Moving the purchasing relationship online was motivated by a desire on the part of both companies to streamline their internal systems for ordering, delivery, invoicing, and settlement. Vendors would provide a secure and private connection to facilitate the automation of the buying and selling process. In this case, salespeople remained in place to run interference on the process to make sure the Internet wheels were well greased.

With the other type of Internet commerce, buyers utilized public Web auctions for spot purchases of raw materials, excess inventory, used equipment, or salvage items. This commerce was not a direct threat to the company's base of suppliers and vendors, because spot purchasing has always been done in the open market without regard to customer relations management. Big companies could save a tidy bundle just by keeping to this semirevolutionary change in the buying process. Under these conditions, vendors and suppliers were quite happy to integrate with their customers, since the efficiencies were taken on both sides.

Then You Start to Change Everything

The world came undone, however, when e-marketplaces tempted buyers with the concept of taking some of their recurring purchasing into an open market. The e-marketplace makers painted a picture of a world in which complex goods that were purchased on a recurring basis could be treated like a commodity if the software platform had programmed in all of the variables required for complex recurring procurement. To the buyer, this meant a break from the often stifling proximity to suppliers and a means for slanting the buyer/vendor relationship dramatically toward the buyer's interests. The low rumbling sound you hear across America is the grumbling from suppliers who have just been stiff-armed by buyers, who are giddy with their new sense of freedom.

As one supplier complained to a software integration service that came calling to hook the company to its customer's e-marketplace, "Now we have an e-marketplace that puts a new distance between me and my customer. I can't tell any longer exactly where I stand. And now you tell me I have to pay for the privilege of connecting my products and services as though they were nothing more than commodities?" The answer to the supplier is, "Well, yes." As an executive of a large steel company recently put it, "If we tell our vendors that's where we're going to buy, I guess they're going to go there to sell to us. When you buy $3 billion in goods, I guess you get to call the shots."

There is a dazzling spectrum of buying and selling opportunities on the Internet. Some companies will retain the direct one-to-one relationship between buyer and seller because of the collaboration needed on complex systems. Even so, complex systems will still take streamlined savings through online connection. But whatever can be moved more efficiently into an open online market will surely move to the open market simply because it serves the buyer. But suppliers shouldn't feel so bad; after all, they're foisting the same revolution on their suppliers and vendors.

TO DOT-COM OR DOT-CORP?

Running an e-commerce operation in a traditional company is not a simple matter. If a company plans to streamline its purchasing by putting procurement through the Internet while also moving its products onto an e-marketplace for sale, it will need to do more than simply create a new department. Successfully implementing buy and sell e-commerce takes a strategic approach, not a tactical one. In order to succeed, a company has to create a new culture as well as develop an internal function.

Most American corporations have made e-commerce their number-one initiative. Those that have not put it at the top of the priority list will soon run into difficulties keeping up with their industries, since virtually all sectors are remaking themselves as Net-ready markets. Once the initiative is given high priority, the changes that move the company into the digital world come in these stages:

- Funding the initiative
- Development of management structure
- Choosing internal or external systems
- Choosing a technology solution
- Recruiting and staffing
- A limited beta-testing phase

The stages are not necessarily in this order, but all of these milestones have to be accomplished. There are usually two initiatives, one for purchasing and one for selling. The same team can conceivably work on both, but often companies move on separate tracks for buying and selling, since each function involves different internal players as well as different external partners. Ford's strategies for connecting with customers over the Internet, for example, is radically different from its strategy for online procurement. The only things these two efforts have in common at the auto maker is the same level of urgency in the mind of CEO Jacques Nassar.

The structure to support these changes varies from corporation to corporation. Forrester Research conducted a study on how corporations organize for e-commerce. The resulting report concluded that companies need to reshape their organizations along one of two lines:

1. Deploy a centralized group within the firm and create a "dot-corp" to take the existing business online.
2. Create a spin-off "dot-com" group within the corporation to pursue new business models and market opportunities.

The essential difference between the two is that the dot-corp's efforts are integrated into the company's existing corporate structure. With the dot-com approach, the company creates what is essentially a maverick team within the company that pursues the Web initiative independent of the corporation's existing structure. Presumably, the dot-com would eventually be reincorporated into the overall corporate structure once the Internet initiatives were established.

Whether the e-commerce effort is organized as a dot-com or dot-corp, it will suffer if it is not adequately funded with capital outlays analogous to new plant construction or geographic expansion. It is also important that the leader of the e-commerce initiative reports directly to a division president or CEO. Companies need to make sure internal turf battles do not interfere with the initiative's potential for success.

The dot-corp organization is appropriate for companies that do not find themselves far behind their industry's move to e-commerce. If the company is a leader on the Web, it can incorporate its Internet development into its overall management structure. If the corporation finds itself in an industry where independent Internet companies have entered the industry with sophisticated online e-commerce options, the dot com approach will be more successful at moving Internet operations quickly ahead.

Gartner Group has studied the challenge of moving a brick-and-mortar corporation quickly to the Internet. The research firm sees the major hurdle for larger corporations is their tendency to move slowly. The report also notes that traditional businesses are constrained by legacy systems, processes, and people. Most of all, Gartner found that many corporations simply don't know what to do. The study proposes three approaches to the problem of independent Net companies that have entered the corporation's turf.

1. *Evade the Net plays.* Although the Internet-based companies, or Net plays, have the benefit of speed and novelty, the advantages of infrastructure, brand, and relationships lie largely with established businesses. Companies may avoid the threat by deepening their existing relationships with suppliers, intermediaries, and customers that are most valuable to them.

2. *Exploit the Net plays.* The Net companies are creating a networked economy offering real benefits for established businesses. Companies can use the Internet to extend supply chain management and buy from new suppliers and intermediaries.

3. *Evolve into a Net play.* Many new opportunities can be exploited by old as well as new business. Established businesses can start selling directly on the Web, become online intermediaries, or create something entirely new.

In many instances, corporations move through these three approaches sequentially. To get to the final stage, where the traditional company becomes an actual innovator, almost always requires that the company CEO becomes a true cheerleader for e-commerce and Internet change. Once the company's top leadership has tipped over to full acceptance of the Internet economy, big, cumbersome, gargantuan companies can become surprisingly nimble and smart.

One company took a novel approach to the problem of becoming a snazzy Net company in the retail sector. Wal-Mart understood that it was floundering in its attempt to create an online presence capable to giving a company like Amazon.com a competitive run. The company knew it had to move fast to create a difference in the quickly-evolving online world, yet running a Net company from the center of the largest brick retailing operation was awkward and ineffective. Besides, it was hard to recruit top people if you couldn't give them a piece of the action and they had to live in Arkansas. So Wal-Mart formed a new company and plopped it down in Silicon Valley. The jury is still out on whether the clever move was sufficient to put Wal-Mart on the cybermap.

However a company organizes its Internet effort, corporations seem to be getting it that the Internet economy has quickly merged with the offline economy. Some analysts are predicting that the terms *new economy* or *digital economy* will slowly disappear as the distinctions between traditional business and online business collapse. Many companies are implementing a number of approaches on their path to Internet commerce. Others are still scratching their heads and waiting for a new model to emerge that shows the most efficient way for a traditional company to step into the bewildering world of the Internet.

SOFTWARE GIANTS: FOUR HORSEMEN RIDE THE WILD RACE

A wide number of software companies are vying for the privilege to help corporate America move its buying and selling onto the Internet. Accomplishing this great task will make fortunes for countless entrepreneurs and early shareholders of the software companies that get the big pieces of this exploding pie. The biggest of the big software companies are rushing to the scene. IBM, Microsoft, and Sun are all reaching out for chunks of new business. All of the big consulting firms are also ramped up for the action, hiring armies of new consultants schooled in the procurement and supply chain management solutions.

In addition to the tech giants, there are dozens upon dozens of companies rushing their nifty new products to market. Quite a number of them argue speed-to-market alone as their competitive edge. But four standouts in the expanding territory of procurement, supply chain management, and integration systems make B2B e-commerce possible: Oracle, Ariba, Commerce One, and i2 Technologies. On any given list of the leaders in putting corporations in cyber-touch with suppliers and customers, you will almost always find these four. Merrill Lynch calls these companies the Four Horsemen of E-marketplaces and though they are the leaders in online exchanges, they all started with direct procurement and supply chain management solutions.

Similar Solutions, Separate Expertise

There is some separation of expertise among these software experts. Oracle produces simply the best database around, and every procurement system or e-marketplace needs a great database. Lately Oracle has also entered the e-marketplace business, most notably as one of the partners in the automakers's exchange, Covisint. i2 Technologies focuses on supply chain management. Its platform helps manufacturers plan and schedule raw materials purchasing, inventory management, delivery fulfillment, and other aspects of the production process.

Of the four, Ariba and Commerce One are the most alike. Although all of these companies compete to some extent, Ariba and Commerce One are in a direct arm wrestle. They both offer a platform that connects buyers and sellers globally. Their systems are also regarded as the top procurement solutions on the Internet. Both companies struggle to improve their systems to accommodate the growing needs of their customers, such as financial or settlement tools and delivery or fulfillment applications. The goal is to give a corporation a one-stop platform for buying and selling goods around the world.

Coopitition Rules Procurement Technology

These players frequently find themselves working together on projects. Commerce One and Oracle work together on the auto exchange. i2 and Ariba have formed an alliance with IBM to bring a full-service e-marketplace platform to industry consortiums. Most of the projects run by Commerce One, Ariba, and i2 utilize Oracle databases. Coopitition is a buzzword closely associated with these players. It's the act of collaboration of companies that are otherwise competitors.

Oracle is already a giant company, but the other three horsemen are growing at a fast pace. The revenue model for these companies involves a combination of project fees, licensing fees, transaction fees, and occasionally equity in an e-marketplace that is operated as a separate company owned by either an independent Net company or a consortium of industry heavyweights. The project and licensing fees are presently the core of the revenue stream for these companies, but as the transaction levels grow, a tiny piece of the action could become considerable.

The prospects for these corporations look good right now, and they very well may own a healthy piece of the future. Imagine if a company building the interstate highway system got paid to design and build the system. Then, the company received a percentage of the sale of all the goods that moved across the highway, and finally, the company also held an equity stake in the highway system. Now further imagine that the company received all of these benefits without investing directly in the cost of building the highway. All this company had to bring to the table was its expertise in building highways. Oracle, Ariba, Commerce One, and i2 Technologies, more than any other companies, find themselves in this enviable position.

EXCHANGES AND AUCTIONS: INTERNET FLEA MARKETS FOR BIG JUNK

If there's an early chestnut in the rush to online trading, it is the world of excess inventory, used equipment, and salvage. Some analysts claim the Internet is better at selling excess inventory and used equipment than any other commodity, product, or service. Auction sites allow sellers to find the best possible buyer for their over-supply while maintaining the anonymity they need to protect their standard prices. For buyers, it's a chance to pick up a bargain. Used equipment and excess inventory sites handle everything from designer dresses to food ingredients. You can even pick up non-performing mortgages.

Some excess inventory traders operate as horizontal sites that sell everything they can find in excess, while others work within vertical markets, getting to know the industry and its players. Horizontal sites usually concentrate on working the numbers of price, while vertical unloaders bring value-added services to the site in order to establish credibility in a slash-and-burn business. All portions of the gigantic world of excess inventory, used equipment, and salvage materials share one thing: a fragmented market. Fragmentation breeds inefficiencies and high prices. Online exchanges are the enemy of fragmentation. Given this market environment, it's not surprising that e-marketplaces are springing up like a thousand tiny toads during a late-spring rain.

E-market Makers Conform to Industry Behavior

Most e-marketplaces design their system to accommodate the particular buying and selling habits of the market. OutletZoo.com meets the special needs of distributors and e-tailers. The site has an automatic price drop system that strategically lowers the prices of the excess inventory until a buyer snatches it up. This concept is difficult to manage offline. Over the Internet, it's a very simple process that is designed to get the optimum prices between buyer and seller.

In their short and happy life, B2B auctions have become famous for defragmenting fractured markets. This has certainly made the sites popular with a market that is accustomed to endless faxes and phone calls to a limited number of players. Solving this fragmentation takes more than Internet connectivity alone; it takes a central electronic clearinghouse. By eliminating the middleman liquidator and bringing buyers and sellers together, all players stand a better chance to reach a price equilibrium that benefits both sides.

Because online exchanges that trade in excess inventory encourage wide participation, they often bring together buyers and sellers who do not have an existing business relationship. Auctions establish credibility through experience in the market. AssetTRADE, an exchange for used industrial equipment and machinery, has strategic partners, Michael Fox International and Henry Butcher International, which provide the assurance of established international asset management companies. When an exchange puts these credibility builders in place, industry leaders will be more likely to do business on the exchange.

Users Can Design Their Own Trading Specs

Most online exchanges in the excess inventory and used equipment arena bring more to the table than simply providing a space for buyers and sellers to shop their wares. XSAg.com uses a blend of services to attract both buyers and sellers. Buyers and sellers can control their trade by a number of control points, including price, geography, credit, timing of delivery, anonymity, and freight. The exchange also offers innovative features such as name-your-own-price for seed and the ability for buyer and seller to haggle over prices.

Most of the industry-specific sites use added-value services as a competitive tool to discourage encroachment from exchanges that trade goods over a wide range of industries. Cymerc Exchange, Inc., an exchange that trades in used communications equipment, uses warranties, inventory, audits, and equipment refurbishing to add value to the equipment that moves through the exchange. The whole idea is to give the market exactly what it needs to encourage the use of the exchange. This almost always requires deep knowledge of the given industry.

In the Internet world, creativity is usually the prime asset a company can bring to market. AssetTRADE has an innovative approach to selling used industrial equipment and machinery. The company is turning its sales effort toward companies that ordinarily buy only new equipment. The idea comes from the awareness that even when a company wants the advantage of new equipment, portions of the equipment and machinery can be supplied by used materials at a savings without compromising quality.

Customized Content

Another aspect of industry-specific exchanges that gives them an edge over horizontal trading sites is industry information. Most industry-based sites offer a variety of customization options as well as streaming news. At most sites, buyers can create their own area of the site that will let them trade with suppliers they have already determined to be acceptable. They can also tailor their unique area to include their particular procurement protocol. If the customization is general, it can usually be accomplished with a few clicks of the mouse. For more involved customization, sites usually offer programming services to help a buyer integrate its procurement with its internal programs.

News is often available on industry-based sites. CloseOutNow.com has added ScreamingMedia custom-filters to provide content to match the needs of its customers. The news includes fashions, trends, fabrics and trimmings, international fashion, and general fashion industry information. Internet communication excels at this type of niche marketing. Industry-specific added value will make it difficult for horizontal sites to retain customers.

E-MARKETPLACES: THE WORLD SHOPPING BAZAAR

The terms *online auction, exchange,* and *e-marketplace* are often used interchangeably, but as the Internet becomes increasingly crowded with a variety of B2B options, these terms are beginning to become more refined. It is one thing for a retail chain to go to an auction site and buy a line of clothing that has been closed out. It's quite another for Ford to go online and buy steel from U.S. Steel. As public e-marketplaces become more adept at facilitating the buying and selling of complex products on a recurring basis, they move further and further from the original auction model that just finds commodities and excess inventory. Distinctions in terminology are developing to distinguish an auction from a large marketplace.

E-marketplaces, which are described in greater detail in the next chapter, are evolving to take on the more complex tasks of online procurement. These public trading sites usually include an auction, but they present a wider range of services than the standard online auction. They usually include industry information and news, product catalogs, auctions, reverse auctions, Dutch auctions, RFQ functionality, and the ability for a company to complete transactions with its regular customers.

A Patchwork of Industry Services

As these sites evolve, they are adding on convenient services such as settlement capabilities and financing, as well as wide choices for shipping, freight, delivery, and warehousing. When working together on an e-marketplace, a company and its customer can track a purchase at every stage of development, from factory manufacturing through packing, shipping, and delivery. The accounting side can also track the purchase from purchase order through invoicing and settlement. This transparency brings enormous efficiency to both the buyer and the seller. Even more, it allows both companies to maintain a lower level of inventory.

When e-marketplaces were first developed in the chemical, metal, and energy industries, they were owned by independent entrepreneurs teamed with venture capitalists. Typically the entrepreneur was a former industry executive who saw the need and teamed up with technology partners and capital partners to make a go of it. When the industry's leaders began to understand that these trading centers were likely to be the place where most future commerce would take place, they decided to get in on the action. "Why should we let outsiders run the trade in our industry?" was the refrain.

The Consortia Are Born

The leading companies in each industry responded in two ways. Their first move was to invest in the entrepreneurial venture that looked poised to handle much of the industry's business. The next step was powerful and, to many, shocking. They launched their own e-marketplaces. The industry leaders understood enough about e-marketplaces to know that if they were going to work, they needed to capture a portion of the market greater than what any one company could provide. So they joined hands with their competitors and created consortia.

The first consortium was the auto exchange launched by Ford and GM, and joined later by DaimlerChrysler. Before the world could fully appreciate the enormity of this move, Sears and Carrefour announced the formation of an e-marketplace. Then came a rush of consortium announcements in every business sector, including chemicals, metals, aerospace, and electronics. Even as corporations put together pacts with diehard competitors, they continued to invest in the independents, just in case.

Our four horsemen have been there every step of the way, from the early auctions (hey, auctions need databases), through the formation of independent e-marketplaces, and on to the consortia. These software players were already installing their procurement systems in the large corporations, so it was an easy shift to move out into the public arena with their customers. Ford brought Oracle into the auto exchange; GM brought Commerce One.

The Trading Sites Sink Deep Roots

E-marketplaces are here to stay, though it will take years to determine whether the best model is the one owned by independent entrepreneurs or those owned by industry consortia. Plenty of doubters are not convinced that long-time rivals can work together effectively, and plenty of suppliers are not happy about their customers ganging up to control the industry. Whatever the outcome, e-marketplaces are clearly the wave of the future. No one is sitting this one out. Virtually every American corporation is involved in one way or another.

YOUR NET STRATEGY:

The migration to Internet procurement will change how virtually all companies buy and sell goods. The savings are so compelling, most large companies have already initiated major shifts to buying over the Internet. This is creating a gush-down effect as the vendors of our major corporations rush online to meet the needs of their customers. If Ford moves to buying online, Delphi, Dana, and U.S. Steel all have to begin selling online. Likewise, auto suppliers turn right around and demand that their vendors also start making their products and services available over the Net.

Some of this procurement is going through auctions, and some of it is moving through e-marketplaces, but the bulk of B2B moves directly from one company to another. Companies are creating their own private purchasing configurations that have come to resemble the shape of a butterfly, with many suppliers selling to one buyer, who then sells to a number of customers. It's many-to-one-to-many. Typically, these companies use a variety of software solutions to accomplish a complicated purchasing configuration.

Most companies will need to use a hybrid of solutions. It is common for companies to use EDI for some purchasing and selling direct materials, while also utilizing browser-based procurement to buy supplies. Then, the company will go to an auction site like FreeMarkets or DoveBid to purchase equipment. The appropriate Net strategy is to stay nimble enough to take advantage of a number of systems for selling and buying. In some cases, companies have to create electronic catalogs to accommodate their customers's automation needs, and these same companies may also pressure their suppliers to get their catalogs into Net-ready condition.

The trick is to automate in such a manner that you don't have to start from scratch for each customer. Software companies such as Poet have come to the scene in order to help companies prepare and present their products in Net-compatible formats. Another major hurdle for many companies is the awkward process of integrating Internet-based procurement into their back-end legacy systems. Integrators are popping up around this need, helping companies tie their Net buying into their ERP systems.

The twin bullets of catalog automation and back-end integration are unavoidable. During the early days of the Internet, many corporate executives resisted these time-consuming and expensive projects, but as more and more of their customers began to demand these changes, purchasing and sales departments have started to change in earnest. This work is transitional. Once integration is in place and the vendor catalogs are automated, the systems that bring the greatest efficiencies will win the day. The best Net strategy is to accept these changes and move aggressively to serve your customers and to pressure your suppliers to make their goods and services available over the Net.

Your Net strategy should also include adaptability. Some Internet trading relationships will remain direct, company-to-company, while others will flow through a public marketplace. Some public marketplaces will incorporate private trading between companies, while some private networks will include direct links to pubic trading hubs for selected items, or for sourcing new vendors. All companies need to remain adaptive as their market sorts itself out online. Many of the consortia sites will never emerge because companies will develop private networks so flexible that the industry sites are simply not necessary. Those who have placed too many chips on the consortium in their sector may find the site never launches.

CHAPTER 9

E-MARKETPLACES

The e-marketplace is a concept founded on the efficiencies available through Internet trading. If you can bring a fragmented industry to a central virtual location, buyers and sellers can meet and shop in ways that have previously been impossible. In response to this reality, companies need to explore the e-marketplaces within their industries. Sure, there will be shakeouts and consolidation, but e-marketplaces will endure, and the better a company understands its industry's trading platform, the better poised it will be to take advantage of the savings and new markets that swirl within these trading hubs.

The development of effective e-marketplaces will likely dominate the first few decades of our new century. A Merrill Lynch analyst correctly called the building of e-marketplaces the largest integration project in the history of humanity. Surprisingly little dissent exists on the prospects of the e-marketplace concept. Despite significant skepticism about which e-marketplace model will emerge as the predominant form, the assumption is that the future of trading between companies will be in one type of e-marketplace or another. No credible voice is calling for a return to offline trading or even for online trading between two companies. There is overwhelming acceptance that over the next few years B2B commerce will mostly take place over public Internet marketplaces.

Half of B2B Will Soon Move through Trading Hubs

A recent study by the Delphi Group found that less than 10 percent of businesses were buying 25 percent of their goods through e-marketplaces in 2000. By 2002, 50 percent of businesses expected to be purchasing 50 percent of their goods through e-marketplaces. The study showed that by 2005, 75 percent of businesses expect to buy over 75 percent of their goods through online exchanges. The overwhelming majority of American corporations fully accept that future commerce will take place over e-marketplaces, even those not already actively engaged in community-based online commerce.

Internet analysts love to make sweeping projections. There is a giddy kind of high that comes when you put out a report that projects the end of the old economy and the beginning of a completely new world in which the leaders are yet to be named. There's a funny kind of pleasure in poking fun at the stodgy world of traditional business. So they claim $3 trillion, $5 trillion, even $7 trillion will move to the Internet, completely toppling the old order of business, and those who are not the first movers in the new revolution will be out of business.

The Revenge of the Bricks

The Internet analysts are a pretty smart bunch, but so are the leaders of the old world economy. If the late 1990s was the revenge of the nerds, with computer geeks taking the lead in a widespread commerce revolution, the early years of the 21st century will be the revenge of the stodgy old crew who still wear ties even on Friday. The oldest of the old world economy are now the ones stepping up to the e-plate, and they're getting ready to hit a few out of the park. After years of snide remarks from the clever bunch in the valley, the adults are walking in to take the business world back.

The numbers have been quietly building for years. Even as the media watched every move from Amazon.com, Priceline.com, AOL, Yahoo!, and eBay, the analysts have been cranking out reports showing that B2B e-commerce would dwarf online retailing by 2001 or 2002. There may be $20 billion, even $30 billion going into CDs,

J Crew sweaters, and airline tickets over the next couple of years, but as that happens, the business world will be trading in hundreds of billions, and it won't be companies whose last three letters are com. It will be companies that are otherwise accustomed to freight cars, massive factory buildings, tons of steel, and oil traded in thousands of barrels.

B2B Commodities Will Spark Increased Global Trade

While Yahoo! tries to figure out how to crack the Chinese market for non-bootlegged CDs, watch out for petrochemicals, plastics, and pesticides flowing back and forth across the Internet, in and out of the Pacific rim. From the media's point of view, entertainment can seem to be America's greatest asset, but the hippest business leaders in the early 2000s may be running companies like Hewlett Packard, Dow, Ford, and Boeing as they spin off Net plays that deliver billions in profits and savings while WebVan is still trying to figure out if they can sell groceries to consumers who are not shut-ins.

The common denominator to this quiet but stunning revolution is the e-marketplace. The world doesn't change when Ford begins to buy parts directly over the Internet from one of its long-term suppliers. Even when you multiply that act by two or three thousand vendors, there are savings, but the basic relationship between customer and supplier stays intact. There are a few new efficiencies, but the world is basically the same. When you take that same act and put it out into a freely spinning public marketplace where a Korean company can bid on the same tool-and-dye work as a Detroit firm, things get a bit dicey.

The Trading Hub Will Become a Sourcing Tool for New Vendors

The big three auto makers tell their suppliers not to worry, but they're very concerned and for good reason. At first we'll see all the same familiar faces on the e-marketplace, but that's just the warm up. These systems are designed to be global, and global they will be. It may take 3 years, or it may take 15 years; at some point the e-marketplaces will open the door to far-distant suppliers that would never have been able to enter the competition in a world of sales visits, faxes, and phone calls.

The proliferation of e-marketplaces will accelerate globalization. More than retail, B2B e-commerce is ripe for global trading. If you're a teen in San Diego and you go online to buy a CD, you're almost certain to buy an American-made product. But if you're seeking a specific grade of petrochemicals, quantity, price, and delivery will ultimately be of greater consequence than country of origin. Even if the foreign suppliers may seem like strangers at first, over time they will become known players who will be able to compete against the traditional suppliers.

This is the advantage of the e-marketplace over an Internet system that merely hooks up a supplier directly with the customer over the Internet. In an e-marketplace, the customer is connected at once to a wide range of vendors, and the customers can use the virtual community to choose among competing suppliers to increase the likelihood of getting the highest quality service and goods at the lowest possible price. If the suppliers feel they're getting squeezed, to a large extent, they're right. But then, they'll be purchasing their raw materials on the e-marketplace as well.

A PARADIGM SHIFT IN AN EYE'S BLINK

When e-marketplaces first appeared selling chemicals, metals, and excess inventory, they were not universally viewed as the inevitable model for future B2B commerce. The new marketplaces were thought to be one of a number of options in B2B procurement. Analysts thought the e-marketplace was a logical development in B2B trading that eventually would evolve into the predominant model as it matured. A mature e-marketplace would include a wide range of services to support the process of seeking suppliers and building business relationships. Most analysts, however, believed the maturation process would take years.

This all changed on February 25, 2000, when Ford, GM, and DaimlerChrysler announced they would team together to build an e-marketplace for the auto industry and that they would push their collective procurement through the new jointly-held company. Three days later, Sears and European retail giant Carrefour announced a similar venture. Then, over the next four weeks, consortium-based e-marketplaces were announced by Sabre, Chevron, International Paper, Georgia Pacific, Boeing, Albertson's, Kmart, and Target, among many others. Overnight, the e-marketplace concept moved to the center stage of B2B commerce.

A Shift Based on an Announcement

For all of the predictions of major shifts to Internet-based B2B trade, the details of where, when, and how had been left in the abstract. The announcement of the auto exchange abruptly made the forecasts concrete, even before the auto makers gave their e-marketplace a name. You could almost hear an audible sigh of relief across corporate America. You could hear every CEO thinking, "Okay, this is what it's going to look like, so let's get moving."

Every corporation knew it was about to move toward a new way of doing business, but until the auto makers announced their exchange, it was not clear what the vehicle for the trip would look like. The idea of a consortium-based trading hub answered a number a questions about how companies would trade over the Internet and who would own the systems by which the trading would take place. Most of the details are yet to be hammered out through trial and error, but the basic models are out on the table for the players to knock around.

No Argument against E-commerce

Most importantly, corporations have accepted that they will buy and sell goods and services in a whole new manner. There are plenty of heated arguments about which e-marketplace model is best for each individual industry or business sector, but no voice argues that a public electronic trading environment will not work. The basic concept of e-marketplaces and online auctions was universally accepted at an amazing speed by very traditional businesses at the center of very staid industries, such as autos, steel, chemicals, and construction.

As a business journalist, I have been surprised by absence of serious doubt. Certainly great controversy brews about the shape of e-marketplaces and whether they will be more effectively run by neutral parties or industry consortia, but the overall direction toward e-marketplaces of one sort or another seems a forgone conclusion. The reason for the quick acceptance of a new way of trading probably stems from general discomfort with existing trading practices. As one corporate executive put it, everyone knows that the pain of moving to a new system can't possibly be matched by the pain of the system that's now in place.

A Natural Extension of Reengineering

I think there's another reason as well. American corporations have remade themselves in fundamental ways a couple times over the past 15 or 20 years. Stunned by the performance of the Japanese in the late 1970s and early 1980s, America's big business woke up to its own complacency and worked aggressively to shed its excess poundage. Corporations have trimmed their management structures and put a high priority on both quality and customer service. They have also turned to technology to become more competitive if not more efficient. They've learned to outsource skills that are not central to developing their core products. Most importantly, they learned to make change a friend instead of an enemy.

Given this major cultural shift in the executive offices of American corporations, the shift to Internet trading is just one more blow that may actually improve the corporation. This isn't to say that large organizations can change quickly. The move to e-marketplaces will move forward in fits, starts, and temporary retreats. But that the change will indeed occur is accepted overall, and most corporations would rather be in the forefront of these changes than in a reaction mode to the efforts of industry strangers.

AUCTIONS, EXCHANGES, E-MARKETPLACES, AND INFORMATION FLOW

We are in an early stage of the development of online trading hubs, and the terminology is still very loose. The elements that make up an e-marketplace are evolving quickly, so terms appear as these elements are added. Ultimately, the trading hubs will be vast and complex, and all of the eventual elements will not be fully developed for 10 to 15 years. The software makers themselves are still furiously working day and night trying to deliver on the promises of their systems.

Some of the elements in e-marketplaces have been developed through retail Internet trading. Most of the auction capabilities have been developing for a few years. Likewise with online catalogs. So even the earliest trading hubs appeared with enough capability to trade materials that can be treated like commodities. Given this, it isn't surprising that the industries that first embraced online trading were industries such as chemicals, agriculture, energy, and metals, which trade substantially in materials of little complexity.

Complex Items Will Move Slowly to the Net

It will take a few more years before e-marketplaces can trade in complex items such as tool and dye, complex machinery, or services. Some sites offer RFQ capabilities, but these systems are not yet widely available or well developed. They are appearing in individual sectors now. The RFQ models are being designed to meet the individual needs of each industry. Perfect.com, for instance, has developed software that enables lumber buyers to qualify automatically and trade with suppliers based on attributes such as wood grade and delivery time. Emerging RFQ software also allows buyers to pre-select vendors based on known quality levels.

The early auction-based exchanges also favor spot purchasing rather than recurring or replenishment procurement. Yet it is the recurring and replenishment purchasing that will ultimately deliver the greatest efficiency savings for corporations. The difference, again, is a matter of complexity. Recurring procurement involves the development and maintenance of a business relationship that goes beyond one-time or occasional purchasing. The relationship in recurring purchasing is still developed offline through interaction that involves sales and service teams. Yet companies are already moving much of their service communication onto the Internet, so it's just a matter of time before the buying and selling also moves online.

Here are the basic elements that usually appear on e-marketplaces:

- *Auctions.* Thanks to online retailers, the auction capabilities of B2B exchanges appeared on the scene as very sophisticated systems. You can find a range of auction types on trading hubs. In the conventional auction, the seller takes the highest bid that comes during a pre-set period of time. In reverse auctions (name-your-own-price), the seller finds the best price offered from various buyers. Then in the Dutch auction, the seller sets a price that drops at pre-set intervals until the goods are sold. Some sites also incorporate shopping bots that travel through a number of vendors looking for the lowest price among like products.

- *Catalogs.* The second level of procurement after the simplicity of auctions comes through online catalogs. For companies that have thousands of products, creating an online catalog that can be fully integrated into a public online exchange is no small feat. But ultimately this is a one-time ramping up. Once the system is in place and meets the uniform requirements of the trading hub, maintenance on the catalog requires little more than the same effort required of a paper or brochure-site catalog.

- *Request for proposals (RFQ).* The RFQ systems on e-marketplaces will handle much of the complex procurement that involves individual project specifications, quality determinations, quantity questions, and delivery timing. Some industries have already rolled up their sleeves and wrestled with the complex considerations involved in online RFQs. Construction sites can enable builders to send blueprints and scheduling requirements to a collection of preselected subcontractors.

- *Settlement and logistics.* In the early online exchanges, the hub was a meeting place for buyers and sellers, but the deal was consummated offline through faxes, phone calls, and mailed invoices. In an effort to automate more of the buy-sell activity, many sites are adding financial institutions and shipping operations to the e-marketplace so goods can be purchased and delivery arrangements can be made online. Platform makers such as Ariba have formed alliances with financial organizations and logistic traders so they can deliver a trading system already equipped to transfer funds and schedule delivery.

- *Industry information.* Industry information was one of the first elements developed for trading sites. VerticalNet began life as a series of sites that presented an information flow developed for business sectors. These sites first showed up in the form of online trade magazines. In time they began to facilitate trade. Meanwhile, the auction sites started to present industry information as a value-added service. Information can include breaking news, features, price listings, or, for agricultural sites, localized weather.

Well-developed information offerings can take on considerable value to the trading participants. The agriculture site, PlanetAg.com, allows farmers to request that the site send a beeper message when the price for a certain crop or livestock hits a particular price. The range and quality of industry information will grow in sophistication as e-marketplaces take on larger and larger portions of an industry's trade.

THE MODELS FOR ONLINE EXCHANGES

A large, sometimes controversial question remains about what e-marketplace models will be successful. Until the automakers banded together and announced their jointly-owned exchange, most business watchers expected e-marketplaces to be owned by independent entrepreneurs who would bring together buyers and sellers from a neutral position. Under this assumption, the big question was: Which player is most likely to attract enough players to reach critical mass? Certainly, to be successful, an e-marketplace needs to gather as many participants as possible.

The underlying assumption was that the leading hub would be the one that could attract the most buyers, since buyers would certainly attract sellers. Early on, industry players made small investments in individual exchanges, indicating their preference for particular players. U.S. Steel invested in e-Steel, and Eastman Chemical invested in ChemConnect. These moves boosted the prospects for e-Steel and ChemConnect because they indicated that big players like U.S. Steel and Eastman Chemical were likely to prefer their investments when they chose to buy or sell goods online.

This all changed when competitors within each industry began to launch their own hubs. Certainly this meant they intended to use their sites as procurement vehicles. When a combination like Sears and Carrefour join together and suggest that they will put a substantial chunk of their $80 billion in combined buying power through their exchange, there isn't much question about whether the e-marketplace will attain critical mass.

Is Coopitition Possible among Bricks?

The big question about consortia becomes: Can competitors change their behavior and learn to work together cooperatively? If the answer is yes, the consortium model will be hard to beat. Yet when big industry players join together within an industry, the Federal Trade Commission (FTC) sits up and pays attention. The feds see a potential for collusion whenever competitors hold hands and work together. The expectation is that the FTC will set specific rules about what can and cannot be done on an e-marketplace, and the consortia will simply abide by these rules.

The neutral players argue that exchanges work best if there is an even playing field of buyers and sellers. Consortium builders argue that if they place their procurement dollars on the table, their vendors and suppliers will follow the money. "And anyway," say the consortium owners, "this is our industry and we're not going to let an outsider come in and run our trading." Analysts tend to say that an independent exchange is best for everyone involved, but the buyer consortia are likely to win. After all, it's the buyer's nickel, so the buyer can go anywhere without devising a system that equally benefits the supplier.

Here's a breakdown of the models appearing as e-marketplaces:

- *Vertical hubs.* VerticalNet is an example of a company that developed a model that can be transported to any industry. The owners of a vertical hub launches in multiple industries in the belief that all industries share the same basic trading and information needs. Many of these hubs begin life as information centers, then foster industry e-commerce as a way to create additional revenue.

- *Independent industry insiders.* Sites launched by independent entrepreneurs who have experience within an industry is becoming the predominant model for independent sites. The entrepreneur is typically a former executive from a company within the industry and so has connections and credibility in the industry. The popular term is *domain knowledge.* Many of these online exchanges were started in retaliation against vertical hubs, with the insider explaining that you simply can't move into an industry and set up shop without a deep knowledge of the industry.

- *Independents with industry investors.* In order to gain funding and credibility within an industry, many independent insider exchanges are turning to industry leaders for investment dollars. These e-marketplaces often are just as interested in the buying power the industry leaders will bring to the hub as they are in the funding. Vertical hubs have not been able to attract the industry leaders to the same extent as the sites that have leaders with domain knowledge. The independents are well aware they are sacrificing some independence as they take money from industry players, but when they're facing consortia, many independents feel they have no other choice.

- *Supply-side exchanges.* Some industries have seen the emergence of e-marketplaces launched by a collection of suppliers. This model may succeed in a very fragmented industry, such as gifts and home accessories, where there are thousands of suppliers and thousands of buyers, but in a tight industry such as autos, a supplier-based exchange is not likely to succeed.

- *Consortia.* Consortia of competing buyers within an industry are hard to beat. Many venture capitalists now look at an industry, and if they find that more than 15 percent of the industry's buying power is concentrated in a consortium, they won't fund any players within that industry. Such is the power of consortia to discourage competition.

So what models are likely to succeed? If the competitors that band together to form consortia really can work together, they'll likely be very successful. So the rule of thumb is that independents will do best in fragmented markets where the top ten companies within the industry have buying power of less than 15 percent of the industry. The consortium in the paper industry, for instance, represents a small enough piece of the overall market that an independent like PaperExchange.com can still do well by bringing together buyers who are not part of the consortium. In a tight industry like autos, however, not much buying power will live outside the consortium.

VERTICAL, HORIZONTAL, OR GEOGRAPHIC?

Another question that is unsettled as online exchanges proliferate is the role the e-marketplace plays within an industry. Just as VerticalNet was setting up numerous industry sites, each one within an individual business sector, a number of online enterprises showed up to trade across numerous industries. Some companies such as FreeMarket.com offered procurement services to any and all industries. The company has been initially successful at offering its purchasing abilities to all takers. So a company like U.S. Steel can say, "We're buying through FreeMarket.com," and its suppliers and vendors will follow the company onto the exchange.

FreeMarkets is a horizontal site that provides for trading of multiple types of goods across multiple markets. Often horizontal sites trade one type of goods across numerous industries. Vertical sites are those that trade many types of goods across a single industry. Selling excess inventory is commonly done by horizontal sites. These sites work across many industries, unloading discontinued lines of clothing to retail chains at the same time they sell an overabundance of livestock feed to agribusiness. Meanwhile, there are vertical agricultural sites that also sell excess inventory of livestock feed to agribusiness. Sometimes you may find that a horizontal excess inventory exchange moves its livestock feed through a vertical agribusiness e-marketplace.

Another example of the horizontal site versus vertical exchange is in the chemical industry. A chemical site may sell goods to a number of industries, including plastics, metals, paper, and agriculture. Would companies in the plastics industry be better served if the chemicals they need were available through a vertical plastics site? Would large farms be more likely to buy their pesticides from an agricultural site or a chemical site? The chemical sites will claim they have a better understanding of pricing and logistics, while the agricultural site may claim to have a better understanding of the needs of farmers.

Local Versions Begin to Appear

To complicate things even more, now sites are appearing that have a geographical orientation. EnergyLeader.com teamed up with the Potomac Electric Power Company (PEPCO) to launch an e-marketplace that is attempting to hook businesses in the Washington, D.C. and Baltimore area to Internet trade. The concept is that the utility company will offer local businesses and institutions the credibility and stability needed to bring them into online trading. The site targets major local organizations such as hospitals and universities.

This geographically-based exchange can hook local buyers to the appropriate vertical sites, so hospitals can buy supplies from health care verticals while also buying office equipment from business sites. EnergyLeader.com is using its co-venture with PEPCO as the first in a series of local sites around the United States. This utility-based model is also appearing in Europe, where the business community is accustomed to working with utilities as network platforms. In Europe, telephone companies are vying for this role, since European phone companies are much more like utilities than in the United States.

Unlike the question over business models for e-marketplaces, little heated controversy exists over whether sites should be vertical, horizontal, or geographic in nature. Some analysts argue that a vertical orientation is usually preferred because the exchange is deeply rooted into the community of its players. Yet a hospital may find that it shares more with its local utility than it does with the healthcare industry at large. Likewise, a retail clothing chain may be more comfortable with sites trading in oversupply of many goods than it is with the exchanges based within the retail industry.

Efficiency Answers Every Question

The questions of vertical, horizontal, and geographic orientation likely will be answered through a combination of sites that deliver the greatest efficiency and trust. The resulting picture may include all three models working together. The horizontal chemical sites may sell their industry-specific chemicals through vertical sites with a split transaction fee. The geographic sites are already negotiating split transaction fees with the exchanges their customers will tap into through the utility's e-marketplace. Though it may look complicated at first glance, a spectrum that includes all orientations may actually be the most efficient way to bring buyers and sellers together. It may be more efficient for an agriculture site to cooperate with a chemical exchange than it is for the agriculture site to tie together the suppliers and logistics companies in the chemical industry.

Likewise with geographic sites. It may be more efficient for a local university or mid-size business to hook into its utility's site than it is to navigate the confusing waters of vertical sites that serve large industry well. But that university or business may have a hard time identifying and serving the needs of organizations that are more a part of their local environments than they are part of a widespread industry or business sector. Ultimately, the sites that succeed will be those that serve their customers most efficiently, which means that all three orientations can coexist.

The Buyer's Gold Leads the Way

The real power in the development of e-marketplaces is the buyer. If an e-marketplace can attract a sufficient number of buyers with a critical mass of procurement spending, the exchange will flourish. Even e-marketplaces formed by a collection of suppliers have to serve the needs of their buyers in order to survive. The weight of the consortia comes from the buying power their owners bring to the exchange. Presumably, the consortia will be built by buyers to serve buyers, and if the e-marketplace is inconvenient for suppliers, then the suppliers will have to adapt, not the buyers. The ultimate mix of e-marketplace styles, whether horizontal or vertical, whether buyer-based or run by independents, will be customer-based. To succeed, an e-marketplace will have to be the most efficient system for the buyer.

SOFTWARE MAKERS DEAL THEMSELVES IN

Imagine a creative construction company that builds a toll bridge to connect two towns. The firm charges each town to build the bridge. Then it takes a small portion of every toll. It also takes an ownership position on the bridge and benefits from the toll profits. When the bridge is ultimately sold to a third town, the construction firm gets a tidy return. The software companies involved in creating the explosion of e-marketplaces are getting a number of revenue streams for their effort and technology.

There are licensing fees for the software, project fees to build the hub, and consulting fees before and afterwards. Because many of the marketplaces are joint ventures between an industry leader and an e-platform company, the software firm gets a minority equity position in the marketplace itself. This can become very meaningful 18 months down the road when the marketplace has an initial public offering (IPO). Also, every time somebody buys something from somebody else, the software company drags a few nickels from the pot. To the industry leader involved in the joint venture, who cares? The eMarkeplace produces such a big chunk of savings in the procurement process, the software company's portion is beneath consideration. Besides, someone has to be at the wheel of the hub, and who better than your partner, the software firm?

The Software Vendor as Equity Owner

The household names in the e-marketplace business are taking the biggest positions in the Net marketplaces. Oracle, Commerce One, and Ariba take partnership positions with their clients in many instances. Commerce One has taken a small piece of equity for its involvement in the aerospace joint venture with Boeing, Lockheed Martin, Raytheon, and BAE Systems, and both Commerce One and Oracle are part-owners of the Covisint automobile exchange.

These giants have recently started working with each other as they serve big clients such as Ford and GM. Sometimes they hire each other as consultants or license specialized pieces of software from each other. An Oracle database is at the heart of many e-marketplaces, even when Oracle is not one of the players in the hub venture, since Oracle's databases are considered the best in the industry.

Licensing May Be a Shortcut to Profits

Some software companies take the more traditional role of earning revenue in the form of licensing and consulting fees on e-marketplace projects owned outright by an industry player. BroadVision and WebVision both use this model, coming in as vendors rather than partners. Microsoft also plans to take a vendor role as it enters the B2B marketplace playing field. Microsoft executives claim this is why Microsoft was included in the aerospace hub instead of Oracle. Oracle executives claim their falling out with Boeing was not based on its marketplace model.

Even if companies do have alternatives to giving their software vendor a piece of the new venture and a cut of the transactions, many still want the weight of one or more major players, such as Oracle, Commerce One, Ariba, and i2. In this fiery race to grab land, corporate leaders want a trusted advisor who knows the strange frontier. A piece of the action is a small price to pay. Yet some software companies would rather take the money and run, in the belief that a licensing fee is the bird in the hand, while the equity is two birds in a very thorny bush.

SHAKEOUT? IT'S NOT AS CROWDED AS IT LOOKS

Almost as soon as e-marketplaces began to appear, some analysts predicted a shakeout for the industry. Other analysts viewed the proliferation of online exchanges as a natural expansion in which most players would find a niche that could support their endeavor. AMR Research predicted that the number of e-marketplaces would swell to over 2,000 in 2001 or 2002, only to shake out to 50 or 100 through consolidations and bankruptcy. The logic is that each industry can only support one or two e-marketplaces.

The Gartner Group, on the other hand, predicted that the number of online exchanges can easily reach 10,000 and that all of these could serve niches and survive. Most analysts fall somewhere between these two extremes, believing that each industry can support more than one or two, but that dozens of e-marketplaces within each industry would duplicate services. The answer will depend on whether online exchanges continue to develop along niche markets, or it becomes more efficient for one-stops to serve multiple niches.

A Patchwork of Niche Sites

Let's take one industry, agriculture. Even early in the development of e-marketplaces, the agriculture industry saw the formation of dozens of online exchanges. Yet few of these trading hubs duplicated the same services. Some sites allowed farmers to buy chemicals on a spot-purchase, or occasional, basis. Others served the farm's need for equipment. Some sold used equipment on an auction basis, while others sold new products which came with ongoing service maintenance agreements.

The agriculture industry also experienced a proliferation of sites that serviced farmers in selling mode. Some sites allowed growers to sell crops through an online auction, while others were set up for livestock auctions. Some sites gave growers the ability to contract with crop buyers before planting, while others bought crops only when they became available. Some sites traded in walnuts, while other sites traded in wheat. Each site served a niche within the agriculture industry with a unique model.

Many analysts agree that an industry cannot sustain much duplication of business models or markets. In other words, the world doesn't need more than one or two sites trading in walnuts. Yet an industry as large as agriculture can sustain dozens of sites that offer a diversity of services, from cattle to equipment, from spot buys in pesticides to recurring purchases of slaughterhouse equipment.

It's about the Savings

The ultimate question of how each industry will be served by e-marketplaces will likely come back to the question of efficiency. Will an industry like agriculture be better served by a wide spectrum of sites that break down buying and selling into niches, such as almonds, harvesting equipment, chemicals, and feed, each served by an individual exchange? Or would the industry be best served by one or two large players that incorporated these niche services into one mammoth site that could sell sheep as efficiently as a tractor.

Most analysts expect niche sites to carve out specialty areas within an industry that allows for high specialization. This would concentrate domain expertise, which serves the buyer with industry information and efficient procurement technology. Over time, it is possible to incorporate the niche specialties into larger, more comprehensive e-marketplaces, but most analysts believe this trend is many years away and that it may not happen at all if niche players can serve their buyers efficiently.

THE COMING IPO BOOM FOR EXCHANGES

At some point, B2B exchanges will become very valuable enterprises. When they first came to light as investments in early 2000, the retail side of e-commerce was experiencing its first serious correction, and the e-marketplace world took the same stock hit. Yet many of the e-marketplaces stand to reach profitability much more quickly than retail Internet companies. They offer companies an efficient procurement option that is superior to traditional purchasing. This money-saving lure is matched with a transaction-fee revenue stream that ensures profitability once the exchange reaches a critical mass of buyers and sellers.

Yes, There Will Be IPOs Again

Still, it has become difficult for online exchanges to attract capital, because the muddy waters in Internet speculation have left venture capitalists skeptical of dot-com launches. Plus, the variety of business models competing for B2B transactions presents a confusing picture to potential investors. At some point, the value of online exchanges will become clear, and a renewed interest in B2B e-marketplaces will produce a boom in IPOs.

The edge in development goes to the consortia, because they are usually well-funded by their industry leader parents. The lack of venture capital pouring into the online exchange market also encourages neutral players to seek support from industry leader investors. This turn of events may ultimately be good for the e-marketplace model because easy venture capital money often supports businesses that have not developed clear business models based on satisfying the needs of a specific market. The bizarre developments in retail e-commerce show how unhealthy it can be for a market when funding doesn't depend on the development of a clear business model.

In the meantime, plenty of opportunity can be found among e-marketplace builders, consultants, and integrators. No matter which model is ultimately successful, quite a number of companies will prosper as corporations in America and around the world move more and more of their buying and selling to the Internet. Companies like Ariba, Commerce One, and Oracle have partnered with consortia as well as independents, claiming they are agnostic when it comes to business models. These companies stand to win no matter which direction the market takes.

The Consultants Get Paid in Cash

In addition to the exchange makers, a small industry of companies provides integration services that tie e-marketplaces into the legacy systems of the buyers and sellers. The integration side of the e-marketplace world is not as well-developed as the builder side of the market. Dozens of firms are vying for pieces of the integration pie, and it is not clear which of these players will emerge with a dominant model. Integration may remain a fragmented market, unlike the e-marketplace builder market, which is clearly dominated by four to six players.

There is also a good deal of consulting work created by the mammoth shift from offline procurement to Internet-based systems. Firms such as Andersen Consulting, Ernst and Young, PricewaterhouseCoopers, and KPGM are training their consulting teams in the software platforms of Ariba, Commerce One, and Oracle so they can send armies of consultants across the globe to teach corporations how to use online exchanges. Some of this work will be temporary in nature, but as with the legacy systems installed at the frontends and backends of large corporations, some of this consulting work will effectively be permanent.

So even if you can't pick the right business model to back right now, you can certainly see there is an emerging industry of service players who are bringing their picks and shovels to do the groundwork of this widespread business revolution. And unlike the move to railroads and interstate highway systems of the past, the new business distribution system will not be a simple set of tracks that require little maintenance once they're installed. The railroad makers of this revolution will not clear the ground, build the tracks, and leave. They're going to move into the large corporations and set up house.

YOUR NET STRATEGY:

Many companies are taking a wait-and-see approach to e-marketplaces. They have popped up in all business sectors, but not all of these public exchanges are creating trading activity. This is particularly true of the consortia marketplaces banged together by industry leaders who want to prevent independent dot-coms from coming into their industry and setting up shop at the center of the trading floor. These industry-owned sites are typically announced many months before they become operational.

Yet some e-marketplaces have created viable trading centers and will clearly be around for years to come. Altra, an energy trading hub, has succeeded in creating liquidity in the buying and selling of electricity, gas, and oil. FreeMarkets is doing well, providing procurement opportunities for a long list of Fortune 500 clients, and Ventro has created a number of viable marketplaces in healthcare, life sciences, and indirect materials.

In the face of uncertainties, the best strategy is to evaluate the individual opportunities for both buying and selling in your particular sector. Keep in mind that the configuration of trading in your industry may go through a number of changes before it begins to stabilize. Companies may spend a few years jumping from technology to technology in order to satisfy the requests of major customers. In some industries, such as retail, e-marketplaces may never quite catch on, while in others, such as automotive, they could become the very center of the industry.

Another thing to keep in mind is that the concept of e-marketplaces may evolve into private trading networks centered around one major customer. These networks may have many of the qualities of an e-marketplace, with many suppliers linking information and sharing technology, while the transaction information remains a closely protected secret between buyers and sellers. If this occurs on a widespread basis, it will prevent public e-marketplaces from gaining large portions of an industry's trade.

Many of the Fortune 500 companies are hedging their bets by forming industry consortia, while also investing in independent e-marketplaces and creating their own private networks. These companies are blending a variety of paths into a portfolio in the belief that they can't miss the e-commerce boat even as it remains uncertain which of the possible boats will actually float. Likewise, their customers will have to be prepared to pursue a variety of potential marketplace solutions.

The wrong strategy is to sit and wait. If you delay your move to automate your catalog or stall in preparing to connect directly to your customers, you may find them happy to connect to a competitor that shows a greater willingness to get hooked into their systems. A number of large companies give their vendors a drop-dead date to get Net ready. If your customers turn to you with an Internet gleam in their eyes, it's best to have your sales effort prewired.

CHAPTER 10

GLOBAL REACH

How many languages can you speak? The Internet can speak any language that two or more people decide it should speak. And how many countries does the Internet reach? If you have a mobile phone, the Internet can travel to every spot on earth. Crews on a ship out to sea use the Internet to arrange for replacement maintenance parts and supplies to be waiting at the dock at their next port city. The Internet is implicitly global. One of the great fears among industrial suppliers is that as industries move to online exchanges, those e-marketplaces can be accessed easily by companies all over the globe. Now that the Internet is becoming the hub of business trading, globalization will reach its full potential.

By the time you read this book, we've already hit that tipping point where English is no longer the language used by the majority of Internet users. For decades, U.S. manufacturers have cast a ravenous eye on China's consumers. China has been called the sleeping giant. Once its population awakes to Western-style consumerism, the companies that can sell to this market will experience explosive growth. Yet China has been beyond reach with its closed culture. Well, the wall came tumbling down when the Internet wires started to spider through China. Don't look now, but the China bear is sipping a cup of coffee and blinking its eyes awake, thanks to the Internet.

Although global Internet usage is still in its infancy, the Web is already growing far beyond its U.S. roots. At the beginning of 1999, most Internet users were in the U.S. By early 2000, Americans accounted for less than 50 percent of Internet users for the first time, according to a study by eTForecasts. The report shows that by 2005, the United States will still be the leading Internet country, but its lead will continue to shrink. The difference between 1999 and 2000 alone was a worldwide increase of 100 million Internet users, moving up to 375 million from 1999's 276 million users.

In 2000, the U.S. had 136 million users, or 36 percent of the global Internet pie. Second was Japan with 27 million users. Next came Germany with 19 million. In fourth place was the United Kingdom with 18 million users. And sleepy China ranked fifth with 16 million users, higher than Canada at 15 million. The eTForecasts tend to be on the higher side of global estimates, but a number of respected firms, such as IDC and Internet Industry Almanac, report similarly high numbers.

Getting Braced for the New Globalization

In one way or another, companies will need to prepare for an increasing level of global trading. E-marketplaces provide many industries with tools to accommodate increased global trade, because many trading hubs incorporate currency, financial, and logistics services to assist with foreign trade. Language and custom differences are the stickier wickets, but vendors are rushing in to help Internet trading companies overcome barriers in language, regulations, and country-centric customs.

It isn't just B2B enterprise that is struggling with increased global trade. An Ernst & Young report shows that Internet retailing is growing internationally, though at a slower pace than in the United States. North America is ahead of all other regions in the percentage of the population that has purchased goods online. The United States reached 17 percent in 1999, while in countries such as Italy and France, only 1 or 2 percent has bought over the Internet. The report also showed a wide variance in usage and purchasing across Europe, with the Scandinavian countries coming in as the most Net savvy, while Italy and Spain lag behind. The United Kingdom ranks below Scandinavia, with Germany close behind, followed by France. Though the United Kingdom and Germany lag behind Scandinavia in Internet adoption, they are the European heavyweights because of the sizes of their populations and economies.

B2B Leads Globalization

Unlike in the United States, for most countries B2B trading will lead the rush to the Internet. Forrester predicts global e-commerce will reach $6.9 trillion in 2004, with a period of intense development beginning in 2001. According to Forrester, North America will lead, followed by Europe. But the Asia-Pacific area is expected to catch up with and pass Europe by 2004. The study sees the Middle East and Africa growing more slowly and not reaching hyper-growth until 2010. In Europe, a good portion of the growth in overall Internet trade will include retail, while most of the e-commerce in Asia-Pacific will be confined to B2B trading.

Even through the hyper-growth, most trading will be among developed countries, with 89 percent of worldwide Net trading confined to 12 countries. Latin America and Eastern Europe still have significant infrastructure problems to overcome before they can reach fast-paced e-commerce growth. Forrester expects e-commerce to penetrate all aspects of business, from industry supply chains to the purchase of household items.

The Gartner Group estimates that B2B e-commerce was dominated by U.S. trade through 1999, with 63 percent of the $145 billion market going to American business. By 2004, however, Gartner expects the U.S. portion to account for only 39 percent as total B2B Internet revenues hit $7.29 trillion. As with the Forrester report, Gartner expects Europe to make the first big move among regions outside North America. The report showed significant movement toward B2B e-commerce by European companies such as BMW, Phillips, KLM, Swissair, British Telecom, and Deutsche Telekom.

The Asian Flu Has Come to an End

The slower adoption of B2B e-commerce in Asia-Pacific is attributed to the region's recent recession. But with the recession past, this region is expected to roar past Europe by 2004 as commercial banks and venture capital funds begin to target Internet companies for direct investment. Gartner is more optimistic about Latin American than Forrester, predicting a move from $1 billion in 1999 to $124 billion in 2004.

Because of the Internet, we have now reached the point that the greatest impediment to international trade is not logistics, distance, communication, language, or currency variances. The greatest barriers to trade are now legal and political in the form of quotas and tariffs. If the political obstructions could be magically removed, a manufacturer in Chicago might be just as likely to buy from a supplier in Singapore or Brussels as from a usual source in New Jersey. As long as all things are equal in quality, stability, and delivery price, the only element holding back the Singapore supplier is trade restrictions. Over the next few years, the Internet will certainly bring pressure to bear on artificial blockades.

EUROPE: TAKING NOTES FROM U.S. DEVELOPMENT

Europe's online development has grown in a much different manner than U.S. Internet growth. For one, there has been no pan-European development on the Internet, even though the European Union has made headway on merging European currencies into the Euro. Each country has its own servers and retailers. Though Europe has watched American development carefully, its own models have emerged that don't reflect U.S. patterns of Net growth. The leading Internet service providers in Europe offer Net access at no charge. In order to compete effectively in the United Kingdom, AOL has had to match the country's free model.

Though the United States got the early lead on Internet business, the number of European Net consumers is expected to grow dramatically during the early years of the new century. Jupiter Communications expects Europe's online market to grow 415 percent from 1999 to 2001. Europe will still lag behind the United States, but its growth rate will surpass the U.S. growth rate. Consumer spending online across Europe is expected to hit $14 billion in 2001, and it will rise to over $60 billion by 2005. The number of online consumers will rise from 20 million in 2000 to 85 million in 2005. The United Kingdom and Germany will continue to lead in overall numbers, while Scandinavia will continue to lead in online penetration.

Pure Plays Lead Retail Growth

Jupiter also expects the Net-only companies to continue their lead in Internet retailing for the early years of the century. But as in the United States, as online shopping becomes increasingly mainstream, brick-and-mortar players have the opportunity to bring their offline consumer clout to the Internet. Jupiter's study noted that to be effective, brick-and-mortar retailers will have to act soon, and the study saw no early movement on the part of European offline retailers that matches the positive Net moves of U.S. brick-and-mortar retailers.

Generally, Europe has lagged 9 to 12 months behind the United States in the adoption of Internet usage and e-commerce. Europe's blue chip companies may be lagging even further behind. The U.K. blue chips tend to be more eager to embrace Internet communication with customers and e-commerce in general than their European counterparts, but even the U.K. companies lag far behind the United States in preparing to integrate the Internet into their business operations. European corporations are repeating the early U.S. mistake of developing its Internet strategies in isolation from existing operations.

Europe Leads in Country-to-Country Integration

A study by Chordiant Software revealed that corporations in Germany and The Netherlands were ahead of U.K. companies in their ability to integrate their customer channels with the Internet. In the United Kingdom, only 16 percent of companies are able to share customer data throughout the company via the Internet. In Germany, 36 percent of companies have integrated information through the Internet, and in The Netherlands, 27 percent of companies have brought the Internet into overall operations.

One area of quick Internet adoption across Europe is the online trading of stocks. International Data Corporation (IDC) found rapid development in Internet trading throughout Europe. Sweden has over ten brokerages offering online trading, with almost half of them online-only brokerages. Germany has also been fast to trade over the Internet, using electronic channels like BTX over their PCs. And, despite their usually conservative approach to financial matters, they have embraced discount brokering, which has resulted in Germany taking the lead in European online trading. The United Kingdom, France, and Switzerland have also moved aggressively to online trading, each through its own national systems and companies.

Forrester Research expects 7 percent of Europe's retail business to migrate to the Web by 2005. Currently, the main online retail categories are media, electronics, and leisure travel. By 2005, the biggest retail categories are expected to be groceries, apparel, leisure travel, and autos. Forrester also expects the emergence of pan-European retailers by 2005, with traditional retailers moving in to claim up to 75 percent of Internet retailing. Forrester also predicts that traditional retailers will support pan-European Internet retailing with brick stores in the countries into which they expand.

EUROPEAN E-MARKETPLACES

As in the United States, the lion's share of European e-commerce growth will come from business trade. While online retailing is expected to hit $8 to $12 billion by 2004, online business trade may hit $1.4 trillion. This trade is coming through e-marketplaces, but how online business trading will evolve across Europe is still unclear. Given the legislative restrictions, tariffs, trade barriers, and language and cultural obstacles, online connectivity may be the easy part, and even that is very unclear.

Though the answers to how Europe will move to Internet business trading remain foggy, the region's corporate leaders are bullish on e-marketplaces. Seventy percent of European corporate leaders expect to conduct more than 25 percent of their business via the Internet by 2004. This figure represents dramatic growth over a four-year period. As of the year 2000, 55 percent of these same firms were conducting less than 10 percent of their business online.

Again, It's All about the Savings

The motivator behind the interest in rushing trade to the Internet is the same as in the United States, the potential savings in procurement process, cost-of-goods, and inventory levels. Corporate leaders expect a wider choice of suppliers that will result in lower product costs. They also expect to lower their transaction costs and increase production efficiency through supply-chain visibility that allows for trimmer inventory levels.

An added benefit they expect from Internet trading is the ability to become more competitive globally. Most corporations see online markets as a tool for expanding their customer base. According to Forrester, 72 percent of European executives expect to participate in four or more online marketplaces to expand their marketing. Much of the interest comes from small-to-medium companies that find e-marketplaces are a way to reach large companies in ways that would not have been possible before the Internet.

Global Companies Have the Early Edge

The rate of adopting e-marketplaces in Europe varies by industry and corporate size. Global companies are much more prepared to expand onto the Internet than localized companies. Large companies also have the IT infrastructure to adopt Internet trading quickly. The difference between early adopters and later adopters in Europe can be a full five years.

The automotive industry is an early adopter, as Volkswagen has partnered with Ariba to create an e-marketplace that will allow the company to buy from its suppliers over the Internet. Electronics corporations are also quick to adopt Internet trading, as are travel, textiles, and telecommunications. Slow industries include consumer goods, construction, and the pharmaceuticals industry. Chemicals and paper products have been slow to adopt Internet trading, which is surprising given that these industries were early adopters in the United States.

Small Countries Will Follow Their Customers onto Global Sites

There are regional variances in how quickly European corporations are embracing online business trading. As with Internet retailing, the United Kingdom and Germany lead the European pack. These two large economies will account for half of European marketplace trade by 2005. Regions that have strong ties to the United Kingdom and Germany, including Benelux and Ireland, will get pulled onto the Net by their trading partners. Italy and Spain will move their business to the Net about two years behind the United Kingdom and Germany. Scandinavia comes to the table with a mature view of the Net, but its impact will be smaller because of its smaller economy.

A good portion of large European companies will be drawn into e-marketplaces simply because they trade with large U.S. companies, most of whom are moving much of their buying and selling to the Internet. The initial moves are in direct purchasing and selling, but e-marketplace trading in the United States is growing quickly. Europe's trade with other countries may take a bit longer, but the first moves to Internet B2B trading in Europe will certainly come through trade with U.S. corporations.

THE ASIA-PACIFIC RIM

The region that includes Asia will move more slowly to e-commerce than Europe, but its effect may ultimately be larger simply because of the vast population of countries like China and India. The early movers in Internet trading are Hong Kong and Japan. Japan was slow to start because of the country's prolonged recession, but the country is quickly making up for lost time. A positive climate for e-commerce exists throughout Asia, because the countries are already deeply involved in global trade and because the governments in the region support e-commerce.

As with Europe, most of the dollars flowing over the Internet in Asia will involve B2B trading. As trade barriers continue to fall, companies throughout Asia will move to the Internet to trade with partners in the United States and Europe, as well as with other Asian countries. Already, 86 percent of Singapore's exports to the United States are in computing and electronics, an industry that is moving quickly to direct Net procurement as well as trade through e-marketplaces. This means Singapore's companies will necessarily follow their trading partners to the Internet.

Trade Barriers Can Slow Down Adoption

Internet trade in the Asia-Pacific region should reach $1.5 trillion by 2004. Yet the region is not likely to develop uniformly. The areas favored by e-commerce will be those with low trade barriers, stable currencies, flexible capital markets, and well-developed technical infrastructure. These qualities put Hong Kong in front of India for early e-commerce adoption. Japan and Australia are also well equipped to begin large-scale Internet trading, while China is hindered by weak infrastructure and mixed signals from the government concerning foreign investment in Internet development. Korea and Taiwan are expected to adopt e-commerce quickly, with more than 16 percent of their total sales going over the Internet by 2004.

Online stock trading in the Asia-Pacific region is set to skyrocket from 2000 through 2004, according to IDC. The brokerages offering online trading in the early stages tend to be Net-only companies, but their offline counterparts are expected to follow suit quickly. In 1999, less than 10 percent of stock in the region was sold online. By 2004 Internet trading will exceed 40 percent of all stock exchanges. During that time, the number of online investors will soar from 2.77 million to over 20 million.

The Winners Will Be Adept at Multiple Currencies and Languages

Like Europe, the Asia-Pacific region will benefit from learning from the U.S. market. IDC also expects U.S. brokerage firms to bring trading to the region, but indigenous brokerages will likely win back lost market share within a couple of years as consumers turn back to the companies with established histories and reputations. U.S. firms will have a more difficult time managing the multiple currencies and languages of the region, skills that indigenous brokerage firms have already mastered.

Retail e-commerce in the region will be a mixed bag, with individual cultures developing retail trade along different models. In China, e-commerce tends to be localized, with consumers purchasing most of their goods from bricks-and-click shops within a few miles of their homes. This trade has created a flourishing delivery business for taxis and rickshaws. Japan also takes a local approach to retailing, with the largest Internet retailing coming through the country's convenience store chains.

LATIN AMERICA'S SLOW EMERGENCE

One of the slowest regions to adopt e-commerce is Latin America. The region got off to a slow start primarily because of infrastructure weakness and high access fees in many Latin American countries. Even with B2B factored in, total Latin American e-commerce will only reach $82 billion by 2004. Of that figure, a full 93 percent will be business trade, leaving retail e-commerce at a paltry $5.7 billion. There are, however, improvements on the horizon in Latin America.

Brazil and Argentina are likely to lead the improvements in the region, as the countries's governments work to stabilize currencies and liberalize trade policies, two of the greatest hurdles to e-commerce in the region. In addition to public policy gains, Latin America will need to reach a critical mass of technological linkages, which includes phone lines, PCs, Internet hosts, and cell phones. Unlike the United States, Europe, and the Asia-Pacific region, Latin

America probably won't have the ability to deliver widespread Internet connectivity until 2003 or later.

Latin America Will Lag for Years

eMarketer has an even more pessimistic view of Latin America's e-commerce future. In its eLatin America Report, the research firm projects Internet retailing to reach $15 billion in 2003. Of this, 87 percent is expected to come from B2B e-commerce, leaving just over $1 billion for online retail trade. At this level, Latin America will fill only 1 percent of the world's e-commerce pie. eMarketer estimates that only 10 to 15 percent of the population in Latin America has the resources to actively shop online. These "Internet elite" users are educated, cosmopolitan, and technologically advanced compared with the region's general population.

Some of the statistics holding back the region will be hard to overcome. Only 18 percent of Brazilians and 22 percent of Mexicans hold credit cards. Tariffs and unreliable shipping logistics make intra-Latin American purchases difficult and expensive. There are only 21 telephones per 100 people in Argentina, 11 per 100 in Brazil, and 10 per 100 in Mexico. Access costs are much higher in Latin America than in Europe, the United States, or the Asia-Pacific region, despite free ISPs in some areas.

Latin Trade Barriers Will Persist

Most research firms do not expect the barriers in Latin America to lift soon. Jupiter Communications believes that breakthroughs will come in Argentina, Brazil, and Mexico during the five-year period, 2000 through 2005. Even with progress in infrastructure, credit, and economic capacity, Jupiter only expects the region to reach $8.3 billion by 2005, with Argentina, Brazil, and Mexico accounting for 80 percent of the total.

Some industry experts see hope in AOL's moves in the region. AOL has launched a joint venture with Venezuela's Cisneros media group to help develop Latin America's Internet industry. Jupiter expects this move to put Latin American on the Internet radar. AOL plans to develop interactive services and content for the region as well as promoting connectivity. The company will begin its Latin American expansion in Brazil, with other countries to follow after Brazil is established. In its early stages, AOL struggled with sluggish sales, aggressive local competitors, and a technical gaffe in which potential users were sent reggae music CDs instead of installation software.

IS ENGLISH THE ONLY LANGUAGE OF E-COMMERCE?

By 2002, the majority of Internet users will not speak English, according to research firm Global Reach. In 1997, only 10 percent of Internet users were non-English-speaking, so the trend away from English is profound. In 1995, non-English-speaking Internet users were a tiny 4 million out of 40 million users. By 2000, the non-English Net population hit 80 million out of a total population of 182 million. Since the increase in non-English speaking users is a diverse group of people speaking Japanese, French, German, and Spanish, the English language will continue to dominate the Web as the language of business. For example, Internet trading between France and Germany is often conducted using English as the common language.

Although English dominates Internet trade, Web sites developed by European corporations offer language choice to customers. A study by U.K. research firm Equipe indicates that an increasing portion of Web users from European and Asian countries are unable to cope with English on the Internet. Productivity suffers when they work with untranslated sites, and thus they are more comfortable with sites in their own language. Leading IT companies in the United States, such as Dell and Cisco, are already capitalizing on this by offering multilingual Web sites.

Customer Service Is Trending toward Multilingual Accommodation

With business trade becoming increasingly global, many corporations see a competitive edge in offering their customers the option to trade in their own language. Developments in customer service and support also favor multilingual Web sites and call centers as a way to capture global business. A trend among U.S. global companies is to match each country with service personnel who are native speakers, in the belief that it is not enough to simply know the language. In order to have good customer relationships, the service personnel have to be from the same country as their customers.

Most large U.S. companies understand that the Internet is inherently global. Forrester Research finds that mid-to-small companies are unequipped to deal with orders coming from outside the United States. A Forrester study found that more than half of U.S. Internet companies turn away non-English orders because they are not equipped to fulfill them. But major U.S. corporations have been working in the international marketplace for many years, so they are well equipped to turn their expertise in communicating with global trade partners to the Internet.

YOUR NET STRATEGY:

The appropriate strategy, given the global nature of the Internet, is to prepare to meet the demands of a steady march toward globalization. We are already a few decades into this trend, and the Internet is accelerating the growth of international business. Technology companies are already rushing in to help American companies cope with increased global trading. Most public e-marketplaces have incorporated currency exchange software as well as set up logistics solutions that allow companies to find shippers around the world easily and track shipments minute-by-minute as the goods circle the globe.

These changes will also provide major challenges to many companies, which will suddenly find that the new e-marketplace allows the formerly loyal customer a peek into prices in Singapore. This challenge may not appear immediately. In their first moves to the Internet, buyers usually reassure their vendors that their intention to move to online buying is just to reach internal efficiencies. But in time, you can be sure that purchasing managers will get curious about what it would cost to buy the same products from a company on mainland China.

The best way to meet this challenge is to take the first peek at competitive potential over the ocean, as well as looking to see if you can buy for less internationally. The move to international buying will come gradually, but it will certainly come, and both buyers and sellers need to keep their eyes open for the opportunities and challenges that will accompany increased international trade.

Many American Net companies, such as Yahoo!, AOL, and Monster.com, have moved quickly and aggressively into Europe, the Asia/Pacific Rim, and Latin America, but these moves have not yet produced any real return. The big story in international trade will likely grow from our traditional industries, such as automotive, energy, chemicals, and metals. In these sectors, low-cost labor will affect prices, and any companies whose products can be commoditized are likely to find challenges overseas.

The solution to global challenges will come in large part from vendors that are rushing in to help companies prepare for Net-based global trade. Vendors have developed solutions in marketing communications, logistics, and financial services as well as customer service. Many of these vendor services have been incorporated into e-marketplaces, allowing companies to gain global reach without developing internal solutions to the problems of global trade.

CHAPTER 11

VENTURE CAPITAL AND INCUBATORS
Funding the Next World

When I launched my first business in the mid-1980s, I did it the traditional way. I used personal savings and family loans. After a few months of producing sales, I was able to secure a bank line of credit and installment loans for equipment. Within a couple of years, I had enough of a track record to obtain a higher line of credit and I was able to attract investors. At first they were family investors, but soon I was also able to bring in angel investors. This was a very typical launch scenario before the Internet changed all the rules of business launches. New companies don't mess around any longer building a track record before they begin selling their ideas to investors.

There are good reasons to go directly to investors. For one, it puts the start-up on the Internet map much quicker than an incremental launch would allow, and for another, plenty of venture capital dollars are seeking new companies. During the first quarter of 2000, venture capitalists invested $17.22 billion in spite of concerns over the future of Internet retailing and B2B e-commerce. The investment level beat the previous record of $14.69 billion invested during the final quarter of 1999.

Venture Investment Is Here to Stay

The Q1 2000 figure quadrupled the $4.31 billion invested just one year earlier in Q1 1999. The total number of companies getting funded during those days when the Nasdaq was turning downward was 94 percent higher than the same period the year before. Obviously, there was still plenty of money out there to back clever new business ideas. Technology, of course, took most of the investment dollars, with $16 billion of the $17.22 billion in Q1 2000 going to Internet-related companies, which comes to a whopping 93 percent of all venture capital invested during the quarter.

These investment dollars don't even take into account the support that was given to start-ups through incubator programs, which often invest in overhead and management support in addition to dollars. Venture capitalists are growing more savvy and careful about the companies they fund, but they are certainly not holding back on the total volume of dollars offered to new and emerging companies. With all of the investment dollars floating around, it's no wonder that most Internet start-ups cruise right along without any debt. It also explains why Silicon Valley couldn't care less about interest rate levels.

THE VENTURE CAPITAL MARKET

There are two ways to get an Internet company funded: venture capitalists and incubators. To a certain degree, the right choice depends on whether a company wants support or autonomy. For the most part, a company that obtains venture capital funding goes it alone with some guidance from the investors. A company that joins an incubator usually receives more management and overhead. These are generalities. Many incubator firms have hands-off management, while a fair portion of companies living on venture money receive considerable direction from investors. Because a very wide range of potential arrangements are available on both sides, an entrepreneur really has to look at each potential funding possibility as a unique opportunity.

Also, a myth persists about the venture capital community. One part of the myth goes that in the period of 1997 through 1999, venture capitalists were eager to fund any idea that came with a *.com* after the company's title. The other part of the myth goes that by early 2000, the venture capitalist community was wiser but sadder about Internet companies, and thus they began to withdraw from Internet start-ups. But as the numbers above indicate, venture capital actually increased after the Internet stock crash in early 2000. What really began to happen is that venture capital firms gained a greater understanding of the future of the Internet and began to invest in earnest according to the Internet business rules that began to emerge.

Here is a quick list of the qualities venture capitalists now seek:

- *Look for management talent.* This rule echoes back to the pre-Internet days of venture investment when the three top attributes venture capital held as supreme were management team, management team, and management team. Every young company runs into trouble, but a company with strong management talent can usually figure out how to get out of trouble. Also, if the business concept proves to be faulty, a company with strong management talent can often refocus the company and forge a more successful path. Without great talent, these hurdles can prove deadly.

- *Look for a sound strategy.* Because venture capitalists are no longer in the embarrassing position of learning about Internet business from college dropouts, they have a pretty good idea of what might or might not work on the Internet. That means a silly idea will not get funded. Venture capitalists are looking for business plans again, and they want to see the strategic advantages of the companies they fund.

- *Look for picks and axes.* The Internet revolution is creating a new highway of business commerce. Venture capitalists are leery of backing the fast cars on the highway, and they're even cautious about backing the land grab necessary to make room for the highway. But they're pretty comfortable backing a company that builds the picks and axes required for the project. It doesn't matter which direction the highway takes, it's going to need the picks and axes. Infrastructure companies will tool traditional industry with the ability to convert to e-commerce. Thus, venture capital sees infrastructure as relatively safe.

- *Look for a pathway to profit.* First-to-market doesn't mean a thing if your company dominates that space and still bleeds red ink. "Show me the money," is the new mantra in the venture capital community. Who cares if you sell more CDs than anyone? If your customer acquisition cost is $60 and your average sale is $25, being first just means you get to lose money faster than your competitors. If you want to get funded, show your investors how and when you'll make a profit.

- *Look for global reach.* Every Internet company is implicitly global. But that doesn't mean every Internet company is equipped to take advantage of its global reach. Venture capitalists understand that if a company is going to really go places, its e-commerce travels have to go all around the world. Make sure your plan includes a strategy to take advantage of the Internet's worldwide reach.

THE TOP VENTURE CAPITAL FIRMS FOR INTERNET COMPANIES

Here is the A-list of venture capital firms. Of course, venture capital is a large universe, and investment possibilities grow even larger if you add in private investment groups or angel investing. Yet these companies send a strong signal in which companies they choose to back and in the way they choose their investments. Any entrepreneur interested in seeking capital for a start-up or a later round of growth is wise to spend some time at the Web sites of these major investors to see what they view as a bankable company.

Softbank Venture Capital <www.sbvc.com>
Fund size: $2.1B
Companies funded in 1999: 52
Sum invested in 1999: $401M
Companies backed: Buy.com, Net2Phone, GeoCities

VENTURE CAPITAL AND INCUBATORS 227

Softbank Venture Capital is part of Japan's Softbank Corporation. It concentrates on early-stage funding. Much of the firm's funding comes from its parent, Softbank. Its portfolio companies speak positively about the firm's close relationship with its companies. Some in the industry, though, see Softbank as too speculative.

Chase Capital Partners <www.chasecapital.com>
Fund size: $1.7B
Companies funded in 1999: 95
Sum invested in 1999: $648M
Companies backed: Kozmo.com, Lycos

Chase Capital Partners is often considered a later-round investment company, but 15 percent of its funding acts like a seed-round investor that concentrates on recruiting, strategic thinking, and advising its portfolio companies. Partners of the firm sit on the boards of only about half of its companies, which is a very low percentage among major venture firms. This is good news for companies that find continual direct oversight intrusive for business operation.

Benchmark Capital <www.benchmark.com>
Fund size: $1B
Companies funded in 1999: 32
Sum invested in 1999: $373M
Companies backed: eBay, Scient, E-Loan

The name of this group has become synonymous with Internet investing. Launched in 1995, this is the place Keith Krach, CEO of Ariba, spent his time before launching his e-marketplace maker. This is a close group of savvy investors who may collectively have the best understanding of Internet business of any investment firm. Some say Benchmark gets the very first phone call when one of its portfolio company CEOs sees trouble coming.

Oak Investment Partners <www.oakinv.com>
Fund size: $1B
Companies funded in 1999: 79
Sum invested in 1999: $454M
Companies backed: TheStreet, Syntra, Exodus

This company has been around for 20 years, quietly funding Internet infrastructure firms. This is a group of investors that get it when it comes to e-commerce. Some say they have been so busy lining up new deals that they haven't been able to spend time helping their portfolio companies as they did in the past, but they still get high marks from their companies, who appreciate the fact that the group keeps a low profile in order to concentrate on funding new companies and boosting its portfolio companies.

Sequoia Capital <www.sequoiacap.com>
Fund size: $1B
Companies funded in 1999: 77
Sum invested in 1999: $536M
Companies backed: Shockwave, BuyProduce.com, BigTray

Like Benchmark, Sequoia Capital is also one of the stars of the new economy. Industry watchers consider it one of the most aggressive investment firms in the Internet economy. They have a reputation for taking a heavy hand with their portfolio companies, which is viewed as producing mixed results. The company often invests counter-trend in a business that usually moves in a herd. They invested in a number of Internet retailers after the sector went out of fashion. The firm is viewed as a bellwether for Internet investing.

Austin Ventures <www.austinventures.com>
Fund size: $833M
Companies funded in 1999: 67
Sum invested in 1999: $209M
Companies backed: Garden.com, Altra Energy

This firm holds the unusual position of being one of the few major venture capital firms that invests primarily in local companies—in Austin, Texas. Though the firm has a strong hold on Austin, many wonder whether it could withstand the entrance of other players into the Austin market. Critics also wonder how well the firm would do if Austin cooled off as a high-tech center. In the meantime, the group is getting most of the strong entrepreneurial action in its home town.

VENTURE CAPITAL AND INCUBATORS 229

New Enterprise Associates <www.nea.com>
Fund size: $825M
Companies funded in 1999: 130
Sum invested in 1999: $510M
Companies backed: 3Com, Carstation.com, LoanCity.com

New Enterprise Associates considers itself a classic venture capital firm, which means it keeps a low profile and requires 100 percent agreement among its partners before it invests. Part of its traditional manner includes a reluctance to invest in unproven technology and its choice to plow its profits back into investments.

Norwest Venture Partners <www.norwestvp.com>
Fund size: $817M
Companies funded in 1999: 73
Sum invested in 1999: $257M
Companies backed: PeopleSoft, Documentum, Vantive

This is a cautious, steady firm that is still very interested in Internet and tech companies. The firm has the ability to turn around a deal quickly—in an average of 15 days, which makes it one of the fastest of the major venture firms. The group specializes in Internet applications software, data and telecom equipment companies, and service providers.

Polaris Venture Partners <www.polarisventures.com>
Fund size: $750M
Companies funded in 1999: 34
Sum invested in 1999: $89M
Companies backed: Aspect Medical Systems, Akamai Technologies

Polaris Venture Partners are known for following their own rhythm. The firm often sets off in directions contrary to street wisdom. The company moved strongly into the medical field while most investors were moving to the Internet. Its goal? To get in on genetics developments. The firm did, however, turn some of its attention to IT companies. Its IT investments delivered a stunning 1,172 percent return in 1999.

J.H. Whitney & Co. <www.jhwitney.com>
Fund size: $700M
Companies funded in 1999: 19
Sum invested in 1999: $158M
Companies backed: Media Metrix, Fogdog Sports

This stalwart investment group goes back to the 1940s. It's an East Coast institution that tends to prefer East Coast companies. Yet it certainly displays some hip tendencies in its backing of Net companies, such as ExpertCentral (now an About.com company) and Media Metrix, which has become the leading traffic measurement company on the Internet.

INCUBATORS: A SLINGSHOT TO LAUNCH

There are two predominant cliches in the world of Internet business. One says that in digital time, fast beats slow. Like most cliches, this one is founded in truth. New Internet companies are rushing desperately into new markets in an aggressive land grab. There is good reason to hurry. The giants of the past look like befuddled dinosaurs as tiny new mammals dash around eating all the available food. Time Warner got gobbled up because it fumbled its Net strategy. The auto industry looks vibrant because it embraces every Internet device or business model that could remotely be used to buy a window wiper or sell a Taurus. Though there is truth in fast-beats-slow, the other side of the story is that you don't help yourself by speeding up the wrong process.

The other Net cliche is that creativity and talent are the twin tools of Net success. It is also rooted in truth. Venture capitalists agree that the most important part of a launch plan is the management team. Yet only blind luck will bless a new Net play with both speed and creativity. To solve the challenge of matching speed with talent, a new Internet business model has emerged, the incubator. Incubators are created to help new dot-coms rush to market in three to six months, a dizzying rate even on the Internet clock. As well as getting a slingshot boost, the new companies get access to training and guidance from experienced Net managers.

The New Incubators Are Designed for Internet Trade

The incubator concept cannot be painted in simple strokes. In the 1970s, business incubators were publicly funded offices that allowed entrepreneurs free office space, phone, and equipment for a few months (or years). Communities invested so new companies could grow and create jobs. Internet incubators are a radically new animal. Most of them do not altruistically encourage entrepreneurs to build companies and create jobs. The Net incubators want equity in the enterprises they launch, and independence is often the last thing an incubator company wants for its hatchlings. Instead, the incubator would rather have its young enterprises hang around and help an even younger generation of companies.

NEW MODELS FOR NET INCUBATORS

Internet incubators come in a number of models. Some are little more than venture capitalists with a hot new name. Others, like IBM's Dot-Com Incubator program, are designed to create future customers. Some, like Divine interVentres, create a network of companies that cross-pollinate and succeed, in part because they become each other's vendors and customers. Still others, like Bain & Company's Bainlab, create ideas for new enterprises by searching the Net for unfilled opportunities.

The early incubators, such as CMGI (nicknamed "The Creature"), Idealab, and Internet Capital Group demonstrated that the incubator is a valid concept for creating new Net plays quickly. Having backed the growth of companies such as AltaVista, GoTo.com, and eChemicals.com, the first incubators put the concept on the map. When a few of these incubators starting showing off stock values that exceeded 1,000 percent growth in 1999, the whole Net economy sat up and paid attention. In the fourth quarter of 1999, incubators began appearing like mushrooms after a rain, fully formed out of nowhere. Go to PRNewswire or Business Wire right now, and you'll find a handful of announcements touting new incubators. They're appearing at the rate of five to ten a week. Surely dozens have appeared since this book went to press.

The emerging models for incubators reveal two Internet strategies. One is based on the urgency to get a company centrally placed in a vertical B2B market before the market gets crowded. This strategy is grounded in the belief that the early plays will dominate. This is a well-founded idea if you look at how the B2C market was dominated by early Net plays like Amazon.com. Speed and deep funding are critical to this strategy.

The Speed-to-Market Concern Will Pass

The model based on urgency is temporary. At some point, the land rush will be over and a few heavy-hitting conglomerates will win the day. This is already mostly complete on the consumer side of the Internet. The ISP wars are over, and the retail players are mostly in place. The B2B land grab favors players who emerge from within their industry, then get deep-pocket backing from conglomerate incubators such as CMGI, Internet Capital Group, and Idealab. At some point in the next two to three years, the majority of the B2B wilderness will be settled by big ranchers.

The other model is based on the incubator as a group of symbiotic companies. The network allows each individual company to forgo the expensive and time-consuming process of developing accounting, legal, marketing, public relations, and human resource departments. Without this overhead burden, the individual companies can stay nimble, light, and maneuverable. Plus, all of their funding goes straight into creating markets.

Network Model Supports Niche Developments

The *keiretsu,* or network, model will be an ongoing factor. This model is tailor-made for niche markets and companies that need strong local involvement with their clients. The conglomerates are blunt instruments. The networks with their collection of nimble companies are more able to pinpoint opportunities and deliver custom services and products. Networks like Divine interVentures will likely be very happy to go on developing their minority pieces of the B2B world. After all, even a small slice of the Internet's B2B pie dwarfs the consumer Internet market.

The hot territory for incubators now is B2B. The early focus for venture capitalists may have been retail e-commerce, but the early focus for incubators was clearly B2B. Most of the new incubators are immediately setting their targets on Net plays that help businesses consummate trade. The B2B market is looking very attractive with its promise of e-marketplaces swinging mega-billions in transactions. All of the research firms show B2B e-commerce hitting $2 to $3 trillion by 2004. Now that it's clear retail e-commerce has inherent limitations, the smart money is going down on the unlimited potential of B2B. The incubator system is designed to make it a safer bet.

As incubators appear daily to push Net ideas like lightning to market, investors are experimenting with a number of different models. Some incubators add companies to the parent company like a patchwork quilt of contrasting concepts. Others add new companies strategically to enter new markets or to fit within a nest of companies designed to buy each other's services and products. Also, the odd incubator gets created to launch ideas brainstormed by the parent company. Still others have been launched with the goal of creating future customers. Incubator models are evolving as fast as they appear. Part of the experimental nature of incubators is that the business models are very fluid. They change with the quick moves of the Net. There may be only one thing common to all incubators: Their capacity to reinvent themselves in pursuit of opportunity.

Here are some examples of the new company builders. But don't hold them to their descriptions, as they're all ready to change.

The Incubator as Conglomerate

Affectionately known as "The Creature" because of its stock's dramatic upswings and downturns, CMGI is an example of an incubator that may become a future conglomerate. As CMGI hatchlings begin to succeed, they stay in the nest, building equity value and giving mama creature market strength as it moves from sector to sector grabbing B2B e-commerce space. CMGI holds equity in more than 60 companies, covering diverse areas of Net business including vitamins, art, auto parts, construction, and seafood. CMGI even bought a chunk of a younger incubator, Divine interVentures. The strategy of being everywhere on the Web at once has been successful. Since CMGI went public in 1994, its shares have increased 71,000 percent.

Is the Incubator Just a Venture Group?

Some argue that CMGI is not an incubator at all because it doesn't provide support services and it doesn't promote future independence. Yet CMGI and its fellow conglomerate incubators, Internet Capital Group and Idealab, are viewed by most as a new model of incubators that strategically foster the growth and development of e-commerce companies. They're considered an incubator because they ensure their new investments will be successful within their sectors. Many analysts see CMGI and its rivals as early-stage conglomerates. The Net street wisdom says some of these companies will emerge as the GMs, GEs, and Proctor & Gambles of the future.

In January of this year, CMGI formed a new fund, @Ventures, designed to nurture B2B companies that are developing e-commerce in their individual sectors. CMGI created a $1 billion B2B fund to strengthen the diversity of its original investment strategy and focus its top investing professionals on the sectors of the industry that present the greatest potential. CMGI intends to grab portions of the B2B market that do not already have strong players in dominant positions. CMGI will use its hybrid incubator to buy equity in emerging companies that are in the best position for sector land grabs. The $1 billion B2B fund comes in addition to the company's standard venture criteria.

The Keiretsu Model

This concept is similar to the Japanese model of a network of businesses that use each other's services and support each other's developments. Chicago-based Divine interVentures prides itself on creating a symbiotic network of companies that support each other and cross-pollinate their fellow hatchlings's markets. Strictly a B2B incubator, Divine prides itself on providing a network of management support for its companies. Within Divine, a series of companies are created to serve the hatchlings. These include Buzz Divine (marketing, advertising, public relations), dotspot (facilities leasing), FiNetrics.com (accounting and financing), Host Divine (IT services), Justice Divine (legal services), and others. These companies were put in place so that the incubated companies would not have to bother with creating a whole series of management departments.

With its management infrastructure in place, Divine focuses on moving into vertical markets with its hatchlings. The roster includes Whiplash (travel), Beautyjungle.com (beauty products), bid4real.com (real estate), BidBuyBuild (construction), Commerx (plastics), and many more. This system lets a company get to market very quickly. Companies can focus on their core technologies rather than worrying about building a full business infrastructure with legal, accounting, human resources, public relations, and advertising.

One incubatee, Andy Parker, moved his company, Mercantec, into the Divine family in 1999 after four years on his own. Mercantec builds Web store platforms for Internet service providers (ISP) to use for their shopping mall merchants. As part of the Divine group, he can cross-pollinate his company with other Divine companies. He gave up 33 percent of his equity for the benefit of funding and support. The management backbone he receives from Divine has allowed him to concentrate on moving his e-merchant platform into the merchant systems of 200 different ISPs in 13 countries.

The Empty-Market Incubator

Bain & Company, a global management consulting firm, has created Bainlab, a venture capital incubator designed to generate ideas for Net companies to fill e-commerce gaps. David Sanderson, head of Bain's e-commerce practice, asked his team to find industries that were not fully on the Internet. The goal was to find an industry that produced at least $10 billion in revenues and still had room for a new Net player. After considering petrochemicals (too crowded) and adoption services (not profitable enough), the Bainlab decided on crafts, including crafts materials, kits, and finished products.

The industry is fragmented, but it trades at the surprising level of $20 billion per year. So Bainlab launched Ideaforest as a greenfield expansion.

In order to gain an insider's knowledge of the industry, Bainlab tapped Jack Bush, the executive who had taken the largest arts and crafts retailer, Michael's, from 200 stores to 500 before retiring in 1995. Bush used his industry contacts to recruit names in the industry that provided both knowledge and credibility. By the time Ideaforest went live with its content, it had an insider's lock on known names. A full line of merchandise will be added to the site this spring.

The Incubator as Customer Creation

Last fall, IBM teamed up with Conxion and Silicon Valley Bank to create the DotCom Incubator program. The nest was designed to allow 25 companies to utilize IBM technology and Conxion's hosting services for six months at no charge and no equity. Why? Because it helps IBM and Conxion build future customers. As well as sharing technology, the incubator puts its entrepreneurs through a training program. The program gives incubator participants the ability to skip the stock car circuit and drive a Porsche at the Le Mans, according to Antonia Salerno, CEO of Conxion.

The incubator program was very successful at attracting quality start-ups, so IBM and Conxion decided to double the program with 25 more companies earlier this year. For the second round of 25, they used the services of fellow incubator Garage.com to make participant selections. Companies participating in the first round include MarketMakers.com (a provider of Web-based marketing events), ienvironment.com (a provider of environment compliance support for small to medium businesses), and Mercanteo (a procurement application for small companies).

An Incubator as Social Change

BLG Ventures aspires to be the Idealab.com for minority Net start-ups. Formed just this year, BLG Ventures is an idea seeking

VENTURE CAPITAL AND INCUBATORS   237

start-ups. Company founder, Julian Barnes, wants to incubate companies with $250,000 to $500,000 as seed. Then the incubator will work to bring in larger capital sources. Barnes is a New York attorney whose clients include PlanningCentral.com and Soulhouse.com. The difference with the BLG Ventures incubator is that it focuses on minority businesses, which includes multicultural, black, and handicapped ownership.

Barnes has put together a grassroots network of support services for start-ups, including legal, accounting, finance, IT, and sales and marketing. He has also established a network of government and nonprofit entities, which have agreed to funnel prospective clients to BLG Ventures. Geographically, he concentrates on the cities up and down the East Coast.

THE CORNUCOPIA OF HATCHERIES

BLG Ventures <www.blgventures.com>
Seeking: Minority, multicultural, handicapped business start-ups
Offers: Seed funding, support services, connections to larger funding
Portfolio includes: N/A

Bainlab <www.bain.com>
Seeking: Launches greenfield ideas to fill industries with Internet gaps
Offers: Complete support for start-up and growth
Portfolio includes: Ideaforest.com (a crafts e-marketplace)

CMGI <www.cmgi.com>
Seeking: Four to six new Net companies each month
Offers: Financial backing in trade for 30 to 40 percent equity position
Portfolio includes: AltaVista, Lycos, iCast, GoFish

campsix <www.campsix.com>
Seeking: B2B entrepreneurs in Silicon Valley and San Francisco
Offers: Funds, management support, affiliate network, facilities
Portfolio includes: Getconnected.com, RedLadder.com, US Creative

Divine interVentures <www.divineinterventures.com>
Seeking: Start-ups and existing Net plays that can cross-pollinate with other companies in the group
Offers: Financial backing, marketing, PR, human resources, legal, and customer service
Portfolio includes: OpinionWare, Whiplash, Mercantec

DotCom Incubator <www.conxion.com>
Seeking: B2B companies in the Silicon Valley area
Offers: Free use of technology and hosting for six months with no equity position
Portfolio includes: Dream Logic, MarketMakers.com, NoNameArt.com

DotCom Ventures <www.peacockfinancial.com>
Seeking: Early-stage companies with IPO potential
Offers: Funding and management expertise in exchange for equity
Portfolio includes: iNetMotors.com

eCompanies <www.ecompanies.com>
Seeking: Start-ups with IPO potential
Offers: Funding and management expertise
Portfolio includes: Business.com, icebox, eMemories.com

Garage.com <www.garage.com>
Seeking: Start-ups seeking $500,000 to $5 million
Offers: Funding and management expertise in exchange for equity
Portfolio includes: drDrew.com, Startups.com, iCopyright.

Idealab <www.idealab.com>
Seeking: Silicon Valley companies
Offers: Funding and management expertise, talent
Portfolio includes: eToys, Tickets.com, GoTo.com

Internet Capital Group <www.internetcapital.com>
Seeking: B2B e-marketplaces
Offers: Funding and management expertise in exchange for equity
Portfolio includes: PaperExchange.com, eChemicals, Vertical Net

Net Value Holdings <www.netvalueholdings.com>
Seeking: B2B networks with IPO potential
Offers: Funding and management expertise in exchange for equity
Portfolio includes: AssetExchange, Swapit.com, Webmodal

Synergy Brands <www.sybr.com>
Seeking: B2B and B2C who have need for strong back-end support
Offers: Funding and management expertise in exchange for equity
Portfolio includes: Cigarnet.com, BeautyBuy.com

YOUR NET STRATEGY:

If you seek funding for a Net venture, keep in mind that venture capitalists and incubators are very subject to trends. They flock like birds, all going for Internet retail companies one year, off to B2B the next. The business idea may be a hot-button winner during spring, fall out of favor over the summer, and come back full steam three months later. Your only protection against the seemingly arbitrary nature of venture capital investments is to fortify your business fundamentals.

Venture capitalists have always put a high premium on the depth of experience in the management team. There was a brief period during the early days of the Internet boom when investors lost their collective heads and forgot this cardinal rule. During the Internet retail shakeout, venture capitalists came to their senses and reemphasized the importance of a solid launch team.

The fashionable launch team now has a few gray hairs. Venture capitalists are looking for launch companies with adult supervision. They also want to see domain experience. If your business concept involves selling to the furniture industry, your investors will example your team bios for gray-haired domain experience in furniture. A common launch team now includes the father of one of the founders, and the industry for the launch is usually dad's industry.

The other area of emphasis is on the path to profitability, which has come to be known as POP. This can be a tough area to address realistically. Even the most successful launches don't hit profitability for three to six years. Yet a plan that doesn't show profits in the first three years may get the big bump. Investors are still stinging from the weak profit potential of early Net plays. If your plan doesn't show early profits, you need to offer credible reasons for the delay and show exactly when the profits will come.

Don't fall for the reverse hype that venture capitalists are gun shy about Net companies. They certainly have become very careful, but they're also continuing to invest with a vengeance. And most of the investment is going into high tech firms or Internet companies. Venture capitalists have big bankrolls to invest and they are not about to back a shoe store. They need to tap Internet and high tech companies in order to obtain the level of return required from their investments.

Incubators have also taken a heavy hit on hype. Yet they remain a viable option for a company looking for support during the start-up years. In choosing an incubator, remember that companies are judged by the company they keep. Not all incubators carry the respect and high regard of Internet Capital Group. Make sure the incubator you choose is well regarded by the venture capital community you hope to reach.

CHAPTER 12

BUSINESS-TO-GOVERNMENT
Finally Some Efficiencies

We all remember the hammer. It was just a simple hammer, like any you could purchase at a hardware store for $10 or $20. The federal government, however, procured the hammer for a cool $700. One elected official devised the "Golden Fleece" award for the most outrageous overpayment to come through the federal procurement system each month. Now we may find the e-commerce revolution could turn our wildly inefficient government into an e-marketplace wizard, taking savings in both process and direct costs. If e-commerce can make the government sit up and act right, it truly deserves to be called a revolution.

When we think of dynamic e-commerce altering the way companies conduct business, the government doesn't come quickly to mind. When corporate leaders in Silicon Valley explain that in the past, big companies ate small companies and that now fast companies eat slow companies, the feds don't look like fast fish. Even within the old economy, the government looks stodgy, slow to adapt to new technology and endemically resistant to change. Yet Internet history proves things are not always what they seem.

The Internet Started as a Government Program

The Internet has become so closely associated with entrepreneurial enterprise, it is easy to forget that it began life as a military initiative implemented by the Central Intelligence Agency (CIA). In the 1980s, numerous successful online companies allowed users to conduct literature searches through "dial-up" services. These services were used primarily by specially trained research or corporate librarians, who conducted the searches on behalf of researchers and analysts.

The military research community was a heavy user of these services, and the government stored much of its information, both public and secret, on internal and external online networks. As the government came to regard its computer databases as increasingly critical to national security, it began to get nervous about the prospect of computer outages through accident or attack. The intelligence community decided to protect itself by spreading content storage and access through a network that had no center that could be eliminated. They wanted access to their information from anywhere at anytime, and they didn't want it stored on one vulnerable computer. So they designed the Internet.

Al Gore Really Was There at a Critical Moment

The system worked very well, and soon government officials saw value in allowing corporations to use the system for their own literature searches. The system would make access to online databases easier, so a research librarian could easily move from Dialog Information Services for business and technical searches to the Nexus/Lexus law library without hanging up the phone and redialing. A bill was submitted to congress to allow corporations and private individuals to access the Internet. One of the sponsors of the bill was a young member of congress, Al Gore, who later claimed he invented the Internet. The statement stretched the truth, but Gore certainly helped to take Internet access to the private sector.

Government involvement in e-commerce has been a late development, even if the government was a first-mover in Internet communication. Part of the problem is that the government feels funny about money. There is so much suspicion surrounding the expenditure of public money, procurement employees are very uncomfortable with innovative initiatives. They tend to hang back until a new technology is tested and known to be sound.

E-commerce Is a Natural for Government

On the side of Internet entrepreneurs, government business was the last thing on their minds. Retail e-commerce made perfect sense, as did the emergence of business-to-business trading. But the idea of government employees taking the Internet for a money-spending spin seemed downright unnatural. Yet the Internet has quite a bit to offer government procurement departments. The Internet is handy for using online auctions to get good prices on used or surplus government goods. Add to this the citizens's ability to pay taxes and parking tickets online, and it becomes clear a wide range of e-commerce services are appropriate for government, even before you start to add up the billions upon billions in recurring federal expenditures that can be made more efficient with Internet procurement.

According to U.S. Bancorp's Piper Jaffray, the public sector opportunity for e-procurement is a $500 billion market. Federal Procurement Data Systems estimates that the federal government spends $200 billion annually through the General Services Administration (GSA) alone to buy goods and services. Entrepreneurial companies have stayed away from this market largely because of the sheer weight of the bureaucratic process required for contract approval that results in sales cycles well beyond private-sector norms. For complex sales such as IT systems, approval can take 18 to 24 months.

Yet the federal government can't ignore the possible savings to be had from e-commerce. On the sell side, the GSA has experimented with online auctions by selling surplus federal property through GSAAuctions.gov. The auction is supported through a joint platform designed by American Management Systems (AMS) and Ariba. The GSA expects to auction up to $10 billion annually in government assets. But procurement is a different matter for the government. Online buying is inevitable, but the form it will take is still unclear.

Citizens Will Demand the Savings

Non-military federal agencies may be the last big spenders to go online, but go online they will over the coming years. As the procurement savings taken by large corporations becomes common knowledge, citizens and their representatives will look to their government to implement the same efficiencies. Don't expect the pressure to come from the bottom up, as it has in many corporations. The procurement professionals on the federal dole are not likely to call a meeting with the boss to explain how online purchasing will bring a 4 percent savings to the budget. The boss is likely to respond that a budget savings will result in a budget cut, which they don't want, and besides, the efficiency will probably mean a loss of jobs.

The changes will probably come from above in the form of an edict. Government agencies will be given instructions through legislation that they must move to Internet-based procurement solutions. Don't expect great results when it happens. Remember the great paperwork reduction act? Those who dedicate their lives to work within bureaucracies develop powerful capabilities of resistance. They gain a deep and detailed understanding of the job-protection laws that give them cover as they dig in their feet and resist any efficiencies that will potentially trim their numbers and diminish their clout. With many federal workers, their budget level is far more important then the quality of their output or its efficiency.

THE FIRST MOVERS: CITY, COUNTY, AND STATE GOVERNMENTS

On the city, county, and state levels, though, it's another story. Workers in local government service share a greater degree of sincere interest in effective government service. This is already beginning to translate into an acceptance of online alternatives in procurement and payment acceptance. Citizens generally expect their city, county, and state governments to be responsive to their needs, and their needs increasingly include the ability to communicate over the Internet.

The first step for local governments was communication over the Internet. All states and most cities now have elaborate information-based Web sites that give their citizens access to agency directories as well as detailed regulations and permit information. The next move, to online transactions, is being led by public-sector entrepreneurs who are eager to help the government accept online payments for taxes, parking tickets, and permit applications. The entrepreneurial sites accept credit cards and virtual checks from their customers and send the government cash, after taking a transaction fee. Other sites are helping governments obtain greater prices for used equipment through online auctions. A few additional sites are beginning to help government agencies buy over the Internet, at least for spot purchases or catalog buying.

It Begins in the Niches

Different entrepreneurial sites offer the government and its citizens a variety of e-commerce transactions. In this early stage of B2G, companies are mostly claiming niche territories within the public sector instead of competing directly with each other. Some concentrate on city governments, while others target the Feds. One venture, San Francisco's Epylon, targets the $144 billion market of school district spending by offering an online exchange that allows schools to move procurement to the Internet.

The Gartner Group is bullish on government e-commerce sites. A study of sites that target government e-commerce found that while niche e-government providers face considerable hurdles in terms of brand recognition and proving security capabilities, their highly innovative, citizen-oriented business models deserve real attention. Gartner explains that consistent themes in government-to-business sites include performance- and transaction-based contracts, public-private partnerships and risk-sharing, application hosting, and zero start-up cost methodologies.

Conservative Buying Is Natural When the Funds Are Public

With its convoluted and seemingly arcane business practices, it's clear that government has a lot to gain from the highly-detailed possibilities of Internet purchasing. Kelly Blanton, co-founder and chairman of Epylon, believes the view of inefficient government procurement is a false image. He claims that government purchasers are not bogged down because they're inefficient, but because they're spending public funds. With government spending, you have to make sure the system has an audit trail, because the people have a right to see how the funds are spent. Though this may seem at first glance an impediment to innovative procurement solutions, the Internet actually helps governments keep their audit trail visible.

Epylon installs a back-end auditing system to give its government clients the audit trails required for the spending of public funds. It also helps with vendors who wonder why they lost out on a bid. When they ask, "Why didn't I win?" the data on the project is available to all bidders. Plus, Epylon's procurement system has been customized to meet the auditing needs of the government office. From Epylon's perspective, the Internet enhances the public's ability to see the procurement process.

THE BIG GOVERNMENT HURDLE: RESISTANCE TO CHANGE

Even if you have a better system, you still have to get people to buy into using it. The adoption rate will likely be the greatest challenge to moving the government to the Internet. Epylon's chairman, Kelly Blanton, spent years as a school superintendent, which gave him a deep understanding of the tactics needed to change the behavior of government procurement employees. As a superintendent, he worked to convert a Southern California school system to an internal, networked computer system. Blanton learned a template for change, which includes bringing a few people into the new system first, then letting them demonstrate its advantages. The rest of the employees will be able to see that the new system is trustworthy.

Part of Epylon's sales strategy is to help individual school systems develop the trust required for widespread adoption. Blanton believes that if a system is implemented across an entire system as a mandate from above, it will likely fail. So he uses the template he used as a superintendent, and it's working. When Epylon attempts implementation in a school system, the company first identifies a small group who learns the system well enough to realize success; then that small group becomes the agent of change within the system. Blanton sees this as sowing seeds of trust.

Buyers Initially Fear Job Loss

Nina Young, director of purchasing for the Orange County Department of Education, ran into some resistance when she introduced Epylon to her staff. Her staff was slow to respond to change. The buyers had held their positions for a long time, and they saw the online exchange as threatening. Young helped her staff overcome resistance by emphasizing that the new skills involved in online procurement would enhance their professional value, and that savings would come to the school system. This helped the buyers overcome the fear that the system would ultimately replace their jobs.

Within a few weeks of using Epylon, Young found she was getting lower prices from suppliers. The bids she was getting on Epylon were the lowest bids she had received from vendors. Plus, she was finding a larger pool of suppliers, a high quality pool. She was surprised by the pricing, and she also found that her staff became enthusiastic about the advantages of online procurement, which meant they were quicker to adopt the new way of buying.

Administrators Are Eager to Buy Online

Blanton finds that school administrators themselves are very eager to move onto the Internet. He notes that they usually ask, "How soon can you get it to me?" because online procurement is a fairly simple concept to understand, especially if you're attempting to deliver on your responsibilities with insufficient resources, the long-term condition of most school systems. It also helps that Epylon is funded through transaction percentages on the buyer's side, which means the barrier to adoption is not financial but rather cultural. For the school district, Internet procurement is risk free. There's no money to allocate on either side. The only barrier is the old-world thinking of the buyers.

The general thinking is that the public sector is hard to change, but Epylon executives note that the old procurement process is painful and time-consuming, which explains why the superintendents are so eager to try a new solution. Surprisingly, Epylon finds that the traction to B2G for school systems is much faster than B2B. Epylon finds that the public sector has a real incentive to adopt the Internet, especially because it's free and it's tailored to their needs.

VCS TURN THEIR SUPPORT TO E-GOVERNMENT COMPANIES

The venture capitalist community has also shown interest in B2G ventures. ezgov.com, an Atlanta, Georgia, site that helps citizens maneuver state and local government sites and allows citizens to pay government bills online, nabbed $28 million from a group of investors that included New York investment firm Warburg, Pincus Ventures. govWorks of New York received nearly $40 million, bringing its total funding to $60 million. Investors included leading Silicon Valley firms such as the Mayfield Fund and American Management Services. govWorks provides an ASP model for federal, state, and local governments to offer payment processing, auctions, and public sector jobs listings.

Epylon was backed by $30 million in series B financing from Highland Capital Partners, Intel Capital, and ITV/Infinity. According to Keith Benjamin, a general partner of leading venture capital firm Highland Capital Partners, the education and government sectors are becoming recognized as important, but largely untapped, areas for expanding e-commerce. In some ways it is not surprising to see venture capital moving into a new avenue for Internet development. With retail sites facing an uncertain future and B2B getting hot and crowded, the B2G market may look like a fresh place to seek e-commerce opportunity.

AUCTIONS AND EXCHANGES

Another side of government e-commerce comes from public sector sales. Government agencies are accustomed to selling used and surplus items through auctions, so it's natural to move some of this activity to the Internet. A number of sites have stepped up to facilitate on some of this business. eCitydeals targets auctions from municipalities, while govWorks aims to build a web of services for federal agencies, states, and cities that includes auction capabilities. Most recently, the GSA has chosen AMS and Ariba to implement an online auction system that will enable the GSA to auction up to $10 billion annually.

eCitydeals also utilizes the Ariba exchange platform. The site targets cities, offering auction and procurement capabilities. The system allows users to aggregate purchases, so multiple cities can buy just one item at a discount. Municipalities use eCitydeals to move everything from motorcycles and school buses to turf mowers and street sweepers. Like most online exchanges, eCitydeals derives its revenue through transaction fees from the sellers. There is no cost to use the system. It's a way for cities to do business in a way they're not doing business now. Plus, the site makes it easy for vendors to access government agencies that they find difficult to access because of bureaucracy and red tape.

CITIZEN PAYMENTS AND PERMITS

At least two ventures are filling a need to make the government more responsive to its citizens over the Internet. Most of this business is oriented toward city, county, and state governments. The concept behind sites such as ezgov and govWorks.com is to give governments improved service and transaction capabilities. Both ezgov and govWorks.com offer government a range of potential services. govWorks offers what they call "three buckets of service." It offers transactional capability, information services in the form of job listings and auctions, and communication exchange between business and government or citizens and government. The portal also offers governments a choice of pricing models that includes a percentage of transactions, revenue sharing, or subscription fees.

Also, ezgov provides a list of potential services for government agencies that includes ezUtility, ezTicket, ezProperty, ezPermit, and others. All of these services are designed to make it easy for citizens or business owners to pay bills, access records, or apply for permits without driving to a municipal building. At press time, ezgov was in 50 states and 3,153 counties. As well as providing citizens easy access to their local and state governments, ezgov also runs a 24/7 service arm that gives citizens immediate payment confirmation on fees or taxes paid to government.

Government transactions may be one of the few areas of e-commerce where new ventures can make a big mark without the threat of large corporations moving in to take over once the market embraces the concept. Unlike Internet retailers or B2B players, B2G players don't have to look over their shoulders to see if Wal-Mart or Ford is about to step in and start claiming market share. Since each of these early players is targeting a niche within the mammoth government market, they may all find lucrative territory in helping governments spend, buy, and take fees.

GOVERNMENT RAMPS UP FOR E-SPENDING

As governments begin to see the advantages of moving their business onto the Internet, they are beginning to spend more and more on the equipment needed for Internet access and for tying Internet-based information into existing information systems. Government spending on equipment and services to make it ready for e-business should reach $6.2 billion in 2005, according to the research firm Gartner Group, Inc. of San Diego, California. The company expects $1.5 billion in online government spending for e-business hardware, software, and related services this year. The study includes federal, state, and local government entities.

Gartner analysts expect the government will run into difficulties in its shift to Internet procurement and service delivery. E-government promises of operational costs savings, improved service delivery, and positive transformations of government workplaces are real, according to French Caldwell, research director for Gartner. But Caldwell also expects a high rate of e-government projects will fail in the next several years. Gartner analysts expect government agencies to look beyond the traditional large professional services companies and system integrators as they choose their e-commerce systems. Gartner expects new companies such as ezgov, FreeBalance, and govWorks.com to benefit from government moves to e-commerce readiness.

B2G E-MARKETPLACES

Just as each business sector has a wide range of online exchanges delivering unique services to different parts of the market, the online companies serving the government are widely disparate in their services. Some exchanges help facilitate citizen payments of taxes and licenses, while others are designed to move government procurement online. Still others help government entities sell their used equipment through auctions. Here's a sampling of the new e-marketplaces that are launching to serve the public sector:

eCitydeals
Potential size: $92.5 billion
Auction and procurement site for cities

The site allows cities to sell used equipment. It is also a procurement tool that aggregates purchasing for numerous cities.

ezgov.com
Site where citizens can access local and state government

Provides information and transaction capability so citizens can pay bills or access government records.

Epylon
Potential size: $144 billion
Procurement site for school districts

This online exchange allows districts to access a wider range of vendors, while also putting procurement into a bidding environment.

GSAAuctions
Potential size: $10 billion
Federal government auction site

Powered by Ariba and American Management Systems, this auction will be used to sell surplus government property.

GovHost.com
Application service provider for cities and counties

Provides a suite of 13 virtual government modules that allows cities and counties to accept citizen payments and apply for permits.

govWorks, Inc.
Enhances interactions between government, businesses, and citizens

Collaborates with local, state, and federal governments to provide Internet-based services including information and financial transactions.

NetClerk
Permit site for contractors

Enables contractors to obtain permits online, even if a city doesn't have an online service.

YOUR NET STRATEGY:

The good news about the business-to-government space is that it remains underdeveloped. The government systems of checks and balances and general bureaucracy have kept government procurement on the slow track toward e-commerce. Most Net plays are too impatient to aim at the government market, especially since most Internet start-up entrepreneurs believe the culture of government purchasing is diametrically opposed to the Net culture, an accurate observation.

Most of the Internet companies serving government entities have been launched by entrepreneurs with some experience in government, either as a participant or a vendor. These entrepreneurs have the connections and general understanding required to interact successfully with the government. Also, most B2G start-ups have aimed at cities, states, and school systems, which are easier to approach and comprehend than federal agencies.

A common strategy among B2G companies that are getting traction in the public sector is to put a politician on the board. Jack Kemp, Bob Dole, and Lamar Alexander all sit on the boards of companies that sell their Internet services to cities, states, school systems, and the federal government. These board members provide two basic services. Their appearance on the list of board members delivers credibility, and these board members often provide the entrepreneur with introductions to potential government clients.

B2G e-commerce is certainly a growth industry, but headway will be made at a slower pace than in private-sector business-to-business efforts. The good news, though, is that government clients tend to be loyal, long-term customers. As hard as it may be to gain the trust of government managers, it will be at least that hard for your competitors to edge you out of position once you convince the government to utilize your services.

CHAPTER 13

THE FUTURE'S FUTURE

Dad picks up the television remote and turns on the set. He clicks to get local weather. While the weather for the next few days is posted, a horizontal scroll at the bottom of the screen shows closing prices on all his individual stocks. He clicks over to sports scores. Each game has a button that allows him to block the score in case he wants to view the game without knowing the outcome. After paging through completed games, he clicks to the status of games in process, then on to the schedule for upcoming games. Each posted game offers the option to download the game to his set's memory for future viewing. Instead he decides to watch a movie. He clicks over to the Blockbuster channel and chooses from a selection that includes virtually every movie ever made.

In the upstairs bedroom, his 11-year-old son has just logged onto Sega's game channel. In spite of valiant efforts by Nintendo, Sony, and Microsoft, Sega still holds the top spot for 3D visuals. He doesn't have to wear those uncomfortable cheap glasses to get the virtual reality effect either. In the next room, mom sits on the bed typing notes onto her laptop as she watches a video of Alan Greenspan lecturing on the mistakes the Federal Reserve made in the early years of the '00s, before they figured out that interest rate levels have no effect on the growth rate of an economy that's racing with productivity gains. This is her last semester of coursework toward her Harvard MBA through the school's e-correspondence program.

Meanwhile, down in the basement, their teenage daughter and her friends are practicing a line dance made popular by a group of young men with bright eyes, crooked smiles, and cool haircuts. They click back over the program again and again, watching each step, then pausing the action so they can try it themselves. When they get it just right, they turn on the set's camera and run through the steps so they can e-mail it to their friend Jacy, who's stuck babysitting her little brothers.

Barely the Future

This scene takes place in the mid '00s, in the fifteenth year of America's longest economic expansion. Things change, and they don't change. Mom and dad still worry about their daughter's taste in boys, and they wonder if the games their son plays on Sega are too violent. Mom struggles to get through her MBA while working part-time with a French investment bank and serving as the local PTA vice president. Dad's wondering if choosing the work-at-home option with the medical consulting firm he joined two years ago was a mistake. His choice allows the family to live in a small town on the shores of Lake Michigan, but sometimes he suspects the decision put him to the slow track with the company.

What does the future hold for the Internet and e-commerce? Mainstream Americans will likely integrate the Internet into most facets of their lives, from television to education, work, and social interaction. Think of the telephone and television. During the 1900s, these communication devices became central to our lives. The dimensions of the Internet are far greater than the narrow scope of the telephone and television, so we can expect it to integrate far deeper into our business, family, and social lives. It will likely change our lives in profound ways for the next few decades.

For one, it will change our need to live in large metropolitan areas. Our migration to cities was founded on the need to process goods that required massive labor and frequent face-to-face communication. Our primary output is now information, and communication, especially in business, is much more efficient through the Internet. We no longer need to work in close proximity, elbow-to-elbow after a crowded and inefficient commute.

SINGING THE MIDDLEMAN BLUES

One of the more profound changes coming to the business world is the threat Internet commerce poses for salespeople, sales rep firms, dealers, distributors, and others in the supply chain who move products from the manufacturer to the end user. If you can connect directly to the manufacturer, who needs someone in the middle? This threat is called *disintermediation*. It can affect businesses as diverse as bookstores and food brokers. The direct connections available between those who create a product and those who use it brings the whole middleman concept into question.

In a business world that praises win-win solutions and coopitition e-marketplaces are just the right systems to make everyone's life easier and every bottom line blacker. They allow competitors to work together for the greater good of all, and they bring buyers and sellers closer together. Sounds great, but in the real world, when an economic shift sends a trillion-dollar diversion into a new procurement channel, there is an accompanying bloodbath. You can't have all this good news without someone getting hurt. The walking wounded and the dead-but-they-don't-know-it-yet in the economic shift to e-marketplaces are the middlemen, distributors, and sales reps.

Some in the Middle Benefit Immediately

Not all of these operators will get their heads chopped off by the brilliantly efficient e-marketplaces. In some industries, they will prosper by the shift to online trading. Automakers are going to considerable trouble to keep their dealers soothed and happy, even as customers rush to retail car sites to get better prices and avoid obnoxious sales bullies. Automakers need their dealers for test drives, product pick-ups, and after-market service, even if the dealer loses the sale to online shopping.

In other areas of the supply chain, the broker or sales rep has been included in the early implementation of the e-marketplace, but their long-term role is anything but stable. Williams Control, a company that produces parts for Hardee Williams agricultural mowers and sprayers, pays its sales reps even when the part is ordered directly online. This solution has become very common for suppliers. Even though the sales force is not directly involved in making the sale happen, sale reps are receiving their commissions and retaining their territories. Suppliers argue that it is important to compensate salespeople because they are still involved in maintaining the relationship with the buyer.

Price-Only Brokers Will Suffer

With independent sales organizations, price is often more important than relationships. Brokers and manufacturers's reps that match product with buyer will probably be the first to go, as e-marketplaces bring buyers and sellers into intimate electronic contact. Brokers have no role in the end game, according to Fulton Breen, CEO of XSag.com, an e-marketplace for excess agricultural products. Breen believes the role of the intermediary is transitory if they do nothing to enhance the product's value as it gets passed along the supply chain.

With e-marketplaces appearing in virtually every industry, the threat to middlemen is widespread. Who needs a broker when you can buy direct from a manufacturer at a lower price and receive equal or even superior service? If the broker provides little more than a way for buyers to find suppliers, the broker loses the race to a superior electronic matchmaker that can provide comprehensive supplier listings indexed by complex specifications.

Value Determines Who Remains in Place

The determining factor that governs the future prospects of intermediaries is value. According to Kevin Surace, CEO of Perfect.com, a company that provides a RFQ application for e-marketplaces, brokers and manufacturers's reps get threatened, but distributors stay in. Surace notes that distributors typically add value to the sale process, while brokers and reps usually just move materials from the supplier to the buyer. As for the internal sales force, Surace expects that call volume will decrease while online business will increase dramatically.

Some intermediaries that deliver more than a matchmaking service will actually benefit from e-marketplaces. Steve Schmidt, founding partner of OfficePlanIt.com, an office furniture e-marketplace, believes dealers will survive depending on the way the manufacturer distributes into the industry. The way he sees it, it all depends on the complexity of the product and how much is transferred by the dealer in the distribution process. If the dealer adds customer support, the dealer stays in the supply chain. If the dealer is doing nothing more than adding a margin, the dealer won't survive.

Schmidt explains that in the office product industry, dealers deliver and assemble products at the customers's sites. Manufacturers increasingly ship products in components that require assembly. Because of this, the dealer's role is increasing. So Schmidt believes his dealers will remain in place because their role is getting enhanced by Internet trading. Because of their role in installation, they actually become the seller, even to the point of carrying the paper.

It's All about the Service

Ultimately, the role of the intermediary in an e-marketplace world is service. The computer can find the suppliers and even conduct complex negotiation on everything from price and turnaround to quality and terms, but the e-marketplace can't deliver it, put it together, or service it on-site. If brokers and sales reps do not alter their traditional role of matchmaking to a new emphasis on service, they will likely be marginalized or driven out of business altogether.

Brick-and-mortar intermediaries will have to shift from providing local inventory and product information to supplying services and delivery. As e-marketplace trade in the United States races to $1.4 trillion in 2004, brick-and-mortar intermediaries must shift both their inventory management practices and services offerings—not just to grow, but to survive.

Some analysts believe that intermediaries only have about two years to remake their operations. There are four areas where intermediaries can complement e-marketplace commerce:

1. They can fine-tune their business models to deliver goods efficiently from the manufacturer to the customer.
2. They can meet time-critical customer demands for delivery.
3. They can support highly complex products with service and delivery.
4. They can respond quickly to customer emergencies and difficulties and help customers diagnose problems.

For most B2B intermediaries, adapting the changes brought on by e-marketplaces requires a shift from being a source for products to being a source for the service and delivery of products. The Net forces intermediaries to choose between products or services. The need for independent brokers to match buyers with available suppliers will fade quickly as online marketplaces create significantly more efficient industrywide clearinghouses.

INTERNET HEALTH CARE: A PHONELINE TO A HEALTHY LIFE

Your doctor examines you while giving notes to a nurse assistant who sits with a laptop. She's throwing off technical terms to the nurse as she checks your pulse rate and listens to your heartbeat. The nurse is furiously typing, focused completely in the screen. After the examination, the doctor makes small talk about how your kids are doing. Then the nurse says, "It's ready, doctor." The doctor takes the laptop and studies it carefully while she moves the mouse and clicks away.

"You have nothing to worry about," she says finally, as she turns back to you. "It seems to be just a pesky cold." This scenario is not very far in the future. The information flow on the Internet is giving doctors a direct connection to diagnostic services as well as templates for care. This allows doctors to be up on the latest research without have to rush away from patients to attend conferences or stay up nights reading journals that are six months out of date when they arrive.

The Patient Gets Educated

The Internet is also providing patients with much greater sources for information. I have an autistic daughter. Our pediatrician suggested a particular medication to help with impulse control. Even though we were facing some behavior difficulties that were very challenging, I was concerned about any side effects, short-term or long-term. So I got on the Internet and started poking around. I went to newsgroups and asked questions. I went to pharmaceutical sites and sites specializing in autism. I posted questions and received responses from doctors. I found studies. I printed out everything I could find and ended up with dozens of pages of detailed information on the medication, its effects, and its benefits.

After a few days of this, I called the doctor and told her about my findings. We discussed the medication and reached a decision. At the end of the conversation, she asked, "By the way, could you drop off your research? We'd like to make a copy of it." That was one of those moments when you realize the world has changed, ever so slightly. As a motivated parent, I was able to gather more information than the doctor had on the medication she was prescribing. She knew the basics on the drug, but she hadn't done the research in the depth I was able to do in a couple of days.

With Education Comes Responsibility

Doctors in all fields have noticed their patients are often very up-to-date on their conditions and the range of treatments. Instead of retaining the role of holding specialized information, doctors have had to move into a more consultative role with patients who walk into the examination room equipped with very sophisticated information. The availability of information on the Internet has shifted some of the control over health care to the patients who are willing to go online and learn about their own health.

This trend has been hastened by the proliferation of health maintenance organizations. Consumers are losing some of their trust in the medical profession now that health care is parceled out and controlled like a commodity. Consumers are learning to research their health and bring up issues with their doctors, rather then depend on thinly-stretched medical professionals to take responsibility for their care. The Internet, of course, makes it possible for the consumer to share some of the responsibility for research and care strategies.

THE PASSING OF THE INDUSTRIAL AGE

The Internet economy has ushered in a new way for companies to do business with each other. In the past, raw competition was the rule of the business jungle. Information was secret. Markets were protected. Successful companies were noted for their skill at domination. These business principles or values produced high productivity and low prices. That is, until a company was so successful it no longer had credible competition. Then, of course, it would drift into slovenly ways.

An information-based economy has been emerging for a couple of decades, but it took the Internet to bring it to the tipping point. This new economy brings a different set of principles to the business table. Information is open instead of secret, and markets are now shared. This change didn't arise simply because Net-based entrepreneurs are nicer or softer. The surprising ruthlessness of Microsoft certainly stops that line of thinking. The change has come about because it's good for consumers, it's good for recruitment, it's good for gaining investment partners, it's good for attracting strategic partners—so it's good for business.

Coopitition Breeds Efficiency

In many instances, companies are discovering that if they work together, they are both stronger for the effort. *Coopitition* is the new buzzword that describes the act of competitive forces that come together for common development. At first it's awkward and difficult to maneuver, but in time, the players become comfortable in new roles. When Oracle announced a suite of business services that would compete directly with many of its own customers, company CEO Larry Ellison was asked if his customers would be uncomfortable with Oracle moving into their business space. He said, "We've been moving into new space for ten years. It's not new and it's no big deal."

The developments in e-commerce will blur the borders between companies. U.S. Steel sells its product over the e-marketplace, E-Steel. Ford asks U.S. Steel to sell its product to the automaker through the Covisint auto exchange. U.S. Steel CEO, Paul Wilhelm, sees no reason why there should be someone sitting at a terminal between E-Steel and Covisint. So does that mean e-marketplaces should hook together into a network going from industry to industry? Will industrial trade move through plastics and steel, into autos and appliances, back to logistics and financial settlements, over to excess inventory and used equipment? You bet.

Spelling Out the Savings

And what will happen to businesses as they move trade through direct Internet procurement, exchanges, and e-marketplaces? Well, they will take some savings. Not just a percentage here and there, but a whole range efficiencies. Here's a short list:

- *Cost of goods.* This may not be a great savings for recurring purchases from vendors with long-term contracts, but it will be considerable for spot purchases and for buying used equipment and excess inventory. Plus, even small savings on recurring purchases can add up to a substantial impact on the bottom line.

- *Process savings.* It will become less expensive to produce a purchase order. Same say a purchase order that now costs $120 to produce will only cost $10 to $20 over the Internet. Even if the savings is much lower than this, it can mean a big difference to the bottom line.

- *Workflow improvements.* Most Internet procurement solutions come with a business workflow analysis. A new workflow system will make sure all purchases move through proper channels, and employees will be discouraged from going off on their own to the office supply store on an inefficient purchasing binge. Some CEOs claim this will be the greatest single source of savings from Web-based purchasing.

- *Market visibility.* Intermediaries will no longer be able to manipulate companies based on their lack of information, selling high-demand product at high prices, despite a matching high supply.

- *Inventory levels.* When the supply chain becomes visible, the suppliers of iron ore will be able to log on and see the inventories of Ford autos to see if there will be demand for their product over the next few weeks or months. They will be able to view the inventory levels of all of the vendors between the iron ore and the finished product. Without this visibility, companies have had to maintain large inventories in case a customer might call. A visible supply chain means that a company that normally keeps $150 million in inventory may be able to cut inventory levels to $50 million and still be prepared to service demand. This frees up $100 million in capital.

- *Corporate lending.* American Fortune 1000 companies are collectively the largest lender on the planet. Thirty-day notes that get paid in an average of 45 to 60 days constitute billions in unavailable assets that earn no interest. On e-marketplaces, financial companies such as Visa, Bank of America, and American Express are eager to step in and say, "I'll pay the rent (for a small finance charge)," taking the burden off corporate America. Corporations will no longer have to build margins into their prices to account for their unavailable assets.

Now let's add up these savings. If a company can save 5 to 10 percent on procurement through process improvement and cost of goods, and it can reduce its inventories by two-thirds, it will deliver a higher productivity level as well as greater profits. This means

THE FUTURE'S FUTURE

that the company is less likely to experience price increases from its suppliers, thus putting downward pressure on inflation. And even if shortages in some areas do cause price increases on the goods it buys, process savings very well may give the company a cushion against the additional expenses that will allow the company to absorb the increases without raising its own prices.

Shorter Recessions

In addition, if a recession happens, the company will be in a position to recover much more quickly, because it will not have to wait until its high inventory levels are depleted before it begins to buy again. In the past, recessions have been prolonged by inventory levels that work as a sludge against the speedboat of recovery. High inventory levels can prolong a recession by 12 to 24 months. Without excess inventory, recessions are likely to be much shorter and more shallow.

All of these changes added together, or even just small parts of these changes, will deliver a much more efficient economy that is far less susceptible to recession. They also create a business environment that is more elastic and therefore able to recover from recessions at a much faster pace. It may take five or ten years, but the results of these changes will likely give America, and later the world, the kind of productivity gains that very well may mean 10 or 15 years of inflation-free expansion.

THE CULTURE CHANGES

Imagine yourself 20 years old. About as far back as you can remember, you've had Internet access, and you've lived in an economic expansion. The only wars you've experienced were on television, the Gulf War and Kosovo. You're two years into college, and you're trying to decide what major to pursue. You like the arts, especially computer graphics, but you're not crazy about the idea of reporting to a middle manager in a corporation. You've considering taking an internship at a Web design company, but that would be a temporary move. You really want to create an Internet start-up, a company that can give creative people like yourself an opportunity to work together and develop new Web-based products and services. Ultimately, you don't want to develop great Web business applications.

You want to create a business rooted in creativity. In your grandparents's day, the main business rule was: big beats small. In your parents's day it evolved to: fast beats slow. But in your day, the mantra has become: creative beats static. It doesn't matter how fast you move if you're not continually recreating your products and services to meet your customers's needs. Your generation is quickly learning that speed doesn't matter if you're speeding up the wrong thing. In fact, a high velocity of change in a company can mask a poorly considered direction, right up to the moment of deadly impact.

Getting Squishy

Unlike your father who worked at home as a research analyst tracking software integrators, or your mother who headed up the design team of a Web clothing retailer, you want to work in a "squishy" environment, like the Web firm in San Francisco where you serve as an intern. The space began life as an edgy restaurant. When the Web group moved in, they kept much of the layout intact, with its open workspaces, high balcony, and the bar in the center of the large, open floor area. The bar remains stocked with beer, which goes with the pizza that's free for all of the designers and engineers who work through the night and go home for a few hours sleep at dawn.

Is this the Paris of Hemingway? Is it the North Beach of Kerouac and Ginsberg? Yes, only instead of writing novels and poetry, these agents of change are creating businesses.

In your next step, you want to work where business applications can be designed with all of the intensity and diagonal thinking of a design team. You want to live with a creative team day and night, pouring over ideas, examining every chunk of new technology for concepts, peeking into the corners of dozens of corporations looking for an opportunity to make a creative improvement. Is there a market for Internet squish-training, delivered through video format? Do companies need multimedia, interactive network templates to create weekly vision meetings that bring hundreds of home workers into the buzz?

What do consumers need to improve their lives? What do corporations need to squeeze even greater efficiencies out of their supply chains? Is there a need for culturally-specific recruitment packages so companies can hire armies of engineers in India? Maybe you could create an idea lab that develops business concepts based on emerging technology for software and middleware companies.

Enterprise as Creativity

Whatever you choose, your life will be different than your parents's, powerfully different. Over the course of your life, the boundaries between countries will start to blur as vertical markets and niche interests become more important than geography. Creativity, especially conceptual creativity, is already growing in importance as a prized quality in a business, as a flood of Net-based applications crave form. Borders between corporations are going fuzzy as affiliations, coopitition, collaboration, and seamless integration bring companies into shared space.

Huge middle classes will form in Eastern Europe, India, China, and Latin America, and with them will rise mammoth demand for consumer products, clothing, and entertainment. Disney will become even more globally oriented as it develops creative teams in China and Latin America. As these continents become more American in their economies, they will turn increasingly to home-centric entertainment as they watch their traditional culture disappear before their eyes in a few short years. Their leaders will study law, medical, and business fields over the Internet, with stripped-down, real-world support implemented locally.

Your life will be a continual process of absorbing and processing information. Though you will own few books, you will spend more than half of your day reading. The text will include breaking news, research reports, Web-based seminars, and the raw ideas and refinements shared by your creative team. Though much of it will be communicated through presentation, it will remain essentially the written word, as the seminars are downloaded to your e-reader while you're watching the presentation.

In the 1800s, the major creative force was the novel. In the 1900s, photography, film, and popular music took center stage, absorbing the greatest artistic talent from each generation. In the 2000s, business will likely draw on each generation's creativity. In the past, creative people have shunned business, because systematic control was essential to profitability. Control is no longer the byword of business. Innovation is. In your future, free spirits may find that business development is the ultimate canvas for creatively altering the world.

YOUR NET STRATEGY:

The appropriate Net strategy is to keep up on the changes ocurring across every industry. Executives are taking a number of different paths to keep up with the changes. One CEO started going out to lunch once a week with his corporation's Web master. Jack Welch, CEO and chairman of GE, asked his Net-shopping wife to teach him about e-commerce. Most executives have started intensive reading programs, buying books and carting around telephone-book sized magazines such as *Business 2.0, Red Herring,* and *e-Commerce Business.* The power lunch has been replaced by the reading lunch.

In the area of Internet education, the executives of brick-and-mortar companies deserve a great deal of credit. During the late 1990s, these executives were ridiculed by Net entrepreneurs for "not getting it" about the Internet. These executives came back with a vengeance. By mid-2000, the bricks were matching the entrepreneurs initiative for initiative. In some sectors, such as chemicals, energy, and metals, the brick companies started to catch up with pure plays, launching sophisticated procurement systems and launching e-marketplaces that challenged the very existence of exchanges owned by independent entrepreneurs.

THE FUTURE'S FUTURE

The quick adoption of successful Net strategies by traditional companies was driven by two realities. For one thing, the bricks were motivated by a powerful self interest. They wanted to take advantage of the efficiencies of Internet trading. Those efficiencies send almost instant savings to the corporate bottom line. For another thing, American corporations were well-trained in change initiation and management after years of downsizing, rightsizing, re-engineering, and quality upheavals.

Top American executives had learned how to change their organizations. These executives were promoted largely based on their ability to change their corporations and point them in a productive direction. Meanwhile, the hot-shot entrepreneurs came to the plate with a bag full of tech know-how and creative guts but with very little management experience, and in their haste to fill their offices with highly innovative and creative professionals, they often cobbled together teams that were unmanageable.

The best Net strategy marries creativity with nimble management skills. It doesn't matter how strong your vision is if you can't get all your horses to pull in the same direction; likewise, it doesn't matter how disciplined your team is if you don't know where you're headed. With this balance in mind, gaining a handle on which way to head the team is far easier than trying to figure out how to run a business, as you head toward your goal in a first-to-market frenzy.

Here's a secret Net strategy: Learn to be second to market with deep domain knowledge. Markets like chemicals, metals, automotive, and agriculture have been around a long time. You can't fool them with a shiny first-to-market portal that doesn't reflect their needs. Go into your markets holding hands with some gray-haired experience. Speed doesn't mean much if you don't know what needs to be speeded up. Companies like Ventro, which enters each of its markets with a brick partner such as DuPont or American Express, are the ones who really get it.

CHAPTER 14

YOUR COMPREHENSIVE NET STRATEGY

So how do you prepare your business for the ongoing changes brought about by the Internet? First off, you accept that continual change may be the most consistent factor in your company's future. On the one hand, you need to assimilate abrupt new opportunities that appear almost daily like a field of mushrooms after an all-night drizzle. On the other hand, you need to blow off the chaff and embrace only the opportunities that clearly will move your business forward. The messages from the Internet revolution are just as mixed as my mushroom/wheat metaphors. How can you tell which changes to champion and which to shun?

The answer is patience. In our fast-to-market, ramp-up-now Internet mentality, this may seem like odd advice, but in reality, you can pick the winning Net strategies as you go along. Many of the large American companies that have the most to gain from Internet trading are moving online over a three- to four-year period. It takes that long to put together a fully operational and efficient e-commerce initiative. Smaller companies can get fully wired much more quickly, because they don't have to tie new platforms into legacy systems.

Most Commerce Will Become E-commerce

Internet-based trading will dominate all future commerce. You may still go to the mall to buy Disney clothes for your kids, but in the near future, those clothes will be designed, manufactured, warehoused, ordered, and shipped to retailers through online systems. The systems and initiatives underlying the manufacturing, sales, and distribution of goods will not be a patchwork of first-to-market packages. The backbone of future Internet commerce will consist of platforms that solve supply-chain problems with durable, complex, easy-to-manage systems. These will evolve over time. The most powerful Net solutions almost certainly won't arrive until mid-decade.

REMEMBER BUSINESS 101

The business principles behind a great Net company are no different than the business principles behind a great traditional company. This fact was hard to see during the early days of the Internet, because easily-available funding from venture capitalists often masked poor business models. Early Net companies could live for years without creating the structure needed to support a company that delivers needed goods or services at an attractive value. Skyrocketing stock valuations distorted the real value of the young dotcoms. This created an illusion that Internet companies succeed in a radically different way from traditional companies, and thus that the Internet business model lives by new rules.

In reality, all business lives by the same rules. Deliver value at a competitive price, and you have a chance to succeed. Once you have your price and value relationship in order, you need to communicate your story to well-targeted customers in a very efficient and effective manner. When the VC money is flowing freely, you don't need to develop the discipline to communicate effectively. The Super Bowl ads in January 2000 were a glaring example. Ad departments believed an edgy image was more important than conveying in a crystal-clear manner the profound benefits of the company's products. A quick study would probably show an inverse relationship between muddy advertisements and business success. A quick read through David Ogilvy's books on advertising could bring any Net company back to earth on the principles of effective advertising.

YOU WILL BUY AND SELL ONLINE

There is no way to avoid it. You will buy and sell over the Internet. Even if you run a retail shop and your customers have no interest in buying from your Web page, you will see eventually that purchasing online saves time and money. If you engage in sales to business, your customers will pressure you to move your goods to a Net-ready format. When the auto supplier, Dana, moved to Internet procurement, the company found that only 15 percent of its 86,000 suppliers were able to present their goods over the Internet.

So Dana put the word out, saying, "We will give you 6 to 12 months to gear up. Then we will either buy your goods online, or we'll seek another supplier." To help facilitate this transition, Dana started holding seminars and workshops to educate their suppliers on the process of converting to Net-ready status. This type of pressure to get wired is being driven by brick-and-mortar companies with leverage unavailable to pure plays. At some point, your company will become involved, certainly on the buy side and most probably on the sell side as well.

The Elevated Procurement Manager

Oddly, the procurement manager is the new corporate hero. Procurement department employees have long been the dull-edged bureaucracy of corporations. In the past, the role of procurement manager has been the position of punishment doled out to executives who fell out of favor with the CEO. The Internet revolution has changed all that. When it comes to massive corporate savings, the action is in procurement. Suddenly the head of purchasing is the new corporate prince.

Not surprisingly, the executive in charge of company buying has been elevated. Many corporations have added the title chief procurement officer, which brings the dusty purchasing manager out of the basement and places him on the board. The reason for this elevation goes beyond a way to reward the position that is bringing powerful new benefits to the organization. The reason for the elevation is that procurement is no longer viewed as a tactical activity. It's now recognized as a strategic activity, and as such, the procurement leader has been welcomed into the inner circle of corporate management.

THE CUSTOMER IS KING

The Internet has allowed companies to serve customers in ways that were not possible in the past. A small explosion is occuring in customer service management (CRM) applications that allows companies to interact more closely and effectively with their customers. Strategically, customer intimacy is becoming a competitive advantage. Though the Internet allows companies to buy their copy paper cheaper from a distant vendor, it also allows them to work much more closely with their core suppliers who produce their direct materials.

Here is a brief list of the improvements that are developing because of the Internet:

- *Shared content.* The Internet allows companies to pass information back and forth very easily. This can take the form of blueprints that need to be revised and redistributed instantly to 20 subcontractors, or it can take the form of a GM engineer who can log on to a supplier's design software to create a needed part.

- *Shared inventory information.* Shared knowledge of inventory levels will allow most companies to trim them to just-in-time inventory, without risking shortages.

- *Multiple contact points.* The Internet makes globalization much friendlier. You can click on your language of choice at the Web sites of multinational corporations. You are also much more likely to speak with a native speaker of your own language when you call into a global company's call center.

- *Collaboration.* The ultimate benefit of close Internet connections between companies is the ability of supplier and customer to collaborate on product development, production, and distribution. In the past, manufacturing struggled with the solution to a design problem, then sent the solution specs to the supplier. In the future, the manufacturer will collaborate with one or more suppliers on solutions, which will greatly improve efficiencies in design, production, and distribution.

THE VISIBLE COMPANY

These changes in shared information, customer intimacy, collaboration, improved communication, and inventory visibility will change the nature of corporations. Many analysts believe that as public and private e-marketplaces evolve, most business functions will be visible along the supplier chain, with only the transactions and contracts hidden. This transparency will give both the supplier and the customer a greater ability to efficiently interact. The savings will come in lower inventories, greater manufacturing and design efficiencies through collaboration, lower procurement costs, lower sales costs, greater sales intelligence and service, and increased efficiencies up and down the supply chain.

Not all of the savings go straight to the bottom line. The Dana Corporation expects to realize $1 billion in savings by moving 100 percent of its purchasing to the Internet. The company intends to use some of its windfall to become more competitive. For a Dana customer like Ford, this means the automaker will receive better service from Dana without increased costs. A manufacturer like Ford will receive these same benefits from the majority of its suppliers. Meanwhile, Ford will also take its own efficiency savings through reduced inventory and lower procurement costs.

THE REVOLUTION WILL CHANGE OUR LIVES

These changes in how businesses operate are occuring simultaneously in most companies around the world. The United States has a big jump on Europe and Asia, but the companies outside the United States are learning fast from their American suppliers and customers. As you add up all of these transformations in individual companies, they accumulate into a vast revolution that will likely deliver productivity gains greater than we have ever experienced. The implications of these gains are unknown. Some economists believe these changes will eliminate the steep downturns in the economy that result in recessions.

Some of the more giddy forecasters, such as Grady Means and David Schneider in their book *MetaCapitalism,* believe we'll see the Dow hit 100,000 and countries such as India and China leapfrog into affluence. The authors also expect government coffers to continue to grow even after aggressive tax cuts, which will allow easy funding of social programs. The savings taken by corporations will flow to the bottom line even as companies keep prices in check.

Savings will flow down to consumers in the form of lower cost of goods as well as increased return on investments. Because over 50 percent of Americans are invested in stock personally, through retirement programs and insurance, the corporate bottom-line improvements will also come to consumers. This will result in greater levels of discretionary income and savings. Americans are already putting more into savings even as they maintain their high spending levels. The savings, of course, will give venture capitalists even more fuel for their brushfire.

Does this mean our long period of economic growth will continue? Probably. Most companies are just beginning their conversion to full Internet trading. The process will take up most of this century's first decade. The returns, though, don't have to wait until the transition is complete. Most companies benefit from the move to online procurement in the first year of their program. This means we are likely to see great improvements in efficiency and performance escalating throughout most of this decade.

It is almost impossible not to be optimistic. We have probably just entered a period marked by long-term economic growth that is both stable and steep. Over the coming decades, our greatest challenges may be social instead of economic. Our political debates will probably center on how best to use our prosperity rather than how to protect it. It may be decades before a politician can again say, "It's the economy, stupid." For the coming decade or so, the economy will probably take care of itself very, very nicely.

RESOURCES

INTERNET NEWS AND INFORMATION

Magazines

Traditional magazines are the source of news for most casual e-commerce watchers. Even those who read a dozen daily online newsletters still turn to magazines for perspective and depth of coverage.

B2B (published by *Advertising Age*)
1520 W. Montana Street
Chicago, IL 60614
773-477-7100
<www.netb2b.com>

Business 2.0
5 Thomas Mellon Circle, Suite 305
San Francisco, CA 94134
415-656-8699
<www.business2.com>

Ebiz (published by *Business Week*)
1221 Avenue of the Americas, Floor 40
New York, NY 10020
212-512-2641
<www.ebiz.businessweek.com>

Ecompany (published by *Fortune*)
101 California St., #2
San Francisco, CA 94111
415-982-5000
<www.ecompany.com>

e-Commerce Business
7025 Albert Pick Road, Suite 200
Greensboro, NC 27409
336-605-1102
<www.ecommercebusinessdaily.com>

Fast Company
77 N. Washington Street
Boston, MA 02114-1927
617-973-0300
<www.fastcompany.com>

I-Marketing News
DMNews
100 Avenue of the Americas
New York, NY 10013
212-925-7300
<www.dmnews.com>

The Industry Standard
Standard Media International
315 Pacific Avenue
San Francisco, CA 94111-1701
415-733-5400
<www.thestandard.com>

Information Week
600 Community Drive
Manhasset, NY 11030
415-538-3217
<www.informationweek.com>

Inter@ctive Week
Editorial Offices
100 Quentin Roosevelt Blvd.
Garden City, NY 11530
516-229-3700
<www.zdnet.com>

Line 56
1 Market St., 36th Floor
San Francisco, CA 94105
415-293-8443
<www.line56.com>

Red Herring
Red Herring Communications
1550 Bryant Street, Suite 450
San Francisco, CA 94103
415-865-2277
<www.herring.com>

Upside
731 Market St., 2nd Floor
San Francisco, CA 94103
415-489-5600
<www.upside.com>

Wired Magazine
520 3rd Street, Floor 13
San Francisco, CA 94107
415-276-5000
<www.wired.com>

Online News Services and E-mail Newsletters

One of the best ways to stay abreast of the lasting moves in e-commerce is to subscribe to a number of e-mail newsletters.

CBS MarketWatch
<www.cbs.marketwatch.com>

Ecommerce Business Daily
<www.ecommercebusinessdaily.com>

Ecommerce Times
<www.ecommercetimes.com>

Emarketer
<www.emarketer.com>

Hoovers Online
<www.hoovers.com>

Yahoo!
<www.yahoo.com>

ZDNet.com
<www.zdnet.com>

Research Firms

A number of research companies provide regular studies on the Internet economy. You can search through the sites of these firms to discover the median income of Net shoppers in India or find out which consortium-based e-marketplaces are likely to reach liquidity.

AMR Research
<www.amrresearch.com>

Cahners In-Stat Group
<www.instat.com>

CyberAtlas
<www.cyberatlas.internet.com>

Deloitte Touche
<www.deloitte.com>

Forrester Research
<www.forrester.com>

Gartner Group
<www.gartner.com>

RESOURCES

Greenfield Online
<www.greenfield.com>

International Data Corporation
<www.idc.com>

Jupiter Communications
<www.jupitercommunications.com>

Keenan Vision
<www.keenan-scope.com>

Zona Research
<www.zonaresearch.com>

BIBLIOGRAPHY

Books

Microserfs
  Douglas Coupland, published by Harper Collins

Marketing on the Internet
  Jill H. Ellsworth and Matthew V. Ellsworth, published by Wiley

Business at the Speed of Thought: Using a Digital Nervous System
  Bill Gates, published by Warner Books

e-Business: Roadmap for Success
  Dr. Ravi Kalakota and Marcia Robinson, published by Addison Wesley

MetaCapitalism: The e-business Revolution and the Design of the 21st Century Companies and Markets
  Grady Means and David Schneider, John Wiley & Sons

Rembrandts in the Attic: Unlocking the Hidden Value of Patents
  Kevin G. Rivette and David Kline, published by Harvard Business School Press

B2B Exchanges: The Killer Application in the Business-to-Business Internet Revolution
  Arthur B. Sculley and W. William A. Woods, published by ISI Publications

E-Tailing
Bernadette Tierman, published by Dearborn Trade

Internet Business Intelligence: How to Build a Big Company System on a Small Company Budget
David Vine, published by CyberAge Books

Research Reports

ActivMedia
"The Longer Online, the More They Spend," April 14, 2000

AdRelevance
"Women Emerging as Coveted Audience Among Online Advertisers," January 17, 2000

AMR Research
"B2B Commerce Forecast: $5.7 Trillion by 2004," April 2000
"Evaluating the Independent Trading Exchanges," March 2000
"Ecommerce Rx for Pharmaceutical Industry," March 2000

Andersen Consulting
"The Net's Big Impact on Selling Insurance," April 7, 2000
"Banner Ads Work!," November 29, 1999

Arbitron Internet Information Services
"Ad Agencies See Value in Webcasts," May 1, 2000

The Boston Consulting Group
"New BCG Research Re-evaluates Size, Growth and Importance of Business-to-Business Ecommerce," December 21, 1999

Business Evolution, Inc.
"50 Proven Tips for E-Service Success," November 1999

CyberAtlas
"Q1 Ecommerce Spending Matches Holiday Season," May 1, 2000

Cyber Dialogue
"Cybercitizen Entertainment Survey: Entertainment Sites Reel in Movie Fans," March 31, 2000

BIBLIOGRAPHY

"American Internet User Survey: Online Info Shifts Views of Brands," February 9, 2000
"Women Are Security Conscious E-consumers," January 12, 2000

Datamonitor
"Paid Content on the Net," May 31, 1999
"Huge Growth for Interactive TV Expected," May 10, 1999

Deloitte & Touche
"Keeping Ecommerce Security Tight," February 11, 2000
"New Ecommerce Study Reveals Key Management Issues," February 2, 2000

@dplan, inc.
"Net Security Still Worries Users," May 8, 2000

Ernst & Young
"Men and Women Have Different Online Spending Preferences," April 12, 2000
"Global Online Retailing," January 31, 2000

eTForecasts
"100 Million New Users This Year," May 2, 2000

Forrester Research Reports
"B2B Auctions Go Beyond Price," May 2000
"Euro Emarketplaces Top Hype," May 2000
"Global Ecommerce Approaches Hypergrowth," April 19, 2000
"$6.9 Trillion in 2004," April 19, 2000
"North America Will Lead Global Ecommerce," April 19, 2000
"Europe Will Deliver 22 Percent of the $6.9 Trillion Global Internet Economy in 2004," April 19, 2000
"After a Slow Start, Latin American Ecommerce Will Leap to $82 Billion in 2004," April 19, 2000
"Ecommerce in Asia-Pacific to Reach $1.6 Trillion in 2004," April 19, 2000
"NFR/Forrester Research's Online Retail Index Advances to Address Big-Ticket Items," April 19, 2000
"Online Business Travel Booking Soars to $20.3 Billion by 2004," April 17, 2000

"Forrester Research Predicts the Imminent Demise of Most Dot Com Retailers," April 11, 2000

"E-Business Demands Online Procurement," April 10, 2000

"European Online Retail Will Soar to $175 Billion by 2005," March 28, 2000

"The Internet Is a Friend to Offline Entertainment," March 23, 2000

"Customer Service Versus Site Uptime Keeps the Web Fires Burning," March 20, 2000

"The Email Marketing Industry to Rearch $4.8 Billion by 2004," March, 8, 2000

"Seventy-One Percent of Companies Will Link to Emarketplaces by 2001," March 1, 2000

"Young Net Shoppers Soar Ahead of Online Adults," February 23, 2000

"Emarketplaces Will Lean U.S. Business Ecommerce to $2.7 Trillion in 2004," February 7, 2000

"Consumer Attitudes Will Shape Ecommerce Success in Europe," February 4, 2000

"Emarketplaces Boost B2B Trade," February 2000

"The Portal Race Is Over—The Race for Online Marketing Dollars Is Just Beginning," January 28, 2000

"Business Trade Will Drive Healthcare Ecommerce to $370 Billion by 2004," January 10, 2000

"Dot Com or Dot Corp—The Right Organization Drives Net Success," January 3, 2000

"The Email Marketing Dialog," January 2000

"Financial Firms Must Reinvent Themselves to Serve Net-Powered Consumers," December 15, 1999

"The Web Will Shift Power from Networks to Professional Sports Leagues," November 24, 1999

"Driving Sales with Service," November 1999

"New Affiliate Marketing Models," October 1999

"Online Retail to Reach $184 Billion by 2004 as Post-Web Retail Era Unfolds," September 28, 1999

"U.S. Online Business Trade Will Soar to $1.3 Trillion by 2003," December 17, 1998

BIBLIOGRAPHY

Gartner Group Reports
"European Businesses Run Risk of Having Excellent Business Processes Supporting the Wrong Business Model," May 25, 2000
"Internet and Electronic Business Europe—It's Time to Take Control," May 24, 2000
"Generation Y Web Shoppers Emerge as Mini-Baby Boomers," May 9, 2000
"U.S. E-Government Transformation Providing Opportunities for New Vendors," April 11, 2000
"Knowledge Workplace is Transforming Organizational Processes," March 23, 2000
"Embracing the E-World—Gartner Group's "Three E Strategy" Paves the Way for Brick-and-Mortar Companies," March 14, 2000
"Gartner Group Forecasts Asia/Pacific Business-to-Business Ecommerce to Reach $1 Trillion in 2004," February 17, 2000
"Business-to-Business Ecommerce Transactions Becoming More Global," February 16, 2000
"Gartner Group Forecasts Worldwide Business-to-Business Ecommerce to Reach $7.29 Trillion in 2004,"
"Online Travel Forecast: $30 Billion by 2001," January 6, 2000
"Traveling at the Speed of Hype," November 1, 1999
"Online Advertising to Reach $33 Billion Worldwide by 2004," August 12, 1999

Greenfield Online
"Online Moms with Babies Prefer OshKosh," April 19, 2000
"Cash Registers Are Quiet for Online Grocers," February 23, 2000
"Fisher Price Is the Most Popular Toy Brand Purchased by Young Mothers Online," February 15, 2000
"Online Apparel Consumers Looking at the Price Tag, Not the Label," February 14, 2000
"Online Public Likes Goody Bag of Services," February 1, 2000
"By Gosh Online Gambling Sites Are Not Attracting the High Rollers," January 31, 2000
"Online Auctions More Popular," January 13, 2000

"Nearly Half of Internet-Active Consumers Have Participated in Online Auction," December 31, 1999
"Today's Typical Internet Family: Meet the Greenfields," October 6, 1999

IMT Strategies
"Marketers to Spend $1 Billion by 2001," November 19, 1999

International Data Corporation
"ICD Expects Internet Commerce to Exceed $1.6 Trillion Worldwide by 2003," June 5, 2000
"IDC Forecasts Online Advertising in Asia/Pacific Will Exceed $1 Billion by 2004," May 31, 2000
"IDC Deems Asia/Pacific Ready for Online Trading," May 17, 2000
"European Online Accounts Will Grow to $16.8 Millions by 2003," May 10, 2000
"E is for Europe—The World's Biggest Economy Goes Hi-Tech," April 18, 2000
"Latin America Internet Services Heat Up," September, 1999

Internet Advertising Bureau
"Banner Year for Web Ads," April 19, 2000

Internet Movie Database
"The Blair Witch Project: An Internet Marketing Success Story," August 30, 1999

Jupiter Communications
"Online Retailers Missing Greatest Opportunity: Web-Influenced Spending to Exceed $630 Billion in 2005,"
"Email Marketing to Soar to $7.3 Billion in 2005," May 8, 2000
"No Easy Way to Customer Loyalty," May 1, 2000
"Triple-Digit Growth Rates to Fade in Internet Travel Market; Suppliers and Agencies Must Lock in Long-term Strategies Now," April 14, 2000
"Jupiter Intensifies Coverage of Wireless Internet Market," April 11, 2000
"Dramatic Growth of European Online Retail Market Threatens to Reverse Dot-Com Lead," March 27, 2000

"$3 Billion on Internet Sports Commerce by 2003; Only Incremental Revenues from Online Programming," March 1, 2000

"Internet Health Commerce to Soar to $10 Billion, but Current Offerings Don't Deliver on Consumer Convenience," January 26, 2000

"$3 Trillion in Online Assets by 2003," September 6, 1999

"Banks Battle Portals for Control of Online Bill Market," February 8, 1999

Keenan Vision
"Internet Exchange 2000," April 24, 2000

Market Tracking International
"Internet Music Sales of $4 Billion in 2004,"
"A Crescendo in Online Music Sales," November 22, 1999

Media Metrix
"Dual PC-TV Use Increasing," November 23, 1998

Myers Group
"MediaEconomics Study: AOL Surpasses Major TV Networks in Brand Value," November 15, 1999

NFO Interactive
"E-Shoppers React to Incentives," June 28, 1999

NOP Research Group
"European Internet Race—Britain, France and Germany," April 18, 2000

NPD Group
"Online Clothing Sales Were Over $1 Billion in 1999," March 13, 2000
"Does Apparel Suit Ecommerce?" November 29, 1999

The Phillips Group
"Study Predicts AOL Merger Hints at Other Deals,"

PhoCusWright
"Flying High on Low E-Fares," May 16, 2000

PricewaterhouseCoopers
"Electronic Business Outlook for the New Millennium," April 15, 2000
"Venture Capital Rockets to More Than $17 Billion Despite Recent Market Uncertainty," May 15, 2000

The Strategis Group
"U.S. Users Want to Be Up to Speed," February 16, 2000

Travel Association of America
"Internet usage by Travelers Continues to Soar," February 8, 2000

Zona Research
"Web Based Procurement of Office Products and Corporate Travel Heating Up," April 3, 2000
"Zona Research Announces Release of Online Brokerage Report: 54 Percent of Respondents Are Not Able to Name an Online Brokerage Firm," September 21, 1999

Magazine Articles, Online Articles, and News Items

Asahi News Service (New York Times Syndicate)
"Tokyoites Remain Wary of Shopping on Internet," April 22, 2000

Bancorp Piper Jaffray B2B Analyst
"B2G: An Emerging Frontier for Web Enablement," June 30, 2000

Boston Globe's boston.com
"Newest Formula for Net Riches: B2B," February 10, 2000

Business Week
"Why the Productivity Revolution Will Spread: The Net's Revamping of Old-Line Industry May Save Trillions," February 14, 2000
"B2B: The Hottest Net Bet Yet?" January 17, 2000

CBS MarketWatch
"Online Bazaars May Become Cyber Ghost Towns," May 14, 2000

BIBLIOGRAPHY

Emarketer (www.emarketer.com)
"AOL Latin American IPO Fuels Net Frenzy," June 14, 2000
"Latin American Ecommerce Expands Despite Barriers," June 12, 2000
"Chevron, Statoil, Shell Lead Oil into Web Age," June 6, 2000
"Email Marketing Spending Will Rise to $4.6 Billion by Year-end 2003," May 29, 2000
"Will Online Travel Leave the Agencies Grounded?" April 24, 2000
"Is the Web Finally Becoming Multilingual?" March 15, 2000
"Building an Online Following: Loyalty in Cyberspace," February 28, 2000
"Barriers and Potential in the Latin American Market," February 16, 2000
"How to Really Market Online," February 15, 2000
"The Six Simple Principals of Viral Marketing," February 1, 2000
"Emarketer Releases the E-Financial Report," January 20, 2000
"Banners and Banner Exchanges," January 10, 2000
"All for One? Auctioneers Unite," September 20, 1999
"The Language of Ecommerce Isn't Just English Anymore," September 6, 1999
"The Worth of the Brand," June 28, 1999
"Brand Building on the Net," April 12, 1999
"International Web Ad Spending Will Grow to $7.3 Billion by 2002," March 29, 1999
"Content Counts—Again," October 5, 1998
"eBay Bags the Long Ball," January 11, 1998

Forbes ASAP
"The Best VCs," May 29, 2000
"Money Magnets: The Top Money-Raisers in Venture Capital," May 29, 2000
"Venture Capital in Crisis," May 29, 2000

Fortune
"The B2B Tool That Really Is Changing the World: Web Auctions Are Revolutionizing the $5 Trillion Market for Industrial Parts," March 20, 2000

Industry Standard
"B2B Exchanges Evolving in Fits and Starts," May 20, 2000
"E-Commerce Loyalty Programs Don't Always Work," April 28, 2000
"Case Study: VerticalNet," September 13, 1999

Reuters
"Believe All the Hype About B2B," March 4, 2000

TheStreet.com
"Listening to CDNow: How Good Retailers?" March 17, 2000

ZDNet (www.zdnet.com)
"American-Style B2B Doesn't (Necessarily) Play in Europe," June 6, 2000
"Meta Networks Will Pull Apart B2B Exchanges," June 1, 2000
"The Great B2B Shootout," May 16, 2000
"Why Some Consortia B2B Exchanges Won't Work," May 15, 2000
"Cooking Up a B2B Smorgasbord," May 8, 2000

INDEX

Accompany.com, 26
Advertising, 64
    banner ads, 18, 19, 142-45, 159
    excess inventory, 138
    expenditures, 137-38, 139
    forms of, 140-41
    growth, 137-40
    pay-as-you-go, 144-45
    viral marketing, 141-44
Affiliation
    marketing, 145-47
    network, 159
    programs, 15, 67, 142, 147
Affinia.com, 26
Age, 99
Agriculture industry, 203
Airline industry, 30, 75
Albertson's, 30
Altra, 207
Amazon.com
    affiliation marketing, 146
    branding strategy, 103-4, 114
    competitive edge, 41
    content strategy, 72, 110
    customer service strategy, 109
    discount mix, 72
    e-tail categories, 69
    information source, 71
    loyalty strategies, 104
    retail model, 44
    returns, 27
    sales techniques, 26
    strategy of, 15
America Online (AOL), 102
    branding strategy, 114
    broadband access, 120-21
    entertainment browser, 118
    partnership, 30, 31
    pricing structure, 15
    retail model, 44
American Express, 36
Apparel, 70
    brick-and-clicks, 78-79
    customer demographics, 79
    sizing issues, 78
Ariba, 62
    collaborations, 178-79
    exchange platform, 249
    focus of, 178
    procurement savings, 7, 8
AssetTRADE, 180, 181
Auctions
    B2B, 179-82
    cooperative efforts, 76
    e-marketplaces, 194
    government surplus, 243-44, 249
    retail, 76-77
    used equipment, 63

293

Austin Ventures, 228
Auto exchange, 30, 62, 183-84
Auto industry, 30-31, 191

Background checks, 63
Bain & Company, 235-36
BainLab, 235-36, 237
Banking services, 83
Banner advertising, 19, 159
    exchanges, 144-45
    market share, 140
    results, 142-43
    success of, 135-36
Barnes & Noble, 15, 28
Bean (L.L.)
    customer service, 32-33
    Web site, 22-23, 68
Beauty aids, 81
Benchmark Capital, 28, 227
Bigfoot Interactive, 153
BizTravel.com, 170
Blair Witch Project, The, 125-27
BLG Ventures, 236-37
Boeing, 62
Bon Appetit, 20
Boomers, 97
BP Amoco, 171
Brand, 28, 29
    building, 102, 114
    consumer confidence, 65
    content and, 114
    core competency, 114
    definition, 101
    for differentiation, 103-4
    equity, 102
    identity, 113
    importance of, 101
    online brokerage, 51
    personality, 114
    shifts, 102
Brick-and-clicks, 28
    advantages of, 31-32
    apparel, 78-79
Broadband Internet access, 115-16
    consumers for, 120-21
    sports and, 128-29
    television and, 116-17
Broad-based portals, 139

Broadcast satellite, 120
BroadVision, 62, 202-3
BulkBuy, 72
Business
    as art form, 6
    leadership, 6
    models, 26
    principles, 272
    productivity, 164
    strategy, 225
    travel, 170
Business-to-business (B2B) commerce
    Asia-Pacific region, 216-18
    auctions, 179-82
    catalog automation, 185-86
    cultural differences, 14
    dot-com or dot-corp, 174-77
    e-commerce, 40
    early days, 41-42
    efficiency, 8, 42
    Europe, 214-16
    exchanges, 179-82
    forecasts, 7, 163-64
    globalization, 211
    health trade, 80
    increased productivity, 162
    incubators and, 232-33
    inflation and, 7
    integration, 185
    Internet initiatives, 169-70
    Latin America, 218-20
    options, 161
    procurement, 42, 163, 170-79
    productivity gains, 42-43
Business-to-consumer (B2C) commerce
    cultural differences, 14
    forecasts, 7
Business-to-government (B2G), 7, 241
    audit trail, 246
    education sector, 245-48
    e-marketplaces, 251-52
    local/state level, 244-45
    niche providers, 245
    strategy, 253
BuyerZone, 71

Cable modem, 120-21
Call centers, 32-33

INDEX

Campsix, 237
Carrefour consortium, 62, 183-84, 196
Catalog, 194
    automation, 185-86
    magazine company partnerships, 23
    model, 21-23
CDNow
    content strategy, 110
    customer retention techniques, 93
    information source, 71
Change
    assumption of, 15-16
    dot-com perspective, 14-16
    effective, 36-37
    speed of, 14-15
    traditional perspective, 16
Chase Capital Partners, 227
CheMach, 60, 61
ChemConnect, 196
Chevron, 62
Chili Pepper, 18
Chipshot.com, 103
Choice, 41
ClickRewards.com, 106
CloseOutNow.com, 182
CMGI, 231, 233-34, 237
Collaboration, 274-75
Commerce One, 62, 171
    collaborations, 178-79
    equity position, 202
    focus of, 178
Communication, 63, 142
Competency, 114
Competitive challenges, 14-16
Competitive edge
    content as, 110-13
    customer service as, 109
Computer hardware and peripherals, 68
Condé Nast, 18-20, 23
Connectivity configurations, 25-26
Consortia
    auto industry, 183, 191
    coopitition, 198
    rules, 196
    rush of, 183-84, 191

Consulting fees, 201-3
Consumer. *See* Customer
Content, 21-23
    branded, 114, 118-19
    customization options, 181-82
    discount mix, 72
    entertainment, 117-19
    industry-specific exchanges, 181-82
    paid markets, 112-13
    partnering for, 111-12
    perceived value, 113
    power of, 110-13
    shared, 274
Convenience, 40-41
Conxion, 236
Coopition, 178-79, 196-98, 262-63
Corporate lending, 264
Corporations, 3, 4
Cost of goods, 263, 275
Cost-per-thousand (CPM), 145
Covisint, 30, 169
Creative thinkers, 5-6
Credit card safety, 53-54
Cross-channel synchronization, 98
Cultural change, 265-68
Customer
    acquisition costs, 32-33, 43
    age, 99
    behavior, 106, 157-58
    branding, 101-4
    buying styles, 99
    confidence, 28, 65
    demographics, 24
    dialog with, 152, 153-54
    digital family, 94-97
    education, 64
    expansion rate, 43
    expectations, 34
    feedback, 26
    gender, 99-100
    generational groups, 97-99
    income level, 100-101
    inconsistencies, 67
    long-term Net users, 93-94
    loyalty programs/strategies, 94, 104-6
    relationships, 152, 154-56

Customer, *continued*
    retention, 92-93, 156
    rewards program, 106
    satisfaction, 32-33
    spending patterns, 69
    targeting, 92
    value offers, 154
Customer service, 22, 32, 105
    as competitive edge, 109
    contact points, 108
    loyalty and, 106-9
    management, 274-75
    mix, 156
    multilingual, 220-21
    proactive approach, 109
    reactive approach, 108-9
    strategies, 108-9
Customer-recognition devices, 54
Cymerc Exchange, Inc., 181

DaimlerChrysler
    consortium, 183-84, 191
    e-marketplace, 61-62
    partnership, 30
Dana Corporation, 273, 275
Data mining, 157-58
Dialog, 152, 153-54
Dialog Information Services, 16
Digital Impact, 153
Digital subscriber line (DSL), 120-21
Direct mail, 47-48, 152-53
Direct marketer, 21-22
Direct sales, 65
Direct-to-consumer retailing, 73
Disney, 118-19, 133
Divine interVentures, 234-35, 238
Document storage, 64
Domain knowledge, 197, 269
Domain partners, 36
Dominos, 31
Dot-com
    abilities of, 14-15
    brick components, 31-32
    business partnerships, 24-25
    change and, 14-16
    connectivity configurations, 25-26
    customer service, 32
    definition of, 14
    experimentations, 25-27
    initiative, 174-77
    traditional company response to, 35
DotCom Incubator program, 236, 238
DotComGuy, 31
DotCom Ventures, 238
Dot-corps, 29, 174-77
Dow Chemical, 62
Downloads, 122-25
Drop-shipping system, 33
Drucker, Peter, 2-4
Dutch auction, 194
DuPont, 36, 62

Eastman Chemical, 196
eBay, 25, 76
    branding strategy, 114
    e-tail categories, 69
    offline venture, 102
    Safe Harbor Investigations, 77
eChemicals, 60
eCitydeals, 249, 251
E-commerce
    Africa, 55
    Asia, 55-56
    Australia, 56
    buy/sell implementation, 174-77
    catalog model, 21-23
    China, 56
    efficiencies, 34
    Europe, 55, 56-57
    France, 57
    future of, 6-7, 271-72
    Germany, 57
    globalization, 54-57
    government and, 243-44
    hesitancy strategy, 10
    holiday sales, 23-25
    Hong Kong, 56
    Japan, 56
    Korea, 56
    Latin America, 55
    magazine model, 18-21
    mainstream, 24-25
    Middle East, 55
    middleman in, 257-60
    multiple strategies, 10-11

INDEX

297

niche sites, 44, 48-50
online brokerage, 50-51
organization for, 175-76
porn, 44-46
prior to, 40
purpose, 39
retail, 43-44
security issues, 53-54
Singapore, 55
shift to, 9-10
Taiwan, 56
transactions, 40
United Kingdom, 57
warehouse sites, 109
wireless, 51-53
eCompanies, 238
Economy
    cultural shift in, 13-14
    economic changes, 4-5
    operational efficiency of, 13
    technical shift, 14
E-culture campaign, 103
E-government companies, 248
Efficiency model, 8, 204
Electronic data interchange (EDI), 39
E-mail
    advertising, 140
    as communications tool, 23, 135
    customer service, 108
    internal system, 63
    newsletters, 111
    offsite access to, 63
    service bureaus, 152
    spam, 46-48
E-mail marketing
    cost of, 152
    customer retention program, 156
    direct mail replacement, 152-53
    growth of, 151-153
    industry, 47-48
    service company, 155
    techniques, 153-56
E-marketplace, 7, 8, 174-77
    advantages of, 62
    auctions, 194
    birth of, 60
    B2G, 251-52
    buyer in, 201

catalogs, 194
concept, 187
consortia, 183-84, 191, 198
content strategy, 110-11
controversy, 164-65
efficiency, 204
elements of, 193-95
European, 214-16
evolution of, 182-84
exchange IPOs, 205-6
geographic sites, 199-200
globalization, 189-90, 221-22
growth of, 61-62
horizontal sites, 198-201
independent industry insiders, 197
industry information, 195
industry shakeout, 203-4
integration services, 206
intermediaries in, 257-60
logistics, 195
models, 195-98
multiple revenue streams, 62-63
for new customers, 63
paradigm shift, 190-92
projections, 188-89
RFQ model, 193, 194
settlement issues, 195
software companies, 201-3
supply-side exchanges, 197-98
transparency of, 183
vertical hubs, 197, 198-201
Encryption software, 53, 85
EnergyLeader.com, 199-200
Entertainment, 115-17
    broadband audience, 120-21
    content, 117-19
    global gaming, 130-31
    movies, 125-27
    music, 122-25
    sports, 127-30
    television, 131-32
    traditional, 121-22
Enthusiast, 105-6
Epicurious, 19-20, 23
Epylon, 245, 246-48, 251
Equity position, 201-3
eSteel, 169, 196

E-tailing
   apparel, 78-80
   Asia-Pacific region, 218
   auctions, 76-77
   boomers, 97
   categories, 68-70
   content/discount mix, 72
   customer inconsistencies, 67
   difficulties, 66
   financial services, 82-84
   future of, 86-88
   gender, 99-100
   Generation Next, 98, 99
   globalization, 213-14
   health care, 80-82
   income level, 100-101
   Latin America, 219
   loyalty strategies, 104-6
   niche sites, 65, 68
   online mall, 71-73
   rules, 65
   security issues, 84-86
   seniors, 97, 98-99
   tech developments and, 69-70
   travel services, 73-75
   value-added sites, 72
   Xers, 97-98
eToys, 28
   consumer demographics, 100
   customer service strategy, 109
Excess inventory, 179-82, 199
Exchanges, 179-82
   government, 249
   models for, 195-98
Excite, 139
Expedia, 30, 74
Experimentation, 64
Exploitation, 142
Ezgov.com, 249-50, 251

Financial services, 82-84
Firewalls, 85
FloNetwork, 154
Ford Motor Company, 4
   consortium, 183-84, 191
   e-marketplace, 61-62
   online procurement, 169
   partnership, 30, 31

   PCs for employees, 169
Forecasts
   B2B, 7, 163-64
   B2C, 7
FreeMarkets.com, 166, 169, 198, 207
FreeRide.com, 106
Free services, 141
FreeWheelz.com, 26
Frequently asked questions (FAQ) section, 108
Fulfillment operations, 22, 33-34
Future trends, 255-69

Garage.com, 238
Gender, 99-100
General Cinema, 31
General Electric, 4
   Net strategy, 64
   online procurement, 58
   procurement savings, 163
General Motors, 4
   consortium, 183-84, 191
   e-marketplace, 61-62
   online procurement, 58, 169
   partnership, 30, 31
   purchase order costs, 165
General Services Administration (GSA), 243-44, 249
Generation Next, 98, 99
Generation X, 6, 97-98
Geographic sites, 199-200
Give-aways, 141
Global gaming, 130-31
Globalization, 64, 189-90, 209-10, 226
   Asia-Pacific region, 212, 216-18
   B2B, 211
   e-tailing, 213-14
   European development, 212-16
   Latin America, 218-20
   multilingual, 220-21
   online trading, 214
   preparation for, 210-11
   usage demographics, 210-11
GO.com, 139
Good Catalog, The, 23
Gourmet, 20
Government
   auctions, 249

INDEX

299

citizen payments, 249-50
exchanges, 249
Internet design by, 242-43
Internet preparation, 250-51
permits, 249-50
procurement, 244
GovHost.com, 252
GovWorks, Inc., 249, 252
Grateful Dead model, 124
Grocery service, 30
GSAAuctions, 252

Health care, 80-82, 260-62
Health maintenance organization (HMO), 81
Hesitancy strategy, 10
Hickory Farms, 93
Horizontal site, 198-201
Household income, 100-101

IBM, 236
    e-culture campaign, 103
    online procurement, 58
icraveTV.com, 131
Ideaforest.com, 236
Idealab, 231, 234, 238
Incubator, 230-31, 224, 240
    as conglomerate, 233-34
    as customer creation, 236
    empty-market, 235-36
    hatcheries, 237-39
    models for, 231-37
    network model, 232-33, 234-35
    as social change, 236-37
    speed-to-market model, 232
Independent industry insiders, 197
Industrial Age, 2-3
Industry information, 64, 195
Inflation, 7
Information
    exchange, 4-5
    free, 71
    magazine model, 18-19
Information Age, 2-4, 6
Infrastructure companies, 225-26
Initial public offerings (IPO), 205-6
Innovation, 35-36
Insurance, 83-84

Integration, 185, 206
Intermediaries, 17, 257-60
    airline industry and, 30, 75
    auto industry and, 30-31
International Data Coporation (IDC), 214
Internet
    commerce shift to, 8-10
    early consumers, 16-17
    education, 268
    future trends, 156-58, 255-69
    government design of, 242-43
    local company interactions, 31
    transformation, 5
Internet Capital Group, 231, 234, 238
Interstate Wire Act of 1961, 130
Inventory, 167-68
    levels, 264
    shared information, 274
i2 Technologies
    collaborations, 178-79
    focus of, 178
iVillage, 81, 100

J. Crew, Web site, 22-23, 68
Keiretsu model, 232-33, 234-35
Kmart
    content strategy, 110
    retail model, 44
Knowledge workers, 2-4
KPMG, 62

Land's End
    content strategy, 110
    customer service, 32-33
    Web site, 22-23, 68
Large portals, 139
Licensing fees, 201-3
Logistics, 195
Loyalty
    customer service and, 106-9
    strategies, 104-6
Lycos, 139

Magazine companies
    advertising, 18-19
    catalog partnerships, 23
    online model, 19-21

Magazine companies, *continued*
   special interest sites, 17-18
   subscriptions, 18-19
   Web based, 20-21
Management, 2-3, 225
Market
   affiliation, 145-47
   fragmentation, 166-67, 180-81
   research, 64
   segmentation, 21-23
   transparency of, 167
   visibility, 264
Marketing techniques, 22
   banner advertising, 135-36
   content as, 111
   e-mail, 135-37
   personalization, 136-37
MarketMile, 63
Mercantec, 235
Microsoft
   Slate, 20, 21
   technological stumble, 3-4
Middleman, 257-60
Mobile e-commerce, 51-53
MoHotta.com, 41
Monster.com, 114
Mortgage services, 83
MotherNature.com, 41
Movies, 125-27
Multiple contact points, 274
Multiple strategies, 10-11
Music, 122-23
   downloads, 122-25
   labels, 123-24
   subscription service, 124
Music Blvd, 25, 93
MyPoints.com, 106

NetClerk, 252
Net gambling, 130-31
Net plays
   definition of, 14
   early attempts, 16
   evasion, 176
   evolution into, 176
   exploitation, 176
   incubators and, 231
   in outside offices, 29
   results for, 28
Net-ready markets, 174-77
Net Value Holdings, 239
New Enterprise Associates, 229
News Bureaus, 119
Niche sites, 48-50, 65, 68
   ad share, 139-40
   auctions, 76-77
   B2G, 245-48
   efficiency, 203-4
   incubator model for, 232-33
Norwest Venture Partners, 229
Nutraceuticals, 81

Oak Investment Partners, 227-28
OfficePlanIt.com, 259
Offline brands, 89
Offline spending, 67
1-800-FLOWERS.com, 25
One-to-one marketing, 26, 137
Online brokerage, 50-51
Online economy, 5
Online mall, 71-73
Online procurement, 5, 42
   adoption of, 59-60
   buying/selling opportunities, 173-74
   commodities, 171
   direct, 171-72
   efficiencies, 165-68
   public auctions, 172
   recurring purchases, 173-74, 193-94
   savings, 7-8
   software companies, 177-79
   spot purchases, 171, 172
   supplier savings, 58-59
   vendor savings, 58-59
Online shopping, 23-25
Online stock trading, 82, 217-18
Operational efficiency, 13
Opt-in programs, 148
Oracle, 62
   collaborations, 178-79
   equity position, 202
   focus of, 178
Organizational leadership, 6
OutletZoo.com, 180

INDEX

Outpost.com, 109
Outsourcing, 62, 63, 155
Over-the-counter drugs, 81

Partnerships
    catalog/magazine company, 23
    for content, 111-12
    dot-com/traditional company, 24-25
Patents, 25-26
Path to profitability (POP), 239-40
Patient education, 261-62
Peet's Coffee, 154
Penny's (J.C.), 28
PeopleSoft, 62
Perfect.com, 193, 258-59
Perfect Storm, 127
Permission marketing, 137, 147-48, 159
    costs of, 150-51
    programs, 149-50
    rules, 149
    self-interest, 149
    spam versus, 148-49
Permission transfer, 149
Personality, 114
Pharmaceuticals, 81
Picks and axes, 225-26
PlanetAg.com, 195
PlanetRx, 81
Polaris Venture Partners, 229
Pornography, 44-46
Post Communications, 155
Potomac Electric Power Company (PEPCO), 199-200
PrairieFrontier.com, 49-50
Preview Travel, 41
Price competition, 41
Priceline.com, 26
    branding strategy, 114
    competitive edge, 41
Price-only brokers, 258
Pricing strategy, 15
Privacy issues, 157-58
Process savings, 263
Procurement. *See* Online procurement
Procurement manager, 273-74

Product
    image, 101
    lines, 22
    sectors, 99
Productivity, 4, 42-43
Profitability, 226
Project fees, 201-3
Promotions, 122, 125-27
Purchase order costs, 165
Purchasing, 63
Pure-play start-ups, 90

Reader's Digest, 23
Recessions, 265
Recruitment, 63
Request for proposal (RFQ), 193, 194, 258-59
ResponseSys, 155
Retail, 43-44. *See also* E-tailing
Retransmittal programming, 131-32
Return on investment (ROI), 275
Reverse auction, 194
Revolution, 1-2
Rolling Stone, 19
Royal Dutch/Shell, 171

Sales costs, 166
Sales techniques, 25-26
Salon, 21
Salvage, 179-82
SAP, 62, 171
Scams, 46-47
Sears, 62, 183-84, 196
Security issues, 53-54, 84-86
Seniors, 97, 98-99
Sequoia Capital, 228
Service providers, 17
Settlement issues, 195
Shared information, 152
Shared resources, 145
Shopping. *See* E-tailing
Slate, 20, 21
Softbank Venture Capital, 226-27
Software companies
    equity position, 201-2
    as partners, 202
    revenue streams, 201-2
    as vendors, 202-3

Sony, 124
Spam, 46-48, 148-49
Special interest sites, 17-18
Sponsorships, 140
Sports, 127-30
Staples, 63
Statoil, 171
Sticky, 26
Subscriptions, 18-19
Suppliers, 58-59
Supply chain management, 178, 272
Supply-side exchanges, 197-98
Synergy Brands, 239

Television, 116-17, 131-32
3Com, 154
TotalMro, 63
Tower Records, 153
Toys 'R' Us
    consumer demographics, 100
    fulfillment woes, 33
    Net play, 28
Traditional company
    change and, 16, 36-37
    dot-com partnerships, 24-25
    innovation, 35-36
    Internet division for, 29
    Net presence, 35
    response to dot-coms, 35
Training, 63
Travelocity.com, 18-19, 30, 74, 171
Travel services, 30, 68, 73-75, 170-71

U.S. Steel, 166, 169, 196
Universal, 124
Used equipment, 179-82

Value, 152, 154, 258-59
Value-added benefits, 19
Value-added services, 181
Vendors, 58-59, 159, 171-72, 202-3
Ventro, 36-37, 207
Venture capital, 223-24, 239-40
    business rules, 225-26

e-government companies, 248
    firms, 226-30
    incubator, 235-36
    market, 224-26
    myths, 224-25
VerticalNet, 61
Vertical portals, 139
Vertical site, 197, 198-201
Viral, 26
Viral marketing, 141-44

Wal-Mart
    branding strategy, 104, 114
    Internet effort of, 176-77
    retail model, 44
    Web site, 29
Warehouse sites, 109
Webcasts, 140-41
Web sites
    banner advertising, 18
    catalog model, 21-23
    content, 22-23
    early, 17-18
    explosion of, 48
    magazine model, 11-21
    niche sites, 48-50
    success of, 48-49
WebVan, 30
WebVision, 202-3
Whitney (J.H) & Co., 230
Williams-Sonoma, 20, 23
Wireless, 51-53
Wireless broadband, 120-21
Women.com, 100
Workflow improvements, 264
World Sports Exchange, 130

Xers, 97-98
XSAg.com, 181

Yahoo!
    branding strategy, 114
    entertainment choices, 118-19
    offline venture, 102
    partnerships, 30, 31